"What is it that transforms inexperienced, naive young women into mature compassionate nurses? Heart, humour, perseverance and courage ~ and these are evident on every page of Donna Yates-Adelman's delightful coming-of-age story *Yes, Sister, Memoir of a Young Nurse*. We laugh and cry with Yates as she comes to grips with the challenges and the defeats of her healing profession. This highly readable, sometimes graphic memoir is heart wrenching and hilarious, filled with medical drama and timeless insights."

Deirdre Gilbert, RN
Past Vice President, Books and Home Entertainment Editorial,
Reader's Digest Canada Ltd.

"The reader comes to apprehend the gravity of nursing, the importance of timing, and the exigency of focus and concentration. But more importantly, Yates-Adelman restores the reader's faith in a profession that has been reputed to lack sensitivity. {She} revives confidence in medical personnel."

Aniko Koranyi-Bergman
President, Canadian Writers Society

"This is the fascinating story of a nurse's training and her diverse experiences ... on almost every kind of medical ward. It is rich in knowledge, personality and anecdote. But most importantly, it teaches stark lessons that apply directly to the state of medicine in Canada today. Meticulously written and often graphic in its detail, this book can be an important contributor to our country's debate on healthcare."

Michael Carin
Editor, Montreal Business Magazine

"A charming memoir of a young woman with a true calling to care. Yates captures the innocence of youth and the coming of age {of the author}, whose life was transformed by caring for and witnessing illness, suffering and vulnerability."

Laurie Gottlieb
M.Sc. in Nursing, Ph.D., Author
Professor at McGill University

"An honest and intriguing portrayal of the nursing world by one who has lived it from the inside. Engaging. Told directly from the heart."

Elizabeth Kane Buzzelli
Writer, teacher, reviewer

Yes,
Sister

memoir of a
young nurse

Donna Yates-Adelman

Shoreline

Copyright Donna Yates-Adelman 2005
Cover design and graphics, Sarah Robinson
Editing, Andrea Borod
Photographs from the collection of the author

Printed in Canada by Marquis Imprimeur
Published by Shoreline, 23 Ste-Anne, Ste-Anne-de-Bellevue, QC H9X 1L1
514-457-5733   shoreline@sympatico.ca   www.shorelinepress.ca

Dépôt legal: Library and Archives Canada
Bibliothèque nationale du Quèbec

This story is true. The characters are authentic, the events real.
The names of several characters have been changed, to protect the privacy of
patients, personnel and of my classmates.

Second Printing, 2006

Library and Archives Canada Cataloguing in Publication

Yates-Adelman, Donna, 1939-
Yes, sister : memoir of a young nurse / Donna Yates-Adelman.
ISBN 1-896754-44-9
1. Yates-Adelman, Donna, 1939- 2. Holy Cross Hospital
(Calgary, Alta.). School of Nursing. 3. Nursing students ~ Alberta-
Calgary ~ Biography. I. Title.
RT37.Y38A3 2005   610.73'092   C2005-904259-1

For you, Mom

Evelyn May Scorah Yates

Acknowledgements

My gratitude to Judith Isherwood and Shoreline Press for believing that this nurse's story should be told and remembered, to intern Andrea Borod for her editing and to Sarah Robinson for the cover and graphic artistry.

To the Grey Nuns from Montreal for their lifetime commitment to giving of themselves to better us all, and to Sister Leclerc for her unwavering dedication to the mission of turning out only the best nurses. To Father Flanagan for his spiritual and emotional nurturing of all Holy Cross nursing students.

To my teachers and all the fine physicians at Holy Cross who gave me an education and a profession that I could confidently carry with me for a lifetime.

To my classmates, my sisters, who have supported me throughout that lifetime and the writing of this book. To all my patients and their families who taught me what it means to be a humane human being.

To these fine physicians who took the time to proof read the chapters pertaining to their specialties and offer valuable suggestions: Nathan Sheiner, cardio-vascular thoracic surgeon, Jewish General Hospital; Eric Lenczner, orthopedic surgeon, Montreal General Hospital; Sidney Pedvis, pediatrician, retired. To Manuel Borod, Site Direcor of Palliative Care, Montreal General Hospital for his time and perspectives on nursing today. Special thanks to Richard Margolese, Director of Oncology, Jewish General Hospital, who read the entire manuscript and offered valuable counsel.

To my dear friend Michael Carin who told me that I could write my own story and then taught me how. I am forever grateful and will always remember his patience, perseverance and expertise.

And to the many angels who helped me along the way:

The Banff Centre for the Arts for accepting me in their Writing With Style program with Eunice Scarfe.

Ann Diamond and her workshops; Eunice Scarfe of Saga Seminars; Lee Gutkind of Creative Non-Fiction, whose mentoring program gave me my mentor, Judith Ketchin; to Judith Ketchin for believing that my story should be published and for her help in making it happen; to Enza Micheletti, Judy Yellon, and Judith Searle for early edits; to Elizabeth Buzzelli for her generous support; to Deirdre Gilbert for her expertise and encouragement; and to Joni Miller for her support and for finding me my publisher.

To my friends who read the manuscript from beginning to end and offered their support, Belinda Tatlow, Madeleine Ritz, Lynda Southam, Myra Firestone, Dolores Nickerson, Louise Goldwax, Sheila Masson, and my sister-in-law Charlotte Yates. My deepest appreciation to Yvonne Callaway Smith, "the Artist," who stayed up all night to help me complete a final edit.

To my brother Allan Yates, Associate Dean for Graduate Education, Director Division Neuropathology, Ohio State University, for his support and invaluable input, and for always being there; to my nephews Robert and Brian for their ongoing interest and encouragement; to my grand-daughter, Gillian, for her interest; and to my grandson and sometimes writing partner, Noah, for his enthusiasm and pleasure in the story.

To the International Women's Writing Guild (IWWG) and Hannelore Hahn, founder, who believes that every woman's story should be told, and who works diligently to make it happen. To Pat Carr, Susan Tiberghien, Susan Baugh and my many new sisters from the IWWG Writing Conference, at Skidmore College in Saratoga, NY, without whom I could not have brought *Yes, Sister* to fruition.

To John Thornton of Spieler Literary Agency, New York, NY, for his years of assistance and encouragement.

To Lane's Studio, Calgary, for the cover portrait as well as the grad photos, reunion photos and Faculty photos. Author photo by Magenta Studio, Montreal.

Especially, my heartfelt thanks to Diane Gallo, editor, teacher, and now friend, who took my manuscript and with her expertise and generosity, helped me to shape it into a publishable book ~ then gave me the skill and confidence to send it out into the world. Without you, Diane, I would not be here.

Last but not least to my husband, Hy Adelman, my best friend and best critic ~ a special "Thanks" for giving me the name of the book, *Yes, Sister*.

Contents

Introduction

I was born at The Holy. My mother never tired of telling me stories of the nurses at Holy Cross Hospital, and of Dr. Richardson who delivered me in the early hours of the morning.

When I was three years old, my mother would take a clean white tea towel from the kitchen drawer and lovingly fold it into a triangle. I would stand perfectly still on the linoleum floor as she tied it over my wild brown curls in a sacred ritual. My skin would tingle and my scalp prickle as the tea towel magically became a nurse's veil. All day I'd nurse my dolls and our cocker spaniel, Sally, who would eventually howl for rescue. In the evening, my father was my patient. I'd stick a thermometer in his mouth and pretend to take his pulse as he listened to Fibber McGee and Molly blaring from the wooden radio console beside his chair.

I started school just as World War II was ending. Now the tea towel ritual included a red cross, which my mother drew on the tea towel and coloured with red crayon. Carrying a pot of leftover morning porridge as nourishment for my wounded patients and scraps of worn-out sheets for bandages, I ran out to play backyard war games on the fragrant grass. The Royal Canadian Air Force, out on their daily training run, roared through the blue sky overhead, providing a realistic backdrop for our make believe games. I would always be the nurse who crawled under the barrage of bullets and dragged the wounded to safety.

So it was only natural when the time came to go into nursing training that I would go to The Holy. *Yes, Sister* is the story of my three years of nursing training at Holy Cross Hospital in Calgary, Alberta, Canada, which was owned and run by the French-speaking Grey Nuns from the Mother House in Montreal.

Even in those days, Calgary was a rough and tumble frontier town. In the 1860s, large numbers of buffalo hunters had moved into the region, followed by traders exchanging "whiskey for furs" with local natives, the Blackfoot, Sarcee, Stoney, Pagan and Blood. In 1875 the North West Mounted Police, now the Royal Canadian Mounted Police, established their second outpost, Fort Calgary. By the early 1880s the railway had reached the town site and in 1884 Fort Calgary became simply Calgary, Alberta's first town.

At two o'clock on the bitter cold morning of January 30th, 1891, Sister Agnes Carroll, Sister Olivia Beauchemin, Sister Elizabeth Valiquette, and the young lay-nun, Sister Gertrude, arrived at the Calgary rail station accompanied by Father Leduc, who had traveled to St. Boniface, Manitoba to meet them. According to the Grey Nuns' Chronicles, the Sisters arrived "with no other resources than their confidence in Divine Providence."

Although they had collected slightly more than $200 canvassing friends and relatives, the Canadian Pacific Railroad refused the Sisters' requests for free fares and charged them $116 for tickets, plus $16 for berths. As a result, the Sisters of Charity had less than $74 to finance the Holy Cross Hospital.

Finding no one to meet them and with no transportation available, the nuns carried their belongings and followed Father Leduc through the snowy darkness to Sacred Heart Convent, where the Sisters provided beds for the night.

The next morning, they moved into their hospital near the convent ~ a two-storey building still under construction. Each floor was 20 feet square, divided into two rooms. The nuns slept on old mattresses, furnished their rooms from purchases at auction sales, and purchased a stove to heat the draughty hospital. They hauled drinking water from Father Leduc's well and laundry water from the nearby Elbow River. It would be many months before the hospital would have its own well.

Two women organized a door-to-door collection of linens and furnishings and Sister Gertrude canvassed the city for donations of food and money.

On April 10th, 1892, Holy Cross Hospital admitted its first patient whom Sister Gertrude described as, "so poor, that all he had was typhoid."

At first, Calgary received the nuns miserably, but in that first summer of 1892, a measles epidemic struck the town of almost 4,000. Tents were set up on the outskirts of town across the river to quarantine the patients. The mayor appealed to the nuns who took up the challenge. They accepted isolation and worked around the clock to nurse these patients back to health, thereby creating a bond between Calgary and the Grey Nuns. One year later, a diphtheria epidemic broke out and another in 1894. Then came the typhoid epidemics of 1901 and 1908, followed by smallpox and the Spanish Influenza in 1918.

In 1892 the Sisters built the first Holy Cross Hospital with 25,000 bricks donated by the Oblate Fathers. And though the hospital was conveniently located within walking distance from St. Mary's Church, Holy Cross did build a magnificent chapel of its own. Through the generosity of C.J. Duggan, a Calgary businessman and devout Catholic, many tons of Carrara marble were imported from Italy for the altars, including the 15-foot-high centre altar and an elaborate balustrade, the communion handrail. To support the enormous weight of the two-storey chapel, whose second floor extended out over the entrance of the hospital, 10 classic pillars had to be erected. Now, Calgarians were referring affectionately to Holy Cross Hospital as simply, "The Holy."

By 1929, The Holy was a source of pride to Calgary. From its humble beginnings, The Holy had grown into an impressive four-storey structure featuring a Roman-style facade and exquisite, stained glass chapel windows. Inside, there was a noble stairway of Tyndale stone and mosaic art, terrazzo floors, elevators, a silent call system for the patients ... and an excellent school of nursing.

From 1907 until the school's closing in 1979, the Grey Nuns at Holy Cross Hospital graduated 2,409 superbly trained, registered nurses. But The Holy did more than turn out good nurses. It changed the lives of the women who trained there.

This story is about nurses being trained in those hospital trenches. It is the story of my patients who taught me about respect and dignity, about living and dying. But, most of all, this story is about how people treat people.

Calgary. Feb. 3rd 1891

Most Honored Mother General

A postal-card which
I addressed to you on Friday last,
acquainted you of our arrival
at the famous City of Calgary,
so long the subject of conversation
and of anxiety to those most
concerned.

When we alighted from the train
at 9½ o'clock Friday morning, the
air was cold, it was snowing
heavily, and we felt very chilly.
Revd Pere Leduc went to the wait
ing

Calgary, Feb. 3rd 1891

Most Honored Mother General ~

A postal-card which I addressed to you on Friday last, acquainted you of our arrival at the famous City of Calgary, so long the subject of conversation and of anxiety to those most concerned.

When we alighted from the train at 2 1/2 o'clock Friday morning, the air was cold, it was snowing heavily, and we felt very chilly. Rev. Père Leduc went to the waiting room to see if there was any one there to receive us: but came back after a few moments, saying we would be obliged to walk over to his house. The Rev Father started ahead, carring (sic) as many portmanteaus and baskets as he could; he walked so fast that we were breathless trying to keep up to him, while the snow came pelting into our faces without mercy.

We soon reached the Convent where we were cordially received by Rev Mother Green. R. Leduc, celebrated the holy Sacrifice in the Convent chapel, we had the consolation of receiving Holy Communion. Our feelings at this sublime moment, can be better imagined than expressed. After a light breakfast we went to bed, in the Convent; but not to sleep, Our poor imaginations wandered back to Our beloved Mother-house, to the dear ones from whom we are now separated by 2.262 miles. After a few hours rest, we arose, took a good dinner, which had been prepared by the kind Sisters, and then went to visit our <u>hospital</u>.

On entering our future residence a feeling of dismay came over me, and I had to use great efforts to restrain my tears ~ A house 2 stories high, and 20 feet square, separated by a partition in the middle, neither lathed nor plastered, with chinks and holes in every corner, through which the cold wind blew freely, there was only one small stove which hardly sufficed to heat the apartment where the men were working. Père Leduc soon joined us, and inquired in a Jocose way, how we liked our hospital? If the trial of beginning in such a house seemed too hard for the Grey Nuns who are so rich now, etc, etc.

I manifested my surprise that the house was not more advanced but he cast all the blame on Rev. Père André, who he pretends, neglected to oversee the men and make them advance their work. Père Leduc then took us over to the Sacristy, and showed us then riches he had in store for us. Six iron bedsteads, some old, disty (sic) looking mattresses; three old, washing stands which needed a good scrubbing, and other bedroom necessities; all second hand articles, purchased at an auction.

We looked at each other in dismay: but seeing there was no remedy for our present position, we set to work at once, Put up 4 beds, washed the old furniture which was indispensable, and placed all in one side of the upper story which we call <u>a dormitory</u>. The Rev. Père then sent us over some dirty blankets which I presume he took from his own beds, some pillows much the worse of use: he got a heating stove put up, so we were ready to take possession of <u>our dormitory</u> that same night. The cold was intense on Friday night Saturday, and Sunday. I wrapped Sr. Beauchimin in all the old blankets we could spare, still she trembled and shivered all night in her bed.

Next morning everything around us was frozen hard. We dressed quickly and ran over to the Convent for Mass. As we had no cooking stove, or kitchen utensils, we were obliged to beg our meals from the good Mothers, who kindly offered to give us any assistance in their power. I thanked them for their offers of hospitality: but as I noticed that their house is very small, and they have a number of boarders to lodge, I did not wish to inconvenience them by taking possession of one of their rooms for they are already crowded with children.

We got up a cooking stove on Saturday, so we were able to prepare a frugal supper in our own home. While doing so, we were agreeably surprised to see our dear Sister Cleary come in, wrapped up in blankets and covered with frost and snow. As you may imagine this dear Sister received a cordial reception: the house was cold indeed but the hearts of those who ran to greet her were very warm. Our kind-hearted Sister shed tears over us and said we should go to High River with her: but after a little consideration, she agreed with me in thinking it is better for us to remain here, now that we have come. The people will be more inclined to give us some assistance, when they witness the hardships we have to endure.

However after having consulted Père Leduc, I decided to send Sister Beauchimin to the Industrial school for a couple of weeks. She seemed to take her new position so much to heart, that I feared it would injure her health. Sr. Cleary promised to take good care of her, and we will be settled down better here when she comes back. Sr. St. Marc feels disappointed, she expected something better than this. However she is cheerful withal. Sister Gertrude takes everything very easy. She sleeps and eats well, and does not seem to be lonesome yet.

Rev. Père Leduc surprises me by his paternal kindness, he sends us plenty of <u>edibles</u> and often comes to see if we are alive. I have already become acquainted with some of the principal ladies in town, and these have sent in donations ~ blankets, quilts, towels, etc. We will certainly have to suffer for some time but there are good prospects for the future. Ask our holy, old Sisters to pray for us that we may be generous in Our Divine Master's Service. Thanking all the dear Sisters for their kindness to me.

I refrain as every, your grateful

(child Sr. Carroll.)

PART ONE

So You Want to be a Nurse

Holy Cross Hospital, Calgary, Alberta, February 10, 1959: My mother sat beside me in the dim, narrow hallway used as a waiting room. A small discreet sign beside the door read: *Sister C. Leclerc, s.g.m.*
          Director of Nursing

An elderly housemother at the reception desk, partially hidden by a Plexiglas partition, quietly answered the telephone and sorted mail. "Nurses' residence," she said softly into the headset. Waiting in front of the partition sat a girl with three battered shopping bags overflowing with clothes. Her shiny black hair was as tousled as her bags of clothes and she looked pale and thin. I felt sorry for her, all alone the first day of nursing training, when Sister had specifically asked all the new students to bring their mothers. I waited for her to lift her head. I would smile at her to let her know, it's okay if you don't have a suitcase, or a mother. But she sat folded into herself, eyes downcast, as if trying to hide from the world.

Above us, the student nurses' quarters were silent. I strained to hear the gentle murmuring of those angels in white, but the only sound was the occasional buzz from the switchboard and the constant hum of the large black-and-white electric clock on the wall behind me. I inhaled deeply, again, and again, hoping for a whiff of the hygienic hospital, but could only smell the freshness of the new building and the waxy, wooden floors, so shiny that when I leaned over, I could see my fuzzy reflection ~ short dark hair, round face, hazel eyes. In a Black Watch tartan kilt skirt that my mother had made, I fidgeted in my chair and smoothed the skirt over my knees, feeling as if I was about to write an exam.

Mom turned to me and smiled her happy-you-made-it-my-little-girl, smile. She wore her Sunday black dress and had her mouton-lamb coat draped over her shoulders. Mom was petite and delicate, angelic looking, actually, with bright blue eyes, high cheekbones and a soft bow to her lips.

Sister Leclerc's door opened. A girl with her black hair combed neatly into a pageboy, and her mother in an impressive red hat with a floppy feather, stepped out. They gave a cursory glance at the pathetic lone girl across from me, the red hat acknowledged my mother with a nod, and they disappeared into the elevator. My heart pounded and my hands shook. I was next.

"Miss Yates," Sister called from the doorway of her office.

Sister Leclerc was a tiny woman immersed in the billowing black and grey habit of the Grey Nuns, Sisters of Charity from Montreal, Quebec. Her face was barely visible beneath a tight-fitting hood embossed with two stiffly starched scrolls of material that stuck out from under her chin like a shelf and rose on each side of her face like blinkers on a buggy-horse, ending in a perfectly symmetrical V above her forehead. Someone had once told me that nuns shaved their heads and I wondered if a bald head truly lay beneath that hood. The large silver cross around her neck reminded me of Ingrid Bergman's cross in the movie *The Bells of St. Mary's*. The association convinced me that all nuns are kind people.

Sister smiled as my mother and I sat down. "*Bon*. This is a really important day for you, Miss Yates," she said, crisply, with a French accent. "You will have to adjust to a new way of living. We have our rules that you must obey."

"Yes, Sister," I said.

Sister sat rigid, her hands folded on her desk. "The Holy Cross Hospital is a most valued and respected institution," she said. "And this hospital offers one of the best training programs available. It's a privilege to train at Holy Cross. We are really proud of our nurses. Your conduct must always bring credit and honour to our hospital and school."

"Yes, Sister."

"Your conduct outside of the school also reflects The Holy Cross, Miss Yates. If you exhibit good conduct outside, then you no doubt will use good judgment on the wards and become a good nurse. The two must go together."

"Yes, Sister." I was so excited and happy, if Sister had told me to jump out of the window, I would have said, "Yes, Sister," and jumped.

Sister's sharp eyes looked hard at me, now, deep into my soul. "Life in residence is very different from the life you have been living, Miss Yates. This is your home now."

Then Sister smiled and said, "*Bon*," again, and gave me two keys, one to my room and one to my mailbox. Mrs. Schriefels, one of the housemothers, was waiting to escort us to my room.

As we left, the girl in the hall was still staring at her hands in her lap. As I stepped into the elevator, I heard Sister call to the girl with the shopping bags, "Miss Kaufmann."

The nurses' residence was a new, state-of-the-art eight-floor building with a science laboratory, gymnasium, beau rooms (for visiting family or beaus), a reception hall, and television room. The student nurses occupied floors two to six, a small group of student nursing assistants lived on the seventh floor and the nuns on the eighth.

My room was on the fourth floor, third from the end of the hall, very small. As I gazed around the room I thought: For the next three years, this will be my home. I had a little sink, and across from a long wooden desk, a single bed with a deep blue, cotton bedspread. A crucifix hung above the bed. An armchair was squeezed in front of two windows that framed the south side of the hospital where the bright, winter sun was turning the stained glass windows of the chapel into a gleaming kaleidoscope. To the east, one short block away, was the curving Elbow River with its shallow rocky banks and willowy trees arching over the clear mountain water. In the distance, the snow peaks of the Rockies stood majestic on the western horizon.

"What a darling little room," whispered my mother, in awe. She slowly moved to the window and gazed longingly at the hospital with its Roman-style façade and classic pillars. Mom had always wanted to be an RN, but the Depression had forced her out of school to work as a practical nurse in a private home. She turned and wrapped her arms around me. "I'm so proud of you, my little girl," she whispered. "I know you'll make a wonderful nurse." Then Mom snapped open her purse, took out her black kid gloves and slipped them on. My door made a soft click as she closed it behind her.

After my mother left, I opened my small suitcase, which we had carefully packed together. One by one, I found a place for my family pictures and favourite treasures. In the position of honour, smack in the middle of the bookshelf above my desk, I placed the heavy metal horse my brother Allan had given me. He'd won it at the Calgary Stampede, knocking down roly-poly pins. I also had a little ceramic skunk with a furry tail my friend had given me in grade six and a small gold plastic horse Grandma Yates had given me when I was a child. On my cork bulletin board, I tacked a large picture of Cisco Kid on Diablo, and a picture of Lester Brennen, my boyfriend, beside the corsage he'd given me for our high school graduation dance last June.

As I hung up my few clothes, the yellow duster, garter belt, white nylons, each garment on its own hanger, and took my nurse's shoes out of the box and placed them on the floor, I thought: These are the clothes I will wear for the next three years. Shopping at the Hudson Bay with my mother, I had even discovered a nursing bra, but when I held it up to show her, she laughed and shook her head and said, "That's not for nursing students, Donna."

When I had finished unpacking, I sat down in the armchair and stared out the window. Now and then a car pulled around the u-shaped driveway in front of the residence and deposited a new student with a suitcase and a mother.

"Hi, there! Up here. I'm up here!" I heard someone shout. The girl who had just stepped out of a car, looked up at the residence. "Welcome to Holy Cross!"

The residence curved slightly to the right; I could see a fair-haired girl leaning out the window, waving a rag. "Welcome!" she called again.

It was a clear crisp February afternoon. Calgary, with almost a quarter of a million people, lay at my feet. I looked down on bare, twiggy elms and evergreens, older clapboard houses in muted earthy colours and grey stucco homes with front porches and picket fences. I turned my gaze to the hospital beyond the driveway. Its windows mirrored the blue sky and gauzy, white clouds of this perfect day. It stood silent, mysterious, secretive. Smoke snaked into the brilliant afternoon like a ribbon of black velvet.

I tried to imagine beyond the windows ~ a nurse in crisp white, laying her cool hands on a fevered brow, a patient propped up in bed with pillows, a relative at the window, waiting, hoping. But somehow I couldn't imagine myself beyond those windows. I was here, just a heartbeat from the hospital, the patients, the nurses, all I had dreamed about for so many years, yet I began to wonder: Had I make a mistake? Could I do it? I'd never lived in a residence before, never left my family. Besides, I was a Protestant. I had never been around nuns before. I began to feel lonely for my mother. I opened my rulebook.

Suddenly shrieks of laughter jolted me back to reality. I followed the sound down to the lounge and was delighted to find real-live nurses. The seniors, also living on the fourth floor, had just come off duty. Still wearing their caps and blue-and-white dresses, they were stripping off their white bibs and aprons and tossing them on the floor.

"That bitch made me stay after the delivery and clean the whole bloody case room," one of the students snarled as she pulled off her white apron. My jaw dropped. Such shocking language. She threw the apron on the floor to join the heap of uniforms growing in the middle of the lounge. "And *I'm* a senior!"

"Yea! Thank God!" Everyone cheered.

These girls were nurses? Angels of mercy? There was nothing celestial about them. Nothing! They were absolutely human.

My realization brought with it a rush of relief. Of course nurses were human. Wasn't it silly of me to have thought all these years that nurses were real angels? Suddenly I smiled. Becoming a nurse as a mere mortal would certainly make my task ahead much easier.

I returned to my room. Wondering how I would ever get up enough courage to go down to the hospital cafeteria for supper, I felt someone's eyes on me. I turned quickly to the door, and there stood a tall, sweet-looking girl with honey coloured hair that hung way below her shoulders.

"Porter," she said shuffling toward me in fuzzy, pink slippers. "Lynn Porter." She peered into my face and smiled. "Hi. Sorry I don't have my glasses."

"Hi. I'm Yates, Donna Yates."

Her deep-blue eyes quickly scanned my room. "Gosh, you've fixed it up real nice. Like your horse," she said. "It's kind of lonesome, eh?"

I nodded.

"You from Calgary?"

"Yeah."

"Me, too."

"Was that you, hanging out your window a while ago?" I asked.

"Yeah," she said, running her fingers through her hair like a comb. "And now I'm in a lot of trouble. Sister called me down to her office and really told me off. But they were awfully dirty, you know ~ the windows."

"I would think she'd be happy to get the windows cleaned."

"It's not professional to be hanging out the window like that, she said. And she was *really* mad. Said I have to always ask before I do *anything* that's not in the rulebook. Golly, I don't know if I'm going to like it here."

"Don't be silly," I said, trying to sound like I knew something about residence life. "Sister wouldn't hold that against you. She's a nun. If anybody will understand, she will."

"Well," Porter hesitated, "I don't know about that. She didn't seem so understanding to me. Anyway ... you hungry?"

"Starving."

"Let's go," Porter said.

After supper, I returned to study my rulebook. *May your three years with us find you fitted not only professionally and physically for your chosen career, but also that you may be morally and spiritually equipped to meet the obligations of a Christian nurse.*

Suddenly my door opened and a blond, winged-capped head slowly peered in. It was a student in uniform with short, curly hair and a big smile. Her entrance was accompanied by an outburst of cursing from the lounge.

"Hi," she said. "I'm Beverly Church, your big sister."

Church held out a small package wrapped in tissue paper, and an envelope. "This is for you," she said. "Welcome. Just remember, I'm always here if you need me, even if you just want to talk. The Holy's a great place, but it can get kind of rough at times. I'm on the sixth floor. Come up any time."

I opened the envelope and read: *Welcome to The Holy. I wish you luck in your training ~ many happy days ahead! Have fun ~ but if you ever need a shoulder to cry on or a friendly chat, I'm here. Best wishes, your "big sister."*

I opened the white tissue paper; it was a small teddy bear with a big smile on his embroidered mouth and "Rah-Rah" written on a banner across his chest.

"I'm six months ahead of you," Church said. "I'm in the September class."

"Were you nervous when you first came in training?" I asked.

She grinned and nodded. "Yeah, petrified. But you'll get used to it. It doesn't take long."

After she left, I sat the teddy bear on the end of the bookshelf above my desk and felt a little less lonely. Then I walked to the phone at the end of the hallway and telephoned my mother.

"I have a new friend, her name is Porter," I said, my news bursting forth in a great breathless rush. "I've got a big sister who's going to watch over me and I had pancakes and maple syrup for supper ~ it's Ash Wednesday. We're the class of February '62 and we're called probies. And I saw the emergency room, Mom," I added excitedly.

"Your Father and I are very proud of you, dear."

"Thanks, Mom, I'll call you in the morning."

And that's what I did at seven the next morning and once a day for the rest of my training.

That first morning I awoke to the visions of patients curled up in little beds. I floated among them like an apparition and they rose from their sick beds, miraculously healed.

I dressed in my class uniform, a grey skirt, white blouse and navy jacket with the crest of our hospital on the left pocket. I pinned my name pin, Miss Yates, on the right lapel, and rushed to breakfast.

Down in the cafeteria, there was a long line. I fell into line behind Hazel White, a tall girl with black hair and pale skin. A small group of seniors arrived and pushed in front of us.

"Hey," White said, turning around. "What's going on?"

"That's the hospital caste system," Porter whispered.

Wilma Niven, a redhead with a face full of freckles, and as tall as White, joined our small but growing knot of probies at the end of the line. "Christ," she said in a loud voice, "I've been in this brainless line since seven o'clock! I was almost up to the food when those damn seniors bumped me back here."

"Shh," said Jean Perry, the girl who roomed next door to me. She held her finger to her lips. "The rulebook says we have to be courteous at all times to senior students and grads."

"To hell if I'll be courteous when they won't even let a person who's been standing here for 20 minutes get near the food." Niven spoke just as loudly as before. "I'm just as good as they are. Aren't I?" She had turned and was speaking to the dark-haired probie who had just rushed up behind us. "Well, aren't I?" Niven repeated like a command. It was Delores Kaufmann, the girl without a suitcase.

Kaufmann quickly pulled her chin to her chest without looking up. She smiled and moaned at the same time, then whispered, "Yeah ... I guess-s-s...."

"Geez, it's almost 7:20," Jean Perry said. "The rulebook said we're supposed have eaten breakfast by the time Sister gets here for our prayer at 7:25."

"Oh, well la-di-dah ~ and I'm Sister Superior," Niven intoned.

Finally we made it to the food. Porter leaned into the glass counter and squinted down at a row of stainless steel containers, steaming heartily ~ but only three had food; stark white hard-boiled eggs, limp toast and slimy-looking porridge.

"Come on, for godsake, shake a leg, Porter," Niven said.

Porter quickly chose a bowl of cornflakes and a glass of milk. We found our table at the back of the student nurses' cafeteria.

Perry sat beside me, nursing a cup of black coffee. "I'm so nervous," she said. "Can't swallow a bite. Sure wish students could smoke in here."

As I took my first bite of cold soggy toast, a loud voice pierced the din of chatter.

"Sister's coming!"

Sister Leclerc had rounded the corner on her way to the cafeteria. Through the open double doors I saw her gliding down the hall looking like a little music box doll. The students pushed their chairs from the table and sprang to their feet in a collective abrasive noise that echoed throughout the cafeteria. We turned to the crucifix on the wall opposite the door. I fumbled in my pocket for the piece of paper on which the prayer was typed, Morning Prayer: To Memorize.

Dear Lord, I begin my day of duty with the hope that I shall serve Thee faithfully. I have consecrated myself to the service of Thy sick and suffering. I have pledged my loyalty and devotion to the noble principles of my calling.

Each task I offer with the sincere hope that it is prompted by my love for Thee. I shall not shirk any duty however unpleasant. When I cool the fevered brow, moisten parched lips or comfort the aching body, I shall remember that I bring comfort to Thee. Help me find in every patient another soul created by Thy infinite love. I pray that my calling may find me always a real lady, kind, courteous and considerate of those who face the trials of sickness. Besides, I shall find hope in the thought that the more perfect my service, the more genuine my sacrifice, the more I shall be like to another Lady – the Lady you honoured in such a striking way as to call her, Mother.

I shivered with excitement as I said the prayer. This was the kind of nurse I wanted to be.

In starched bibs and aprons and blue-and-white striped dresses, the student nurses, wearing impressive winged, white caps, began their morning march in single file past Sister Leclerc. Sister was ruler supreme with the eye of a hawk. Students' hair must be at least one inch above the collar, no runs in nylons and the seams absolutely straight, shoes polished, bandage scissors in back waistband, and except for a light-coloured lipstick, no makeup. Long hair must be kept in a hairnet. It was considered unclean by hospital nursing standards, as were rings with stones. Clear nail polish was permitted, except in the operating room. If the polish was chipped, it would trap bacteria and carry infection to the patient. The graduate nurse was allowed a plain wedding band. Student nurses wore no rings.

In this world of rules, Sister could, and did, cancel late leaves – if our uniforms were not complete, clean or orderly at morning inspection, if we came into the residence late (we had three minutes grace), if we had lights on, or were in someone else's room after lights-out.

Now with an almost imperceptible nod, Sister pulled a few nurses out of the line. After the last student disappeared down the hall, Sister turned and spoke to each delinquent girl before allowing her to continue to the ward.

Twenty minutes later, I was at my desk. We had 36 girls in the class and we sat in alphabetical order. I sat next to White – where else, but the last seat.

White leaned over and whispered, "Did you fill your fountain pen? We're not allowed to bring ink bottles into the classroom," and I nodded.

After class, I retreated to my room to continue reading the rulebook: *... For the next three years, your life will be intimately bound with that of the Sisters who conduct this Hospital and School of Nursing. They will be your friends and your guides....*

After supper that night, I sat in the lounge reviewing the rulebook with the girls from my class. We were on page four – *Discipline* – when Perry asked, "Hey, what's a misdemeanour?"

"I think it's a crime," said Porter, holding up her book within an inch of her face. "It's like breaking the law."

"It is," said Marie Guenette. She tapped the rulebook in her lap. "You pay dearly if you break one of these laws." Guenette was 33, old for a student nurse, with reddish hair and pale freckles.

"It says here," Perry said: *Any misdemeanour committed by a student while away from the school but which reflects on the good name of the school....*"

"Aw, garbage," Niven said. "Who the hell would know if you commit a misdemeanour while you're away from the school? I live in Saskatchewan. You think Sister would hear about me down here?"

"It says right here that each student is on her honour to report any infraction of the rules that she's committed to the Honour Board," Perry said.

"Well these rules are stupid-crazy," Niven intoned.

"These rules are what makes Holy Cross the best nursing school in North America," Guenette said with authority. "I *know*. I checked them all out." She had been in the U. S. Navy for many years before moving to Canada to become a nurse. "Now if you want to know what happens if you break the rules in real life, I'll tell you. Look at Discipline again ... *3. If a student marries during her course, she is automatically dismissed from the school.*" Guenette looked around at us; we stared back.

"Yeah, so?" Niven finally said.

Guenette lit a cigarette. "Last night Sister got this anonymous phone call about one of the seniors ~ the one who was supposed to give the valedictorian address at the graduation ceremony." Guenette took a drag on her cigarette and pursed her lips, slowly releasing a thread of smoke that curled across the lounge.

"Well, the squealer told Sister that the girl had secretly married two months ago and she wasn't even pregnant."

"You mean the girl's gone? Out of the residence?" Porter asked, squinting at Guenette with her myopic blue eyes.

Guenette lifted her hand and studied her fingernails for a moment, then looked up, and said, "You bet. And Sister's mad as hell. Won't allow the girl to participate in the graduation ceremony. Even wants to rob her of her RN but she's already written and passed the Canadian and State Board exams ~ thank God ~ so Sister can't take that away from her."

Niven suddenly stood up and without even asking, snatched up Guenette's lighter and lit her own cigarette. She blew the smoke out in a gruff puff. "Shit," she said. "That bitch of a Sister gave that poor senior the royal shaft."

Wow! She used Sister's name in vain. I had never heard so much swearing in my life. I looked round the room and thought: These are the people I will live with for the next three years. Then my eyes fell on the open rulebook on my lap: *Good manners are the criterion of a well-educated lady....*

Possessed Probies

And so my life as a student nurse began with five intensive months of classes ~ seven hour-long blocks per day, five and a half days per week.

8 a.m. <u>Anatomy and Physiology</u>. Mrs. Meeres. Jasper lived in the narrow closet at the front of the classroom. In the evening I would go down to study his wired bones, always with White or Perry or Niven for courage and company. He hung

there, grinning ~ no tongue, wide-open mouth full of teeth. And he would stare right through me from two dark sockets that once held his eyes.

Who had this man been in real life? We knew he was a man, because his pelvis was narrow and funnel-shaped, not broad and deep like a female. One night during our study, Niven stuck her arm through the pelvic basin and said, "Hey, Big Daddy you gotta be a guy, 'cause you got no room there for babies."

"Dem bones, dem bones, dem dry bones," we sang as we studied Jasper upside down and backwards. *"The foot bone connected to the leg bone."* There were long bones and short bones, *"The knee bone connected to the thigh bone,"* carpals and tarsals, *"The thigh bone connected to the back bone,"* the frontal bone and flat bones, *"The back bone connected to the neck bone,"* the cranium's parietal bone and irregular bones of the vertebrae, *"The neck bone connected to the head bone"* ~ clavicle, femur, tibia, fibula, carpus, metacarpus, and six auditory ossicles. *"Oh, hear the word of the Lord."* Two hundred and six bones in the human body. I memorized them all.

"Dem bones, dem bones gonna walk aroun'," we sang as we jived in front of Jasper, holding his metacarpal phalanx, twirling under his ulna, which articulated with his humerus and radius. *"Ohhhhh, yeaahhh."*

9 a.m. <u>Nursing Arts</u>. Mrs. Whitford. It was here in nursing arts that I felt like a real nurse and Mrs. Chase, named from the Chase Company that manufactured her, was the true, perfect patient. I spent many enjoyable hours nursing this voiceless, life-size doll. I sat her up, laid her down, turned her over and lifted her on and off the bedpan. I made an occupied bed with her in it and pulled the bottom sheets so tight I could bounce a dime off them ~ there could be no wormy wrinkles to cause bedsores.

In Nursing Arts lab we practiced many of the patient care procedures on each other in the classroom ~ a mockup with all the equipment we would find on the hospital ward. Working in pairs, our class took turns giving each other bed baths and heavenly back rubs with alcohol and powder.

We took each other's temperature. And every day we'd climb into bed to be rolled up and down, gently turned and positioned with pillows. One day Perry fell sound asleep nestled in fluffy pillows.

And each night after classes, we continued to study.

"Okay, Perry," I said. "What's the purpose of a bed bath?"

"Purpose: *To make the patient clean and comfortable,*" Perry read from the rulebook.

White continued: *"To enable the nurse to observe the patient.* And don't forget to chart your observations."

"Don't forget to immerse your hands and feet in basin if possible," said Porter. She shrugged, puzzled.

"Porter, that's the patient's hands and feet, not yours," White said

"Oh, is that what that means." Porter squinted down at her book again and continued, *"Clean nails. Clean glasses. Brush hair.* That's the patient again, right?"

"And what if he's bald?" Niven asked, her hand on her hip.

"Come on, Niv," White said. "Get serious. And don't forget: *A bed bath is a good time for health teaching.*"

First it was oranges, then our partner's arm and finally, "the other place." My partner, Marlene Brown, had a wonderfully large buttock for me to pop my needle into. But I can't say the same for poor Brown.

"Gosh, I hate this," she muttered as she slowly ground the needle into my flesh. Then after she yanked it out, asked, "Did it hurt?"

"Naw," I said stoically, trying to hide the pain. Though I thought she'd come very close to the vital sciatic nerve we had been warned to stay away from.

After class I rushed up to my room to look in the mirror. Sure enough, I had a big bruise the size of a silver dollar on my left buttock.

Two days later, I was shocked when Mrs. Whitford assigned me a new partner. Brown had quit. She was the fourth to go ~ we were down to 32.

The pink-tangerine sun was bursting forth splendidly over the dark peaks of the Rockies one morning when Mrs. Whitford said, "Turn to procedure number 24." Perry who sat in front of me, turned around with flushed cheeks.

"Holy shit," she breathed. "Preparing the body for the morgue!"

"First we give the body a complete bed bath," Mrs. Whitford continued. "Then we pack all the orifices with gauze, using the long forceps provided in the morgue pack."

"I'll be goddamned," shot Niven, the tall, tomboy. "No one is going to pack my orifices."

The class snickered, and Kaufmann lowered her chin to her chest and daintily cupped her hand over her mouth.

Mrs. Whitford ignored the commotion. "There will be no lab for this procedure." Thank goodness for that, I thought. "The nurse has an important role in the care of a dying patient. You must keep your finger at the wrist and monitor the pulse until it stops. You must chart the *exact* time that the pulse and respiration cease. The chart is a legal document and can be used in a court of law.

"Now be sure to put the teeth into the mouth before sending the body to the morgue," Mrs. Witford said. "Otherwise you must go down to the morgue, by yourself, and unwrap the body and put the teeth in. By then rigor mortis will have set in and you'll have a frightful time to get the mouth open."

How would I ever touch a dead body? I ran my father's words over and over in my head. "Why are you afraid of the dead? They're the only people in the world who can't harm you."

Maybe he was right, but I wouldn't trust a morgue full of them.

The buzzer buzzed, class was over. I quickly made a large note in my exercise book ~ *mouth ~ morgue ~ rigor mortis ~* and crossed my fingers.

Each day, Mrs. Whitford inspired a desire in us to nurse the whole patient, mentally and spiritually, as well as physically. "These are indivisible!" she would stress over and over again. She explained the golden rule of Holy Cross: "You must answer the call bells *immediately*. A Holy nurse never walks by a patient's room with a call bell light on ~ no matter how busy you are ~ whether it's your patient or not!"

Answer the patients' calls quickly, cheerfully and quietly.

"Nothing can substitute for good nursing care," Mrs. Witford continued, "not even drugs. If the patient can't sleep at night, you must first give a back rub and a cup of hot milk before resorting to a sleeping pill. Your obligation to the patient is to comfort and alleviate fear, not to knock them out with a pill." She paused for a moment, then smiled and said. "I remember a student nurse who sat down and had a quiet talk with her elderly, belligerent patient who wasn't responding to treatment for her pneumonia. The woman finally admitted that she was worried about her cat that had been left alone in her house. The student told the Head Nurse who arranged for the patient's neighbour to care for the cat. Lo and behold, the patient suddenly made a remarkable recovery.

"You must think of it as though you were the patient. To lie in bed month after month is a terrible thing. A little goldfish in a bowl is fascinating to watch and can do wonders to perk up a lonely patient." Then Mrs. Whitford smiled and I thought she was the kindest nurse ever.

These were the values instilled in us each day. "A Holy nurse must be one cut above nurses from the other hospitals."

10 a.m. Professional Adjustments. Mrs. Croft taught this class. She was not a model of what we were supposed to be. Her cap perched precariously atop her carrot-red bun and her pink-rimmed glasses sat just below her black eyebrows. She wore bright red lipstick and her uniform hem usually hung in a bit of a wave.

Always late, she would fly into the classroom in high plumage. "Splendid, splendid, girls," she'd say, reaching to push her crooked cap back up on its bun.

"You are Holy girls, and you must never bring discredit to your hospital ~ on or off duty." She paced back and forth in front of the class fingering a piece of chalk. "Remember, do not sit in parked cars. That's only for *racy* girls." Niven turned around and rolled her walnut-coloured eyes at White and me as Mrs. Croft continued. "Our late leaves are midnight in your first two years and 1:00 a.m. in your third year, more than enough time for a movie and a Coke afterwards. What could one possibly do after 1:00 a.m.? Everything is closed!"

White jabbed her elbow into my ribs, leaned over and whispered, "Think she ever heard of back seat bingo?"

Mrs. Croft's cap had slid to the side again, one wing pointed to the ground. She stared blankly at us, then returned the cap to its perch. It was still crooked.

Another jab from White. "God, what a goofball."

"I'll tell you what will happen," Mrs. Croft continued, "You sit in a parked car, one thing leads to another, and first thing you know your career is over."

Niven covered her mouth and said in a coarse whisper, "Oh, for godsake, she's worse than my mother."

The electronic buzzer sounded.

"Splendid. Splendid." In a fluid motion Mrs. Croft gathered her books and swept out of the room.

White closed her books and said, "There's something wrong with that woman, Yates. Definitely, something wrong."

11 a.m. Sociology. My last class of the morning ~ a fun class given by Father Malo. Dressed in the traditional black suit and white priest's collar, he would bounce into class, a thin, black spiral notebook under one arm. We all sprang to our feet, as we did whenever a lecturer or instructor entered the room ~ but we did it with a little more oomph for a priest.

"How are we all this morning?" He would say, rubbing his hands together. "Scintillating and salubrious? Yes? Good!"

Father talked about the norms of society and wrote notes on the board.

"To be or not to be, that is congestion. Can something be done about it? Of corpse, of corpse!" We laughed.

"Wouldn't that just jar your mother's preserves."

We laughed again, then the buzzer buzzed.

"This has been absolutely scintillating and salubrious. My sufficiency has been suffoncified. More would be obnoxious to my consumption," he said with a straight face, but always with a prankish glint in his eye.

"And be sure you know how to spell scintillating and salubrious," he added. "It will be on the exam." Then he picked up his black book and walked to the door, turned and waved, "Ciao."

We waved back and watched his bouncy walk disappear down the hall.

Sure enough, scintillating and salubrious were on the exam. I was surprised to find priests so human.

Ethel Robbins taught us how to play bridge. We spent our 10-minute class breaks pouring over our bridge cards. As we changed partners, we began to form friendships.

Robbins was a tall, voluptuous, platinum blond from Moose Jaw, Saskatchewan. Half her face was concealed by her long, Veronica Lake hairdo and she walked with more swing to her hips than any of us would dare to show. Robbins loved bridge. She was not only the most serious player on our floor but a sore loser. When she went down because of Perry's ill bidding, her eyes would narrow to slits, she'd flick ash from her cigarette, and then she'd explode.

Perry's cheeks would turn cherry-red and she'd say in a manner that led one to believe she was about to break into a laugh about the whole situation, "Oh, for gosh sakes, Robbins, don't take it so seriously. It's only a *game*." But the day finally arrived when Robbins refused to play with Perry or anyone else who wanted to play bridge just for fun, which pared her partners down to one ~ Riley.

Lilly Riley was a tailor-made partner for Robbins. She was pleasantly pudgy with jet black hair and a strawberry birthmark that covered a good part of the right side of her face. Polio had left Riley's right leg shorter than her left and she had to wear a wicked-looking heavy elevated boot that did not completely correct her limp. Yet with all this, she had developed a vivacious personality that overpowered her physical defects. Riley came from Cranbrook, British Columbia, but had lived most of her life in a children's hospital.

Even though it had been more than four years since Jonas Salk had discovered the vaccine to prevent polio, children's hospitals were still crowded with children who had contracted the disease before the vaccine was invented, and the children of parents who had refused to allow their children to be vaccinated.

That opposites attract may be why Robbins and Riley became constant companions ~ and permanent bridge partners.

12:00 Noon Lunch. Cafeteria. Last in line. The rule of bumping probies prevailed not only at breakfast, but lunch and supper as well. Now the steaming stainless steel was filled with overcooked brownish-green beans, sloppy mashed potatoes and very dried up roast beef. Dessert was yellow pudding with a thick scum on top and a dollop of the red, red strawberry jam in the center.

1:00 p.m. Etiquette. Mrs. Bass's class exceeded any form of education we had previously received from our mothers. She was no more than 4' 10" tall, even in her spiked heels, but what she lacked in inches she made up for in volubility.

"Panties changed every day, bras every two days, slips every three days," Mrs. Bass would expound, standing on her little box behind the podium. "And, girls, we must take a bath *every* day."

Mrs. Bass was our expert on femininity. Dressed in a baby-pink suit with purple trim, she smiled and said in her perky voice, "If you ever have a problem, girls, don't suffer, come and tell me. Why, one day a little student came to me in tears because she had hair on her legs. Well, Dearie, I said, that's not a problem at all. We have razors now. You can have silky, feminine legs like all the other girls."

She often held up her marriage to a doctor at Holy Cross as an example of a perfect marriage. "One little tip, girls. Never let your husband see you dressed sloppily. Now, when Dr. Bass leaves the house every morning at six o'clock, I've been up for an hour." She paused to finger the roses spilling over the wide brim of her mauve hat. "I've taken the curlers out of my hair, I'm dressed, my makeup is on, and I kiss Dr. Bass good bye at the door. *Every morning.* I wouldn't dare send him off to the hospital with the image of me in my curlers, only to greet you girls who are cheery, starched and wide-awake at 7:30, would I?

"One last thing, girls," she chirped. "Be sure to shave under your arms and wear deodorant. There is nothing worse for sick patients than to have a smelly nurse reach across their face."

There was no exam for this course.

2:00 p.m. Physiology, the function of cells, tissue and organs. *Dem bones* again. Mrs. Meers gave us each two beef bones ~ one sawed in half longitudinally, one horizontally ~ and a beef knuckle sawed in half, which we used in the lab to study the skeletal system. Next we had to dissect a beef eye to identify the cornea, lens, iris, conjunctiva, vitreous, vitreous chamber, sclera, optic disk and nerve, retina, and all the other specificities of the eye.

Then the fascinating sheep brain, which I had to handle very carefully, as it could be easily torn or broken. It was mind-boggling that this small mass of grey matter with just 16 structures which I identified on cross-section, could perform such vital and complicated functions. My brain defined who I was ~ and thankfully it was safely housed in my thick skull.

Finally, because pig's organs are similar in design and function to ours, we had to dissect fetal pigs. At first I was a little uneasy, but I soon became absorbed in the tiny pink, kidney bean-shaped unborn piglet. The mystery of my own body unfolded as I traced the minute blue veins that trickled through paper-thin, peritoneal tissue as delicate as a butterfly wing. And it had a perfect little pink snout.

It was Friday, the beginning of May and I had the weekend off. I sat in the lounge after work, glancing through the *Calgary Herald*: The Hudson Bay was having a sale of crinolines, Shop-Easy had bread, two loaves for 37 cents. "Hey, does anyone want to go to a movie?" I asked. "Gigi is playing at the Tivoli Theatre, not far from the Lotus Cafe."

Nobody took any notice of me, but White looked up from her coffee and said, "Got something to ask you, Yates. Want to hitch home with me?"

"Hitchhike? Are you crazy? My mother would kill me."

"Come on, Yates," pleaded White. "I haven't seen my father since he's been home from the hospital."

"What will I tell my parents?"

"Gad, you're such a chicken liver, Yates," snapped Niven. "Tell them White's uncle is going to drive you there and back. It's no sin to tell a little fib."

White was intently filing her nails but she looked anxious. For the out-of-town girls, hitchhiking was the only way to get a visit home. Her father had Raynaud's disease, which caused poor circulation in his hands and feet, and his right leg had just been amputated.

"Okay, okay," I said. I got up and reluctantly telephoned my mother. As I spoke my lie about White's uncle, I felt as though I had swallowed a rock.

I walked down to White's room. She'd begun to pack. "Okay, I'm going," I said, "but I want you to know I felt like a real grunge."

White's face relaxed. "Gee thanks, Yates ... really." She stuffed her babydolls into her suitcase, then looked me in the eye and gave a broad smile. "Aw, don't look so worried, you'll be okay. I'm very selective about the cars I get into."

The spring sun finally felt warm. White and I had our jackets tied around our waists by the time we opened the wooden door of her meagre home. The cozy aroma of freshly baked bread greeted us. Little squeaking noises came from a box on the floor beside the wooden stove where several newborn piglets were struggling to survive. The skinned carcass of a freshly killed deer lay on newspaper on the floor beside the table waiting to be cut up.

I followed White through a small dining area; she pulled back a blanket that hung for a door and we stepped down into the warm living room. Her father sat on the couch, crutches propped beside him, mourning his loss, his leg gone below the knee. He was a tall, ruggedly handsome man , cowboy handsome, actually, with strong features and a set jaw. Years of toil had etched deep furrows into his leathery face. He was a dominant difficult man, weakened by intemperance and adversity, barely able to eke a living from his small farm.

"Hi, Dad," said White. "Who got the deer?"

"I did. Same as always ... on ol' Blackie."

. "Dad, you shouldn't be riding that horse. How did you balance?"

Just then there was a bang from the front door.

"Go help your mother. The sow's farrowing."

I followed White back to the kitchen. Her mother rushed in carrying a piglet wrapped in a towel. She held its breathless body over the stove and began to blow down its throat with short quick puffs, desperate to kindle the small spark of life that might still be there. There was a gasp from the tiny snout. Mrs. White jiggled the little mass of pink skin in her palm and blew down its throat again. It sputtered, gave several laboured breaths and began to whimper in weak wheezy grunts. Then she gently placed the piglet in the box with the rest of the litter.

She could not afford to lose one. By the fall they would be mature enough to send to the auction to be slaughtered. That would bring extra money so the family could live a little easier during the cold winter months. They would keep one sow for their freezer. Still, it would not be enough. Mr. White would have to ride up into the back hills to hunt.

White's mother turned, her thin face drawn and pinched from the cold, her long blond hair hanging in limp curls. Though still young, the strain of her life was beginning to show. She pushed her hair from her face with her forearm, wiped her hands on her jeans, and embraced White in a tearful reunion.

It was late when White and I sat at the kitchen table eating the fresh hot-cross buns her mother had made before retiring.

"I remember how, after the pigs were auctioned, all the women would line up at the door of the Farm Board hoping to collect their cheques while their husbands were crowded in the beer parlour drinking with my father." White licked the icing from the bun. "But the Farm Board refused to give the cheques to the wives. They gave them only to the men. Isn't that ridiculous?" I nodded.

"From the time I was three," White continued, "my poor mother used to send me into the bar to beg my father to come home ... he would drink away all the money we made from the pigs." White poured herself another glass of milk. "My mother's such a strong woman," she said in a whisper. "I hope I can pay her back one day for all she's done for us kids."

After we got back to the residence that Sunday evening, I called my mother and told her about my weekend, about White's parents, whose very existence depended on whether the piglets lived or died, about White's father with one leg, forced to ride his horse and hunt wild animals all year to feed his family, and how the RCMP would look the other way when they saw him hunting out of season.

I didn't tell my mother about standing on a cold highway and climbing in and out of strangers' cars. That night I tossed and turned but I couldn't sleep. This was the first time I had ever seen such poverty. I finally fell asleep thinking of how grateful I was for my bourgeois upbringing, and for my parents who equally shared the ups and downs of married life.

3:00 p.m. Pharmacology: Drugs and Solutions. Miss Lynch, a dark-haired nurse with a bright, broad smile, taught pharmacology, the last class of the day. Many drugs didn't come in pills or vials, they came in packets of powder, which we had to dilute in sterile water. By using a formula of *desired* over *available*, we would work out the correct dosage for each patient.

Dr. Dory, an anaesthetist, came twice a week to recite in a monotone hypnotic voice the generic name of every drug, the trade name chosen by the manufacturer, the drug action, adverse reactions and the antidote, and I took notes.

The room was warm and the sweet smell of lilacs drifted in through the open windows. With my chin resting heavily in my palm and my eyes half open, I tried to concentrate on Dr. Dory. "Chlorpromazine ~ promachlor: uses schizophrenia, mania, dementia; side effects nausea ... Percodan ~ narcotic analgesic: oxycodone ... an opiate. Adverse effects when combined with anticholinergics ... Phenobarbital ~ belladona alkaloids, atropine, hyoscyamine, scopolamine ..." His da-da-da-dah monotone anaesthetized me. I'd watch Perry's pen leave a line on her page at the exact place that she slipped into dreamland.

A Cap and Real Patients

It was the end of June and it definitely felt almost like summer. Robins scurried about the grass outside our classroom window, pulling up worms for their young. Exams were upon us with Pharmacology the most difficult and important of the tests. If I failed Pharmacology I would fail the whole probie block, and risk immediate dismissal. I devoted every spare minute to study.

While we studied, the number of empty desks grew, adding poignant pressure to our efforts. Four girls just couldn't take it any more ~ the pressure of exams, the nuns, the difficult work in the hospital. Five students had been asked to withdraw, three because of their marks and two for no reason apparent to anyone except Sister. Now our class was reduced to 25.

As we doggedly memorized belladona alkaloids, the seniors prepared for graduation. They rushed past us to the sewing room for last minute adjustments on their all- white grad uniforms, to appointments with Mr. Lane, the photographer downtown, to the York for a beer to savour the last drop of precious time they had left together, and ~ the most painful to us probies ~ the intermediate and grad students dashed this way and that preparing for their final dance.

Feeling like oppressed Cinderellas, we crammed for Pharmacology while enviously watching their preparations, their dresses, their excitement. Soon the lure of the dance, a date and a chance to mingle with the senior students and instructors became an obsession. And so it was that when Judy Tanner flew into the lounge, her blue eyes flashing with excitement and said, "I have an idea how we can go to the dance." We all perked up. "We can take benzedrine when we get back and then study all night. We'll be fresh as a rose for the exam."

"If Sister finds out we'll all be expelled," I said with authority.

"Aw, cut the crap, Yates," Niven said roughly. "Everyone takes Benzedrine, don't you know that? It's absolutely safe. For godsake, it used to be kept in the health office right next to the aspirin. They dished it out to students who wanted to study all night." Niven paused. "But I don't think Mrs. Cherry has it any more ... wonder why?"

And so it was quickly settled. We would go to the dance, take the little wonder pill, study all night and be in tip-top shape for the exam the next morning. What could be simpler?

We girls from Calgary called up the old boyfriends who had long ago stopped calling us. Lester Brennan, my high school boyfriend, had joined the RCMP ten months before, and was stationed in Regina. He would be in town that weekend on a pass and would scrounge up enough boys to make blind dates for the out-of-town girls. Presto! A flawless collaboration.

Lester and his friends were waiting at the reception desk when White, Niven and I stepped off the elevator at seven o'clock. Lester eyed me up and down with an approving smile, then bent down and whispered in my ear, "Like your dress." I had borrowed the jade crêpe de Chine dress Mom had made for herself for Christmas. The dress had airy, gold leaves and a mandarin collar that gave it an Oriental look. "Very chic," Mom had said. Whereas it hung loosely on my mother's tiny frame, the dress touched the curves of my body. I felt good in it.

The dance was held in the residence, we headed down the stairs ~ boys were not allowed in the elevator. As we walked toward Waterloo Hall, our excitement rose when we heard ... *Chantilly Lace, with the pretty face ...*

But our spirits soured a few minutes later as we realized: This was not our dance, it was theirs.

Lester and his Mountie friends stuck out like sore thumbs in crew cuts while the other guys constantly preened their Brylcreemed ducktails. We listened to the boys' corny stories about life in the Mounties barracks. And as we sipped bland Cokes, the intermediates and seniors slid from bubbly to silly-high on their forbidden bottles concealed under the tables in brown paper bags.

"Why didn't *someone* tell us to bring a mickey of rum?" Niven complained. *Splish splash I was takin' a bath / Round about a Saturday night* ... "Hey, Donna, let's dance," Lester said, jumping up. Lester was a really good jiver and we danced a few. Bobby Darin was really hot ... *A-well-a, I forgot about the bath / I went and put my dancin' shoes on* ... But the dance floor was terribly crowded, and I felt like I was getting in the way of the seniors, so we sat down again.

Our stark evening slowly dragged on ... and on ...

"And now for all you Donnas out there," the DJ shouted. "Here's your song!"

Everyone gasped. It was Ritchie Valens, the last song he'd recorded before the Iowa plane crash that killed him only a few weeks before. *I had a girl / Donna was her name / Since she left me / I've never been the same / 'Cause I love my girl / Donna, where can you be?*...

"So tragic, I can't bear to listen," Perry said. "They're all gone ... Buddy Holly, Ritchie Valens, 'The Big Bopper' ... I wish they would play 'Chantilly Lace' again ... I loved 'The Big Bopper.'"

I nervously checked my watch ~ 11:15. The dance would end at 11:30. The test would begin in a little more than eight hours.

The home waltz began to play, The Platters ... *They asked me how I knew / Our true love was true-ooooo-ooo-ooo* ... Lester was tall and I lay my head against his chest ~ I didn't quite reach his shoulder. His jacket smelled of warm wool, perspiration and Old Spice. I pressed my face to his lapel and breathed in deeply. Would we have time to go somewhere and park? After all, I had all night to study ... *I of course replied / When a lovely flame dies / Smoke gets in your eyes....* We all swayed to the music on the tiny square of dance floor ~ steamy, moist bodies jammed together like a mass of dying sardines.

At 11:35 when the dance was over, Lester and Clifford, White's date, ran to get the car. White and I got swept up in the stampede of students galloping out the front door and leaping into cars that raced around the horseshoe drive and out into the night. Lester drove down to the Elbow River, The Holy's favourite parking place, and joined the pack of cars. He parked under a low hanging willow swaying in the soft night breeze.

Wow, Lester certainly was a good necker and his wool jacket heated quickly from his hot, sweaty body. Moist wool and Old Spice ~ it set me on fire. I was getting ready to go up in flames when my eye caught the glow of my nurse's watch ~ 11:57. I gasped. "Hey, White, we've got to go. It's almost midnight!"

"Oh, God, you nurses," Clifford groaned from the back seat.

The moment the car stopped in front of our residence, White and I jumped out. Rumour had it that Sister Superior sat in one of the dark hospital rooms with binoculars, counting the minutes. If we sat in a parked car for more than two minutes, she'd report us to Sister Leclerc.

34

By 12:15, I had thrown my yellow duster over my pajamas and skipped down the hall to join the other girls only to discover there would be no magic pill. Our supply person had discovered benzedrine was now a controlled substance.

"Holy shit," Perry said in a panic. "What do we do now?"

Stunned by the news, we sat in silence. White began pacing back and forth. Finally she said, "Well girls, put the kettle on ~ it's going to be non-stop coffee tonight." Then she chuckled as if it was a big joke, and I tried to smile.

Throughout the long night, we drank coffee, double and triple spoons per cup ~ and took turns asking each other questions.

"Okay, White," I said, "give me the name of a barbiturate."

"Pentobarbital," she said, sleepily.

"Cor-rect," I said, "Perry. What's the trade name?"

"Shit, Perry's asleep," Niven said. "Give her a poke, Porter. And cut the crap about sleeping pills, Yates. Ask some questions about stimulants like caffeine ~ stuff like that."

At seven I took a bath and dressed in my class uniform. The caffeine had worn off and I felt like a zombie. But I stuck to our strategy and took a brisk walk down to the Elbow River with the other girls. The air was fresh, and in the early morning stillness, the soft gurgling of the water rushing over riverbed stones was soothing. Suddenly a little terrier raced down the opposite bank, barking excitedly. His owner obliged and threw a twig into the river. A black and white blur plunged into the clear, mountain water and retrieved the stick.

As we walked back to the residence, the nauseous aroma of brewing coffee wafted from kitchen windows. But the fresh air had sent a trickle of energy through my weakened body and at eight o'clock I entered the classroom with my fingers crossed and a prayer on my lips.

The girls who had slept all night looked as frightfully efficient as the girls in Miss McNabb's grade three class had looked on test day. Miss McNabb would smile and sit them on the piano and talk sweetly to them. The only time Miss McNabb smiled at me was when she handed back test papers ~ from best and first to last and worst. My face would feel hot and flushed, my hands sweaty and shaking, my heart throbbing in my throat, waiting for her to call my name. That's when she would smile and say, *"And of course, Donna is last."*

To a chorus of class snickers, I'd slide out of my desk and slink to the front of the room to get my paper from her outstretched hand. Oh, how I wished the floor would open wide and swallow me up.

As I slid into my desk next to White, she gasped. "Yates, my God, don't look so scared. You can do it." She winked. "Take a deep breath and relax. We know all this stuff." I took a deep breath and began.

While we waited for the results of our tests, we began two weeks of clinical exams. For two hours each day I would be on the ward to be tested on the procedures I had learned in class. Mrs. Chase had been returned to the storage cupboard. Now I would have real live patients. My heart skipped a beat, just thinking about it.

My hands trembled as I carried my tray of thermometers. They made a sort of Jingle Bells rhythm as I walked down the hall to my first patient's room.

"Under your tongue, Mrs. John," I said, trying to sound confident as my trembling hands slid a thermometer into her mouth. I reached for her arm to take her pulse ~ but there was no pulse. I moved my fingers up and down and around her wrist. I could feel nothing. I quickly switched my focus to her face. She was smiling. She exhibited none of the routine symptoms of death, but maybe she was *about* to die. My upper lip broke into a sweat. I glanced up at Mrs. Whitford, hoping for a hint. Have you noticed that she's dying? I wanted to ask as I groped about Mrs. John's other wrist, praying for a pulse.

Finally Mrs. Whitford rescued me. "Let's see, Miss Yates." She put her hand on Mrs. John's wrist. "Sometimes it is hard to palpate. Ah, here it is."

I placed my finger on the spot, trying to steady my shaking hands. "I feel it."

My patient gave me a motherly grin ... and I tried to smile.

Monday afternoon at five o'clock we were sitting in the lounge having a cup of coffee. I was flipping through my nursing arts procedure book. Robbins and Riley had continued the bridge game they'd begun during lunch hour with Porter and White. Perry was reading out loud, her rulebook, " ... *Open and close doors noiselessly and avoid loud chattering in corridors, utility rooms and Nurses' Unit.*"

As though on cue, Lucy Hawkins silently appeared and calmly said, "Well girls, the results are up for Pharmacology." She began to slowly pull out a paper from under her bib. "I have the results here."

An ominous pause filled the room. We stared blankly at her. My heart began to pound ... *And, of course, Donna is last ...*

"I *borrowed* the results sheet," Hawkins said.

Tanner shot out of her chair like an arrow. White grinned extravagantly and said, "Hawkins, you beautiful little snitch." We fell into a huddle around Hawkins.

Wedged among my classmates, my face flushed warm, my heart thumped wildly in my chest. My eyes dropped to the last name on the list ... it wasn't me, thank God. I slowly moved up the column of names and marks. I was half way up; I must have missed my name. I began at the bottom again. By now the others had moved away, chattering loudly about their marks. Only I remained.

"For gosh sakes, Yates!" Hawkins said. "What's the hold-up? I've got to get this back on the board, pronto."

"Wait ... wait ... " I breathed. "Just one more minute." I began again at the bottom, slowly moving up the list, line by line ... up ... up ... up ... then, YATES. I suddenly felt faint. It might be a mistake....

"Way to go, Yates," White said, slapping me on the back. "Told you, you could do it."

I smiled at White and gave a weak shrug. It must be true. I turned abruptly and ran to the phone on the wall, to call my mother.

The others were jumping up and down, bumping into each other and screaming, "We passed! We passed!"

"Mom," I shouted over the pandemonium. "I'm third from the top in Pharmacology!"

"Oh, Donna, I always knew you could do it! I'm so proud...."

"Shut up, you damn probies. Shut up!" A senior stood at the door of the lounge. Her face was white with cold cream, her hair in bright orange rollers. Her words hit us like darts, and we stood pinned to the floor.

"Don't you have any consideration? I have a red tag on my door ~ I'm working nights!" She wore a green shirt from the operating room, the trademark of a senior's wardrobe. By the third year, their pajamas had worn out.

We all stood perfectly still. "I'll call you back, Mom," I whispered into the phone, and quietly hung up.

"God damn it, you woke me up. I have to work tonight." Then the senior turned on her exasperation and paddled back to her room, muttering. "You spoiled rotten brats ... no consideration ... wait 'til you get on nights...."

We tiptoed back to our chairs, stifling the giggles that kept bubbling up. Niven raised her hand for silence.

"This calls for a celebration," she said, making a poor effort at trying to be quiet. "Let's hit the York!"

"Groovy," Tanner said, her lips curled, a cigarette clenched in her teeth.

"Settled," said Niven. "We'll meet here in five minutes." She turned and step-hip-nudged back to her room.

I rushed down the hall to Kaufmann's room.

"Want to come to the York with us?" I asked.

She looked up from her New Testament and squinted at me through her thick, black-rimmed glasses. Then she shook her head.

"You don't have to drink beer, Kaufmann. Just come and celebrate with us."

"Nooo," she said tucking her chin to her chest.

"Move it, Yates!" White shouted from the elevator. "We're leaving."

The York was a dingy old hotel on the east side of Calgary, the favourite watering hole for Holy Cross students. We sat in the smoke-filled tavern, pooled our money and ordered a round ~ two frosty glasses of beer each and two glasses of tomato juice for me. I wouldn't be legal for another two years.

"Geez, Yates," Perry said, with a nervous laugh, "I hope we don't get caught, being under 21 and all."

"Oh, Perry, don't be silly." Tanner said, clenching an unlit cigarette between her teeth. "They're used to student nurses coming and going here. They won't ask you guys for ID. Anybody got a match?"

Perry gave her a light. Tanner took a puff, slowly letting the smoke out in a perfect ring. She curled her lips and clenched the cigarette in her teeth again.

"Well, what would you think if you couldn't get a pulse?" I asked the girls. "No pulse means dead, right?" Everyone nodded. "But there she was, breathing ... and smiling at me. I wondered how long it would take for her to keel over, because with no pulse, her heart must have stopped."

"But good ol' Mrs. Whitford saved Yates' day," White said, slapping me on the back.

Perry raised her glass. "To our instructors."

White stood up: "To all of us! We're now *officially* nurses in training at Holy Cross. I sure as hell hope they're ready for us."

We giggled and drank up.

Capping marked the beginning of my life as a real nurse, a life in which there was no tolerance for errors, oversights or misbehaviour. One more girl dropped out. We had lost 12. The 24 that remained would receive our caps.

The capping ceremony took place in the magnificent hospital chapel. As we entered, the impressive 15-foot marble altar, carved from many tons of Italian Carrara marble, held my attention. An aroma of incense filled the air. The pathos of the crucifix reached out before us, a reminder that no one is exempt from suffering, and in one corner candles flickered in little red glass containers for those who were gone, but not forgotten.

Wearing white skullcaps and our navy melton capes, with gold H✝H emblazoned on the collar and a splash of red lining over our right shoulder, we entered the chapel. Two by two, we proceeded down the aisle, each carrying a small ceramic lamp with an unlit candle in its spout. Sunshine streamed in through the stained glass windows, crowning family and friends, instructors and nuns in a rainbow of colours. From an elm outside an open window, a robin's song filled the air.

My mother, father and my brother, Allan, had turned to watch our procession and smiled proudly as I walked by. Lester, my Mountie boyfriend, had flown in from Regina and now sat beside Allan. I smiled at Mom. Her bright blue eyes were tearing and I knew she was living in this moment with me. We passed our stoic nuns and devoted housemothers and moved toward the altar.

Father Flanagan stood near the altar, waiting to welcome us. He was a tall priest with russet hair and a perpetual smile on his round, boyish face. He was hospital chaplain, spiritual leader, and friend to all. Despite the boyish grin, he was regal looking in his impressive green and gold robe. He waited as we settled in the first two rows, then he spoke.

"Today marks a turning point in your young lives. The road you have chosen to walk is not easy. There will be days when you will question your calling. But if you truly aspire to ease pain and suffering, then God will give you strength. For your duty is not only to your patient and God, but also to yourself. With these ideals that have been diligently forged by the dedication of those gone before you, foremost in your mind, then dignity, grace and respect will be with you."

I believed this with every bit of my being.

Then we walked solemnly past Father. He whispered a prayer as Mrs. Meeres, our anatomy and physiology instructor, placed the winged cap of Holy Cross Hospital on my head.

The Virgin Mary stood on the left of the altar looking serene and compassionate. To the right was a smaller statue of Mother d'Youville, founder of the Sisters of Charity, in the habit of the Grey Nuns. Her soft eyes gazed at me, and I suddenly felt gratitude for this eminent woman without whom, there would never have been a Holy Cross Hospital. The cap on my head felt like a feather and goose bumps shivered up the back of my neck. Then the senior nurse beside Mrs. Meeres lit each of our lamps from the large candle she held. Our little lamps blazed with earnest expectations as we recited the Nightingale Pledge.

I SOLEMNLY PLEDGE MYSELF BEFORE GOD AND IN THE PRESENCE OF THIS ASSEMBLY TO PASS MY LIFE IN PURITY AND TO PRACTICE MY PROFESSION FAITHFULLY. I WILL ABSTAIN FROM WHATEVER IS DELETERIOUS AND MISCHIEVOUS AND WILL NOT TAKE OR KNOWINGLY ADMINISTER ANY HARMFUL DRUG. I WILL DO ALL IN MY POWER TO ELEVATE THE STANDARD OF MY PROFESSION, AND WILL HOLD IN CONFIDENCE ALL PERSONAL MATTERS COMMITTED TO MY KEEPING, AND ALL FAMILY AFFAIRS COMING TO MY KNOWLEDGE IN THE PRACTICE OF MY CALLING. WITH LOYALTY WILL I ENDEAVOUR TO AID THE PHYSICIAN IN HIS WORK AND DEVOTE MYSELF TO THE WELFARE OF THOSE COMMITTED TO MY CARE.

I wholly embraced the pledge. Father raised his arms for the benediction and we bowed our heads.

"God, grant these women strength, compassion and humility as they daily face the joy and pain, life and death of those committed to their care. And may they carry out their daily duties with the dignity and grace befitting a Holy Cross nurse." Father then raised his head, and stretched his arms toward us. "To you young nurses, wear your cap proudly. It is the symbol of caring. And carry your lamp high."

We walked out of the chapel two by two, now full-fledged student nurses. Following the ceremony, Sister invited our families to the residence for tea. My mother poked me as I was about to pick up a chocolate chip cookie, the first I had seen since entering training.

"Look at that poor dear," she said tilting her head toward Kaufmann. "Isn't she the one we saw on your first day with all those bags of clothes?"

I nodded. "The nun beside Kaufmann is her sister from Saskatoon. Kaufmann's mother lives somewhere in northern Saskatchewan. She's too ill to travel."

"You'll have to bring her home for supper one Sunday," Mom said, sipping her tea. "She must get very lonely." She slipped her arm around my waist. "Well, my little girl, you've made the first step," she said. "Keep that picture of the nurse in your mind. I know you'll make it all the way."

"I will, Mom."

After five months at Holy Cross, I was now a junior. I would be working an eight-hour shift six days a week with real patients in the real hospital.

Butterflies danced a jig in my body as I dressed in my uniform. The blue-and-white striped dress and apron were easy, but I had a dreadful time with the bib and the collar which were so starched they could stand by themselves. Each time I thought I had myself securely pinned together, either the collar would pop or the straps from my bib, which were supposed to cross over my back, would come undone and flip over my head. I dashed next door to Perry for help, and found her tangled in her bib straps. We pinned each other, then I dashed back to my room and stepped into my white, cushioned Clinic shoes with two-inch-wide heels, "old lady shoes," I had complained to my mother. But the salesman had said, "I'll personally guarantee that your daughter's arches will never fall." So now I laced up the old lady shoes and darted out of my room, almost colliding with Perry, who, I was pleased to see, also wore Clinic shoes.

Perry stood in the elevator like a zombie, biting her nails. "Geez, Yates, I can't remember a thing," she mumbled.

"Don't worry," I said. "I'm sure you'll get nice patients."

Mrs. Whitford escorted our class through the tunnel that snaked its way to the hospital. What a delightful swishing sound we made in our starched aprons as we walked. So this was what it was like to be a nurse!

Though it was a bright, hot July day, the tunnel was cool and dim. A heavy, grey, cloth-like insulation covered the walls and the low ceiling was dotted with weary light bulbs that hung naked from their sockets. We marched silently in starch and sobriety. My chest heaved with timid curiosity. My knees felt weak, and my heart pounded in my ears. I wished my mother could be here to see me in my uniform and share my first day as a nurse.

I glanced at Perry; she looked like she might faint. "Perry," I whispered, "you're going to be okay. Just relax!"

Kaufmann hugged the wall by herself, rubbing her shoulder against the grey insulation, head tucked to her chest.

White was deep in her own thoughts, staring straight ahead, looking quite sure of herself. She walked beside Niven, who wore her look of nonchalance like an armour and did her step-nudge walk of indifference.

After breakfast, when I recited our prayer, I thought: This is not for class, this is for real ... *Each task I offer with the sincere hope that it is prompted by my love for Thee. I shall not shirk any duty however unpleasant....*

After prayer, we filed past Sister, wearing our caps proudly on our heads for the first time. I couldn't stop smiling. Everyone passed Sister's inspection except Robbins, the voluptuous redhead. Sister sent her to the bathroom to remove her bright orange lipstick. Riley limped behind her like a little puppet ~ big Robbins and small Riley.

Perry and I ascended the magnificent staircase, the center of the lustrous marble steps worn to a dull depression by doctors and nurses long before me. Suddenly I became aware of a distinct odour: a combination of alcohol and ether, of steam kettles, compress carts, and autoclaves. This was the antiseptic odour I had been seeking! The aura of the hospital. I found it intoxicating, enchanting. It embraced me like a loving mother and carried me to its soul.

Perry and I found the nursing station on St. John's, a women's medical ward on the second floor. I had been waiting five long months to stand behind the nurse's station and what a peculiar feeling it was as I peered out at a maintenance man across the hall. He was looking back at me as if I were a nurse. A framed motto hung on the wall in three places: *The Patient's Record Is a Sacred Trust*.

Now that I had my cap and was responsible for my patients, I would give injections unsupervised. My knees shook as Perry and I stood with the day staff, listening to the report from the night nurse. After a brief orientation to the ward by Miss Horne, the clinical instructor, Perry and I marched off to our patients.

Full of energy and enthusiasm I bustled into Mrs. Bud's tiny single room but almost gasped out loud when I saw her. Her skin was mottled with messy sores and her mousy brown hair sprouted in every direction. Two stumps protruded over the bed where her legs should have been and the room was in shambles, strewn with newspapers, orange peels and cigarette butts. She sat slouched over the side of the bed, her elbow propped on her arm, her face in a cloud of smoke that rose from the cigarette held between fingers dark yellow with cigarette stain. Her dull watery eyes stared straight ahead with a look of surly indifference.

Both her legs had been amputated at the knee many years before as a result of overeating, smoking and neglect in caring for her skin. Mrs. Bud was a diabetic who had never heeded the warnings from her doctors about the complications from uncontrolled diabetes. Because diabetics had poor circulation they had to prevent the skin from becoming dry and cracked, which would lead to infection, and in many cases, amputation.

"Good morning, Mrs. Bud," I said bravely. "I have your insulin injection."

She didn't move, and after several seconds I thought she was probably fed up with injections and I should just get it done without chattering. So I stepped over the garbage on the floor and gave the injection in her arm ~ perfectly. When she still didn't react, I filled a basin with warm water and left her to bathe.

When I returned some time later, the basin of water was untouched. She sat in the same position as before, smoking another cigarette. I noticed a vacant look to her murky eyes. I picked up the washcloth to help her bathe, but with one swoop of her hand she knocked the cloth from my grip.

"NO!" she shouted.

My mind flashed to Mrs. Whitford's lecture about the cantankerous patient ~ ~ the little old woman who worried about her cat. This woman looked deranged. Her

"No," sounded definite, so I quickly threw out the wash water, made a brief effort to pick up the litter on the floor and left. All the while, Mrs. Bud quietly watched me, never breaking the rhythm of puffing on the cigarette butt pinched between her thumb and forefinger.

My other patient, Mrs. Morrison, was friendly, though she couldn't talk much because she had suffered a stroke two days before and was quite drowsy. Her right side was paralysed and though her speech had not been directly affected, she seemed too exhausted to talk. As I finished bathing Mrs. Morrison, Perry poked her head around the curtains.

"Hey, Yates," she said, softly. "Can you help me with my patient?"

"Sure."

"She's got diarrhea."

Perry's patient was an enormous woman who had suffered a stroke a week before and was still unconscious. The odour was ghastly as we heaved and shoved and cleaned this poor woman over and over again.

All morning long we trotted back and forth to the hopper room with bundles of dirty linen and the unsavoury bedpan. Then late in the morning, Perry ran into trouble at the bedpan sterilizer that sat in the wall, at chest-level, beside the hopper. She called to me as I was stuffing another round of smelly linen into the hamper.

"Hey, Yates, can you help me? The sterilizer doesn't work."

I gave the floor pedal several bangs, then suddenly it kicked into gear just as Perry's hand reached the handle and opened the door. I lunged to slam the door shut again, but it was too late.

"Oh, my God, Perry ... " I whispered. She was dripping in brown flush. Then my heart began to pound when I thought of hepatitis, or some other disease even more deadly that we hadn't even learned about yet.

I didn't mention this to Perry, she was frightened enough, but I used a whole bottle of rubbing alcohol to decontaminate her.

"Geez, you think this will kill all the germs?" Perry asked.

"Oh, yeah," I said, trying to sound positive, as I dried her hair.

As the morning progressed, Perry took on a frayed appearance. Her hair had lost its puffy look after the bedpan flush, it drooped from under her cap and she'd turned very pale. Just as we both were tucking her large patient into a fresh bed for the umpteenth time, Miss Horne appeared at the door and told us to go and eat.

"When you come back, it will be time to pass out the lunch trays." She said with a gratuitous smile. "Have a nice meal."

It was Wednesday, beef stew day. The soft meat was almost purée and the thin juice trickled in all directions over my plate. I had to swallow hard as it oozed into the mashed potatoes.

"It smells funny," I finally said.

"Mine too," Perry said. "I really can't eat it."

We ran to our rooms to change our uniforms We couldn't be sure if the splotches were beef stew or not. Perry quickly washed her hair in the sink and pinned it up under her cap.

When we arrived back on the ward, it was time to pass out the lunch trays, which I was now able to balance proficiently on my right shoulder ~ an accomplishment of which I was very proud. But all afternoon, each time I went into the hall, there was Perry, in search of me. Once I tried to hide from her by squeezing myself behind the linen closet door, but I couldn't stand to watch her pitiful search for me up and down the hall and finally gave myself up. I ended the first day of the rest of my life feeling triumphant that I hadn't made any major mistakes and very sad for my sick patients.

The next morning, Miss Horne gave me a third patient. Mrs. Mack was 82 years old, and unconscious. She had suffered a stroke.

She seemed to be asleep but my eyes were drawn to her chest. It moved up and down, up and down, and then it stopped. I blinked. I stopped breathing. I must be wrong, I thought ~ she can't be dead. Then her chest moved again, she definitely was breathing. I took in a deep breath and felt myself relax, but again her breathing stopped.... Was she dead? I couldn't be sure of anything. Every hair on my back and scalp prickled. I turned and desperately pawed at the curtains.
I couldn't find the opening.

After several frantic moments I finally broke out and bolted for the door. I rushed down the hall toward the stairs with only one thought in my mind: Leave the hospital. Get out! Get away from this dead woman.

"Miss Yates."

I turned. Miss Horne stood at the door of Mrs. Mack's room. I kept going.
"Miss Yates!"

I stopped at the stairs and waited breathlessly as she rushed toward me.

"Where are you going? What's the matter?"

"It's Mrs. Mack. She's dead," I said. "I can't look at her. I can't be a nurse."

"I don't think she's dead, Miss Yates. Come back with me and we'll take a look."

"I don't want to look at her," I said in a forced whisper. "I just can't do it."

"Okay, then *I'll* look at her. Just come back with me."

We walked back to the room and I waited as Miss Horne separated the curtains and peered in. She turned and smiled and motioned for me to come over.

I walked stiffly to the foot of the bed. "The patient has Cheyne-Stokes respirations," Miss Horne said. "Do you remember what that is?"

"Yes, when the patient stops breathing for a few minutes and starts again. But she had really stopped, Miss Horne. She wasn't breathing at all."

"It's normal to have 10 to 20 seconds of apnea before carbon dioxide builds up in the body and the patient begins to breathe again," Miss Horne said.

So I gave Mrs. Mack her bath, and each time she stopped breathing, I told myself, *she will breathe again. She will.* But I left the curtain open a safe distance behind me for a quick get-away.

After lunch, I dashed to the residence to read about Cheyne-Stokes respiration in my Webster's Medical Dictionary. It said:

JOHN CHEYNE, SCOTTISH PHYSICIAN, 1777, WILLIAM STOKES, IRISH PHYSICIAN, 1804. AN ABNORMAL PATTERN OF RESPIRATION, CHARACTERIZED BY ALTERNATING PERIODS OF APNEA AND DEEP, RAPID BREATHING. THE RESPIRATORY CYCLE BEGINS WITH SLOW, SHALLOW BREATHS THAT GRADUALLY INCREASE TO ABNORMAL DEPTH AND RAPIDITY. RESPIRATION GRADUALLY SUBSIDES AS BREATHING SLOWS, AND BECOMES SHALLOWER, CLIMAXING IN A 10 TO 20 SECOND PERIOD WITHOUT RESPIRATION BEFORE THE CYCLE IS REPEATED.

Well I *knew* that. Why hadn't I remembered?

Over the next two weeks Mrs. Morrison improved dramatically from her stroke. One morning, she became indignant about using the bedpan. I wheeled her into the bathroom, but she refused to use the commode over the toilet.

"I don't want to sit on that awful thing," she said. "Please, help me onto the toilet."

I finally gave in and with much difficulty hauled her up on to the toilet. Then Mrs. Morrison begged me to leave her alone. The rulebook said: ... *Never leave children, or weak or irresponsible patients alone ...* But Mrs. Morrison's pleas were pitiful, and I found it difficult to say "no," especially to an adult.

Check patient frequently and remain within calling distance ... "Don't lock the door," I said as I leaned against the sink to await her call. After several quiet minutes, I began to worry. "Are you okay, Mrs. Morrison?"

I heard a muffled grunt. I waited, not wanting to embarrass her by opening the door, I bent down to have a look under it. My heart wrenched when I met Mrs. Morrison's eyes. She was looking back at me ~ upside-down! She had tipped over sideways.

"Oh, my God," I breathed as I lunged for the door. But I couldn't get it open. When Mrs. Morrison toppled over, her feet rose and were now jammed against the door. This was not in the procedure book.

"Don't move, Mrs. Morrison," I shouted, trying to sound calm. I bent down again. Yes, she was still there. I had two choices ~ go over or under. I crawled under the door.

"Oh, poor Mrs. Morrison." I struggled to get her upright. "Are you okay?"

"Yes," she gasped. "I'm fine."

I waited until the purple colour faded from her face.

Later, when I told Miss Horne about the incident, she said, "But you're the nurse, Miss Yates. You're the one who must make judgments for your patients. Mrs. Morrison is a sick woman, and at the moment, is not able to think as a well person. Her reasoning powers are affected by the stroke. You must remember that."

"Yes," I whispered. "I will never forget it."

Disobedience

August, one month after capping. I began to lust after patients with more complicated illnesses, eager to experience the entirety of nursing in one fell swoop.

Miss Quick was in her mid-50s, suffering from advanced multiple sclerosis. She had developed severe complications due to lack of proper medical treatment during the three years she had been confined to bed at home. As a devoted Christian Scientist, she believed that faith alone would heal her. It didn't.

I was allowed to feed Miss Quick lunch. I looked forward to my daily visit with her. "Oh, here's my little student," she would say cheerfully with a big smile, as I carried in her tray on my shoulder. "You are such a kind nurse to stand here and feed me, especially when I take so long to eat. And you never complain."

"Why would I complain?" I asked, glancing down at the frozen tangle of her arms. They were twisted like a rope with two knots of bony fists under her chin. She couldn't move, not a muscle.

I spooned a small portion of pureed mush into her mouth, and even that she had difficulty swallowing. After she did, she sipped a drop of milk from the straw in the glass I held, looked lovingly up at me and smiled. "You are so, so good to me, Miss Yates" she said. "God will be good to you, too."

I smiled back and wondered: What could she be like under those covers? I knew her condition was so severe that only senior students and graduate nurses were allowed to nurse her. But how bad, was severe? Up to now my only reference was skinned knees of childhood and five months of classroom study.

When I asked Miss Horne, my clinical nurse, she answered softly. "Unfortunately, Miss Quick remained at home too long. Her sister tried to nurse her but she didn't turn Miss Quick often enough to prevent pressure sores from developing over her bony areas. Now Miss Quick has decubitous ulcers (bedsores) on her hips, her ankles and shoulders. They had reached grade IV by the time she was admitted to hospital and that's the final stage. That means that the skin and subcutaneous tissue beneath the skin is destroyed and the connective tissue, muscle and bone are exposed."

Now I really wanted to look beneath Miss Quick's covers.

One afternoon I cornered her senior nurse, Dooley, in the treatment room as she gathered the sterile bundles needed to change Miss Quick's dressings.

"May I come and watch you change her dressing?" I asked.

"I don't think you should, Yates," she said gently. "It's pretty gruesome. You're only a junior. You might not be able to handle it."

"Yeah, I know it's gruesome, but I'll be fine. Really I will." We stood and stared at each other for a few moments until she finally gave in.

"Okay, here." She handed me two cloth masks. "Put both of these on your face. The smell is unbearable."

I followed Dooley to the room and bravely helped remove Miss Quick's covers. Her arms and legs were rigid ~ folded and twisted and fixed in the fetal position, interwoven like a wicker basket. I couldn't tell where one leg began and the other one ended. My sweet, smiling, gentle Miss Quick was an inextricable frozen tangle of arms and legs. Behind the drawn curtains, I watched Dooley remove the dressing from Miss Quick's hip. My mask hid the reaction that must have appeared on my face, but my eyes were exposed and grimly fixed on the horrible sight ~ a cavernous hole in Miss Quick's hip that was filled with purulent, putrid fluid, from which her large hipbone was protruding.

I fought back nausea as the smell of warm, rotting flesh oozed into every inch of our secluded enclosure. Miss Quick's eyes were now closed. She began to whimper like a beaten puppy as Dooley pulled out reams of fetid, gauze packing from deep around her hipbone. A knot swelled in my middle. It circled my stomach, squeezing tighter and tighter with each beat of my heart. Before me was a blur of arms and legs, pus and bone, moans and stifled cries of pain. Suddenly I could stand there no longer. I frantically groped for the opening in the curtains, dashed across the hall to the hopper room and threw up in the huge toilet.

Miss Horne, as usual, silently appeared from nowhere. "There are many sad and difficult duties we must perform as nurses," she said soothingly as she held my head over the hopper.

"But I can't do it, Miss Horne." I sobbed. "I can never be a nurse."

"Yes, you can ... and you will. You will be a good nurse one day."

"No, no, I can't!" I cried. "I'll never be able to do what Dooley is doing."

"I used to feel the same way myself when I was a junior. But in time, I learned to cope with unpleasant tasks, as we've all learned to do. This is our job."

"But how could Miss Quick end up like this?" I blubbered, as I blew my nose. "How could anybody let her go so long? That's inhumane."

"We must not judge others, Miss Yates. Our job is to care for the patient no matter what their problem. God knows, it's not always easy." She waved her arm toward Miss Quick's room. "Look at Dooley." I could see Dooley's white legs and shoes below the closed curtains. "I'm sure this bothers her, too, but someone has to help this poor woman. And that someone is a nurse, Miss Yates."

Miss Horne gently took my arm and helped me to my feet. I followed her numbly into the little kitchen next to the medication room. She gave me a glass of lemonade, and I went back to work.

Still shaken from the shock of Miss Quick's hip I couldn't go to the cafeteria for supper that night. I could still smell that pungent odour. I could taste it in the knot in my stomach.

"Come on, Yates," White said, giving me a gentle slap on the back. "Let's get you out of here. We're going to the Lotus. My treat."

White and I sat in the black vinyl booth at the back, where it was quiet. I had a toasted butterhorn ~ a Calgarian Danish pastry ~ and a Coke and we played Elvis records. It was only a nickel a play. I guess the Lotus felt sorry for us. It was a dime everywhere else.

The main Wurlitzer, just inside the door, played the records, but each booth had its own small machine mounted on the wall above the salt, pepper, ketchup and vinegar. Elvis had such a sexy voice the way he slurred his notes. I dropped another nickel in and pushed number five, again, Love Me Tender, his top hit of 1956. The first time I saw Elvis was in September, 1956, at my girlfriend, Sandy's house. Neighbourhood teenagers crowded in to see "Elvis the pelvis" on the Ed Sullivan Show. They showed him only from the waist-up ~ what could he possibly be doing down there? He hardly smiled, just curled his lip and tossed his shock of black hair forward over his eyes, his fingers chording the strings of half a guitar. And when he gave that wounded expression everyone screamed and some girls in the audience fainted.

Now, that September night seemed so far away. While I had been watching Elvis, Miss Quick was out there somewhere, shrivelling up into a twisted heap of unusable parts. My world had been Elvis and dances and Sandy. Now I lived in a world of suffering and rules and discipline. I didn't want to grow up, not yet.

That night when I called my mother, I was on the verge of tears. "I don't know if I can be a nurse, Mom, I really don't."

"Listen, dear," she said soothingly, "Sister Leclerc will ease you into difficult situations gently and gradually prepare you to be a good nurse. You're in good hands ... they know what to do. Just trust them. There are many people who need you, dear." She gave a little sigh. "Now go to bed, and don't worry, you'll feel better in the morning."

My mother was right.

The next morning brought forth in me a deeper commitment to nursing. In the cafeteria, I felt Sister's eyes inspecting my back as I closed my eyes and recited our prayer: *I shall not shirk any duty however unpleasant. When I cool the fevered brow, moisten the parched lips, or comfort the aching body I shall remember that I bring comfort to Thee ...*

I marched back to St. John's ward after prayer: ... *I shall not shirk any duty, however unpleasant ...*

I didn't volunteer for any more dressing changes, but Miss Horne did compliment me on my patient report on Mrs. Morrison.

At the end of the day, I rushed back to the residence, anxious to tell my mother about my renewed confidence. But when I stopped to check my mail, I found a note in my mailbox. *Miss Yates, see Sister Leclerc immediately.* I felt a nauseous knot in my stomach again.

That's it. I'm going to be expelled because I threw up in the hopper.

As I walked around the corner to Sister's office, my mind whirled. Clutching the note in my shaking hand, I knocked on Sister's door.

"Come in," she said curtly.

I opened the door.

"Hello, Sister, you wanted to see me?" I said trying to sound cheerful ... and humble at the same time.

Sister was not smiling and her icy blue eyes looked straight through me.

"Miss Yates, I have a really serious matter to discuss with you."

"Yes, Sister."

"Nurses must be responsible and reliable. We trust them to be honest."

My God, I thought, I must have killed someone! My heart began to pound.

"There was a sign on your floor clearly stating that you were to throw your dirty caps down to the laundry on Wednesday before 12:30."

"Yes, Sister."

"You threw down your cap late!"

"I ... I'm sorry, Sister." I was stunned. I couldn't believe Sister was so upset about such a trivial matter. Well, the sign on the wall had said, caps in laundry before 12:30, but what difference would a few hours make to a cap? It wasn't a *life*.

"Miss Yates, if we cannot trust you to do a simple procedure, how are we to trust you with the responsibility of patient care?"

Not knowing whether to answer yes, Sister, or no, Sister, I stood silent.

"How are we to trust you to give medications on time or perform procedures on time? How are we to trust you to follow doctors' orders properly?"

"I'm sorry, Sister."

"You must always carry out orders as they are written, Miss Yates."

"Yes, Sister."

"*Bon.* I hope I do not receive other reports of your negligence. That is all."

As I walked back to the hospital, I realized why everyone was so frightened of Sister. What on earth would Sister have done if I'd made a real mistake? I promised myself I'd never find out.

Wednesday after work, Perry invited me to have dinner at her house to meet her parents and sister. They lived in a small dark apartment in the industrial section of town, on the third floor of a building that looked like a warehouse.

Perry's father was sitting in a big armchair in the cramped dim living room. His face lit up when we entered the room.

"Jeannie, my pet," he said with a small gasp. "Come over here and let me give you a big hug."

"Daddy!" Perry rushed to him, knelt down and threw her arms around his neck. "Daddy, how are you?"

"No worse than I was half an hour ago," he said with a chuckle. He looked up at me and nodded toward his daughter. "You know she calls me all day long, just to bug me."

Perry lit a cigarette. "Oh, Dad, I do not."

Perry's father had chronic lung disease. From the time he was a young boy, he'd worked in the coalmines in northern Alberta. When he couldn't swing a pick anymore, he drove a coal truck. The emphysema worsened and finally he moved his family to Calgary. He took janitorial work, but it was too late.

Mr. Perry shook his head, and said, "Don't believe her. She calls every hour." Then he turned to me. "So this is Donna." I nodded. "I've heard so much about you, and it's all bad." He grinned.

"It's good to see you, Daddy," Perry said. "Geez, I miss you and Mom."

At six o'clock, Perry's older sister, Joan, burst in and greeted her dad in the same manner as Perry had. She was a secretary in a big oil company downtown. "And she's a damn good one, too," Mr. Perry said.

As I helped set the table for supper, a weary Mrs. Perry shuffled in from her long day at Colonel Belcher Hospital where she worked as part of the support staff. She was short and plump, legs were swollen way beyond her shoes. Perry, Joan and their father greeted her as if they hadn't seen her in a month.

I glanced around at the meagre apartment, a simple table and chairs in the small kitchen, two skimpy bedrooms. The building next door blocked what little light might have squeezed in through the narrow window behind Mr. Perry's chair in the living room.

Once her daughters had her comfortably seated in a chair next to her husband, legs propped on a stool and a cool beer in her hand, Mrs. Perry looked up at me and said, proudly, "Can you believe our Jeannie is going to be a nurse?"

"And a damn good one, too," Mr. Perry added.

Later, as we walked back to the residence, Perry said, "Poor Dad, he never got his pension. Sad, isn't it? He worked all those years in that damn mining town, it kills his lungs and he doesn't even get a pension." We walked a couple of blocks in silence. "You know, Yates," Perry said, with a worried look, "I just hope my Dad lives long enough to see me graduate."

At the end of each month, Sister would review the case study of each student nurse working on the wards and then present her with a pay envelope.

As Sister Leclerc thumbed through my case study about Mrs. Morrison, I waited nervously. She turned the pages, nodding approvingly. I had researched absolutely everything I could find on CVA (cardiovascular accident, or stroke). Miss Horne, our clinical instructor, had graded the case study.

"Did you enjoy St. John's, Miss Yates?"

"Yes, Sister."

She picked up another paper from the right corner of her desk. "Have you weighed in, Miss Yates?"

"Yes, Sister."

"Ah yes, here it is, 127 pounds. I am sure you will work hard on your next rotation."

"Yes, Sister."

She handed me the envelope that held my $10.00. It was the ritual.

Oh, Men! Ah, Men! Men!

September. St. Joseph's Ward: "The family are on their way to the hospital," the night nurse said. "I've prepared the body and pulled the curtains round his bed. Mr. Parson, the dead man's roommate, didn't sleep well with all the commotion. He's still upset and won't go in the room as long as the body is there. He's sitting in the hall."

Though the dead man had thoughtfully gone one hour before I came on duty and was not my patient, I felt compelled to glance at a dead body. Thus I was lured to the dead man's room.

His roommate sat in a chair in the hallway nervously smoking a cigarette. I gave him a solemn nod and hesitantly entered the dreaded room. As I stood at the foot of the curtained bed, my knees trembled under yards of starched apron. Out of the corner of my eye, I saw Mr. Parson peering round the doorway, watching me. I could not back out. I took a deep breath and opened the curtain wide enough to peek in. There'd been a mistake. There lay a black man sleeping, his hands were folded neatly over his chest. I closed the curtains and returned to the hall.

"Too bad about the man in there," said Mr. Parson, tilting his head toward the curtained bed. "They worked very hard on him last night."

"Oh, don't worry," I said, reassuringly. "That man is okay, he's sleeping."

"Sleeping? They told me he died!"

"No, he's not dead," I said, finding my newfound authority quite pleasant. "He's just asleep." I gave Mr. Parson a confident smile and went off to my patients.

Mr. Ross was a 72-year-old man, who only the day before had suffered a coronary thrombosis, or heart attack. I entered his room, where he lay encased in an oxygen tent made of thick, clear plastic that extended from the head of his bed to his waist. An oxygen tank, cradled in a metal stand on wheels, stood beside his bed, looking like a rocket about to be launched clear through the ceiling.

He was rubbing the left side of his chest in pain. I quickly offered him an injection and hurried off to the desk to find the head nurse who held the keys to the medication cupboard where all narcotic and sedative medications were stored. The Royal Canadian Mounted Police controlled the dispensation of these drugs and would review all the medication books. Occasionally, they would visit the ward to verify these records.

It was ten o'clock, morning rounds, and several doctors stood at the nursing station studying their patients' charts. Mrs. Black, the head nurse, bustled around them, stiff with starch and desperately efficient. With layers of spray, she had tempered her steel grey hair into a crisp flip. As usual, her pointy nose was up in the air, especially around students.

"May I have the keys to the medication cupboard?" I asked in a thin voice. Mrs. Black gave me an arrogant look as if she'd never seen me before, then reached in her pocket and slapped the keys into my hand.

"Make sure you give them back to *me*," she snipped.

I prepared the injection and signed for the morphine on the narcotic sheet, recording Mr. Ross's name, his doctor and the time. Then I returned to his room carrying the injection on a small medication tray. I walked gingerly, balancing the sterile needle on a sterile cotton ball, along with another ball dipped in alcohol to clean the skin. If the needle slipped off the cotton, I would have to go back and change it.

I managed to get to the room without contaminating the needle and gave Mr. Ross a perfectly smooth injection in his arm. Then I carefully folded the plastic oxygen tent and tucked it neatly back into the sheets to form a tight seal around his waist.

On my way to my next patient, Mr. McPherson in 272, I bumped into a senior. "You'll need help with Mr. McPherson," she said. "Poor guy is riddled with cancer and can be difficult at times."

She caught my worried look. "Just make sure you give him his shot when he asks. That's all we can do," she smiled reassuringly. "Call me if you need help."

"Don't want a bath, gir-rl," said Mr. McPherson in a broad Scottish accent as I walked into his room with a basin of warm water. "I need a shot ~ and quick!"
... Never run in the halls; it might frighten the patients ...

I walked as quickly as I could in search of Mrs. Black. She gave me a look as if to say: You again? I cringed and looked away from the glare of her eagle eyes. Then she slapped the medication keys into my hand without a word.

When I returned to Mr. McPherson's room he said, "I suppose you're another junior who is going to use me for a pin cushion," his voice weak and defensive. "Hope you've had enough practice ... and don't hurt me!" He added as I turned him on his side.

I gave a sudden gasp. The man was a skeleton. Nothing but skin stretched over bones. There was no flesh on his body. He looked like Jasper!

"Come on, come on, girl," he said impatiently with his whirring burr, "get this over with."

I searched frantically for an area to inject the Demerol, now the sole purpose of Mr. McPherson's existence. My hands were trembling as I traced a line from the upper crease of his bottom horizontally to the iliac crest, and one line vertically down the middle of what should have been his buttock, in order to steer clear of the dreaded sciatic nerve. This was a sure way to identify the upper outer quadrant ~ the safe spot for an intramuscular injection. Unable to find any muscle on his bones, I pinched his skin between my forefinger and thumb and with a quick, descending blow, plunged the needle ~ through the flesh of my forefinger.

Now I was skewered to Mr. McPherson's right buttock, or what there was of it.

Oh, God! I tried to remain calm. This situation was definitely not in my procedure book. I began to reiterate sterile technique. The needle is sterile. The solution to be injected is sterile. My finger is not sterile. The needle that was sterile is not sterile now because it went through my finger

"Come on, girl, come on!" he seethed through his brogue.

51

I had to make a quick decision. I yanked the needle out and immediately felt a throbbing pain in my finger.

"Are ye finished?"

"Well ... er ... ah ... no," I said sheepishly, wrapping a piece of gauze around my forefinger. It was bleeding profusely.

"What the...."

"I am sorry, Mr. McPherson," I quickly interrupted, "I have to change the needle."

Before I could flee down the hall in search of a new needle, and a Band-Aid for my finger, a tornado blew in through the door and swept me into the hall.

Mrs. Black was in a frenzy ~ her arms flailing, red lips raving about keys and jail. We bumped around in the hall for a few minutes as I tried desperately to juggle the syringe and needle on my little brown tray. Finally, she grabbed me by my ear and marched me to the nurses' station, making little hissing noises as we passed the doctors who stood around the desk watching us. She pointed frantically to the little metal box on the wall. Then she exploded.

"Do you want to go to jail? Do you know they could lock you up for this?"

I raised my eyes to the medication cupboard.Hanging from the door, still in the lock, were the keys.

"Maybe you don't care if you go to jail," Mrs. Black spat at me, "but I'm responsible for those keys and they'll lock me up, too! Do you know that? Do you?"

"No," I whispered. I honestly couldn't remember anyone ever telling me.

"I don't want to go to jail, Miss Yates, not for you or anybody else. Is that clear?"

"Yes," I mumbled, hanging my head in humiliation. "I'm sorry."

"Take those keys out of the cupboard and give them to me!"

I slunk to the cupboard and handed her the keys.

"Now get back to work!"

I made a quick retreat down the hall.

"Hey nurse!"

It was Mr. Parsons, still sitting in the hall beside his room. He frantically motioned for me to come over.

"What the Sam hell is going on here?" he bellowed. "First one nurse comes and tells me this poor guy is dead. Then you come and tell me he is asleep. Just asleep, you said. Then another nurse comes and tells me he is dead. Finished! Kaput!" He turned and pointed to the curtained bed which now seemed to emit an unsettling silence. "Now I want to know," he said, carving his words in a chesty whisper, "is this man dead or not!"

I quickly turned to see Mrs. Black strutting in front of the doctors. She filled her bosom with air, and said in a breathy wheeze: "These students must be taught responsibility!"

I turned back and glanced at the closed curtains. "I'll go and check," I said, and made a quick retreat down the hall, to find anyone but Mrs. Black.

I found the clinical instructor. "The man did indeed die at 6:30 this morning," she said. "But because he is black, mottling of the skin would be difficult to detect. You should have checked his nail beds, Miss Yates," she said, gently. "They would have been cyanosed. You saw only what you wanted to believe," she smiled. "This phenomenon is not unusual with young nurses. Eventually you will come to terms with death and understand that it's a part of the cycle of life. One cannot be separate from the other."

Humiliated, I started for his room, rehearsing what I would say. I noticed all the doors to the patients' rooms had been closed. "Fire drill," we had to tell the patients, but everyone knew it wasn't fire drill. An orderly came by pushing a stretcher with a sheet draped over what was unmistakably a body.

"Is that the man from 219, bed B?" I asked.

"Yup."

I did eventually master a painless injection for Mr. McPherson, which I gave him every three hours. Without a word, he'd curl up on his side and patiently wait for the drug to course through his veins and ease his pain. Then he would succumb and drift into a delusory paradise where he could run, laugh and eat again.

One day when I returned from my day off, the nurse reported that Mr. McPherson had died during the night. "No fuss," she said. "His breathing just gradually slowed until it stopped at 4:23 a.m." And I knew she had held his wrist and waited for the exact time his pulse and respiration ceased.

Death had finally liberated Mr. McPherson from his withered, pain-ridden body, but I had an ache in my chest. I would never see him again.

My naïveté had started to fade. We student nurses were locked in a rigid life, a difficult life. Illness and death surrounded us. Out of uniform and exhausted, we found solace in each other during our four o'clock bitch sessions that often lasted well into the night.

"Mrs. Black is a witch," White said, after listening to my humiliating experience with the medicine cupboard keys. "Witch, witch, witch! I had her for my first rotation. I was scared to death and she made me feel like an idiot. God knows the agony I went through with that bloody woman!" White threw herself into a chair and then began to chuckle. "God have mercy on us."

Perry sat hunched with her chin in her palms, staring into the distance. "I thought my patient was getting better," she said. "Her poor husband was so excited about her going home next week."

"They always seem to get better before they go. I wonder why?" Kaufmann said in a small voice.

Porter, in her pink fuzzy slippers, was performing her evening ritual of brushing her hair 100 strokes. She turned to Kaufmann. "Come over here and sit with us," she urged.

But Kaufmann just grinned, shook her head and pulled her chin to her chest.

"Anyway, I waltz into Pops' room, right up to his bed. I throw the covers back and say, 'Okay, Pops, time to get out of bed now,' and up he gets, just like that." Niven snapped her fingers.

"Oh, that's great, Niven," I said. "How would you like to take my place? I hate the men."

It was the end of September and Sister had just assigned me to St. Charles, another men's ward. As the girls shared their experiences on the men's ward, we ate the hamburgers and french fries we'd ordered-in to celebrate my 20th birthday.

Niven bit into her hamburger. "Sure. Bring on the men. I love 'em. I hate those damn women. Always complaining."

"Come on, Niv," I said, "the women are great. They don't tease and they don't joke. I can't joke with the men. I prefer the women."

"Aw, bullshit. Bloody women bitch all the time."

White appeared with her radio blasting out Fats Domino singing: *I Want to Walk You Home. ... You look so pretty, babe / ooh-ooh-wee ...* I loved his cool piano, the way he banged out the notes over and over again.

We began to jive, fully aware that we were performing for the men's surgical ward, whose windows faced front row centre to our own brightly lit windows.

"Come on, guys, close the drapes," Hawkins pleaded. "It's not nice."

"Aw who gives a shit," Niven said. She snatched a french fry from Perry's plate. "Why not give those men on St. Charles something to watch?" Niven turned round to face our floor-to-ceiling windows. She smiled and waved the french fry, "Hi, Pops!"

Porter stood up, tall and angelic-looking, her fair hair shining like a golden halo in the bright ceiling lights. Her eyes were like powder blue pinwheels with brilliant-light spokes, her pupils large and black, the rims almost navy. She shuffled over and squinted into my face with her beautiful, myopic eyes. "Gee, Yates," she said in her soft voice. "If you think St. Joe's is bad, wait 'til you get to St. Charles."

"Why?" I gulped.

"Well, first of all, the men are younger and not as sick as the men on St. Joe's, and with one thing and another ... " she drew her face into a scowl. "I just thought it was an embarrassing ward."

Hawkins giggled. "Yeah, I know what you mean," she said. "They all have those catheters hanging. And they sure do know how to embarrass a gal." She covered her mouth as if she was embarrassed just talking about it.

I knew what she meant. Nursing men was so mysterious and secretive. We had to get the orderly to finish their bath, to help them use the urinal, to insert a urinary catheter. The first time I turned Mr. Ross on his side, I thought he had a tumour between his legs. I'd never seen testicles before.

Niven twirled Perry, but Perry lost her balance and fell over Kaufmann who sat in her corner, eyeing us over the top of her New Testament. Housecoat wide open exposing her underwear, Tanner mimed Elvis, wiggling her hips and pretending to play the guitar as the radio blared out *You Ain't Nothin' but a Hound Dog / Cryin' all the time ...*

Suddenly, the elevator door opened, and Mrs. Schriefels, the housemother, blew in like a gale.

"Girls ... girls!" she shouted. "Miss Tanner ... really!"

Tanner turned around and began to giggle like June Allyson. "Hi, Mrs. Schriefels," she said with a languid wave.

"Close those drapes. Immediately!"

Niven slunk across the room and turned off the radio. Hawkins closed the drapes, her mouth drawn into a thin line as if to say, "I told you so."

"For goodness sake, do up your duster, Miss Tanner," Mrs. Schriefels muttered as she waddled out of the lounge. It's not ladylike to go about showing your bra and panties." She stepped into the elevator, and as the door squeaked closed we all burst out laughing.

"But Charlie the orderly is good," Porter said, picking up her hairbrush again as if nothing had happened. "He'll do anything for you. And he knows his stuff, too."

"You're damned right he's good," said Tanner, flipping the cigarette clenched between her teeth up and down. "He was a trained surgical nurse in the war, but because the poor bugger's a guy, he can't get registered as a nurse in Alberta. That's why he's working as an orderly. Now isn't that just the horse's ass?" She blew a huge smoke ring and watched it float off toward the open window.

"So, Yates, when you get into trouble," Hawkins said, with a serious face, "just find good ol' Charlie. And watch out for those horny patients."

Armed with these helpful hints from my classmates, I began my first day on St. Charles, the men's surgical ward. At morning report I noticed Charlie standing opposite me. Medium height with dark brown hair, he wore a white V-neck shirt and white pants that hung loosely on his thin frame. I cornered him in the hopper room as he emptied a bottle of bloody urine.

"Hello, Charlie," I said, as I approached him.

"Hello. You are ... " he leaned forward to read the name pin attached to my uniform, "...ah, Miss Yates. Very nice to meet you, Miss Yates." He smiled, showing a collection of gold teeth. "First time on St. Chuck?" I nodded. "Well, I'm at your service. Come and get me any time you need help."

My first patient on St. Charles was Mr. Reese, a 25-year-old single man who had just had a circumcision. His constant requests for attention embarrassed me. Because he was an adult, I had to do what he asked. "Please roll up my bed," he'd whine. "Could you give me a backrub?" It seemed that every time I turned my head, he was standing there.

Two days after his surgery I asked Charlie to change his dressing. "Believe me, it will be a pleasure." Charlie's gold teeth glistened through his prankish grin. "This guy is beginning to be a royal pain in the butt, pardon the pun." He bounded off to the treatment room for a dressing tray, and I chuckled.

Charlie drew the curtains around Mr. Reese's bed. I waited in the doorway, watching the bright morning sun cast brilliant hues on the sloping, brown linoleum floor. The room was quiet. Two men were reading the morning newspaper, one was asleep, all unaware that Charlie was about to remove a piece of dried-up bloody gauze firmly stuck to Mr. Reese's raw penis.

Suddenly, a scream pierced the air which sent a shock wave through the three roommates and shattered the silence all the way back to the desk. Mrs. Lee, the head nurse, shot down the hall to Mr. Reese's room as Charlie emerged carrying a used dressing tray.

"It hurts to change your religion," he said flashing his golden smile as he passed the group of stunned nurses gathered beside me.

A few minutes later, a pale and shaken Mr. Reese appeared in a wide-legged monkey stance and asked for a glass of juice. He looked at me like a wounded puppy and stumbled back to his bed oblivious to the smirks and chuckles the nurses cupped behind their hands.

His deflated ego did not droop long, however, and soon he was following me around the ward again. Every time I turned he was either beside me or behind me demanding back rubs. I was afraid someone would report me to Sister for fraternizing with my patients. He was beginning to get on my nerves. I was delighted when his discharge order finally arrived.

Three weeks later, the housemother buzzed my room, "Phone call for you, Miss Yates."

Probably my mother, I thought, though I was really hoping for a long distance call from Lester in Regina. I dashed to the phone on the wall, of breath.

"Hello, Miss Yates ... er .... ah ... Donna?" said a male voice. "This is John ... you know, John Reese."

John! I breathed. "Oh ... ah, how are you feeling?" I said. Then wished I hadn't asked that question.

"Much better, thank you, Donna." God, he used my first name. "Listen, I'd like to take you out for dinner Saturday night."

"Oh ... I can't," I stammered. "We're not allowed to go out with patients."

"But I'm not a patient any more."

"I ... I have to work on Saturday night."

But he called again, and again. I was running out of excuses and the girls began to tease me.

"Come on, Yates. Who's going to know he was your patient?" Perry said.

"Yeah," Niven said. "How would Sister find out?"

Finally, they convinced me that going out for dinner was not a crime, and I was desperate for a good meal.

Saturday night, my buzzer rang at six. John Reese appeared for our date, standing by the reception desk along with several other boys. Surprising how different he looked in a shirt and trousers. As we drove away in his navy blue Oldsmobile 88, I glanced up at the fourth floor and saw my classmates waving to me, their faces pressed against the lounge window.

We dined on steak and baked Alaska at a lovely restaurant overlooking the Elbow River, not far from the hospital. Although he was a perfect gentleman, I was not comfortable. The image of his poor limp penis swathed in gauze remained firmly in the forefront of my mind.

Why couldn't I date a patient from orthopedics like some of the other more fortunate students had done, maybe a handsome quarterback with a broken leg.

When I returned, the girls were waiting in the lounge. I told them I would never see John Reese again.

Day by day, I learned how to handle the male patients, their teasing and their jokes. I tried to stay prepared by always having a supply of answers ready.

"Bet you have lots of boyfriends."

"Wouldn't you like to know."

"What do you do on your day off?"

"I go home to eat and sleep."

"Do you have a steady boyfriend?"

Even though Lester would be locked up in the RCMP barracks in Regina for the next three years, I'd always answer, "Yes!"

The Power of Suggestion

The leaves along the Elbow River now sported vivid shades of yellow and orange, and there was a crispness to the October evening air. I had been at The Holy for eight months. It was time again to leave the wards and go back to the classroom for eight weeks of junior block. This meant being able to sleep half an hour longer in the morning and every Saturday afternoon and having Sunday off. Best of all, I would study the effect of disease on the body, which would be much more interesting than the plain old normal body we just finished studying.

Learning about disease had a strange effect on all of us and we began to develop the symptoms of new diseases we discussed in class. Every day someone had a new complaint.

The large glands in White's neck became leukemia. The lump in my groin, a hernia. But Perry was hopeless. Everyday she had another symptom. "Honestly, Yates," she would say, "when I push on my stomach here I have a pain ~ there in my neck." The next day it was a lump in her thigh. Then her eyes twitched. The following day she was dizzy. "Brain tumour?" she muttered, nervously chewing her thumbnail.

Each time a new symptom appeared we'd run to see Mrs. Cherry, the nurse in the health office down the hall from Sister. She would give a knowing look with her chocolate brown eyes and say, "You're all normal. Our class went through this in our junior block too." Then she would examine the place where the lump was supposed to be, take our temperature and send us back upstairs. "Come back if it's still there in a couple of days." It never was.

My flu symptoms, however, were real, with aches, pains and a high temperature. Twenty minutes after White reported my symptoms to the health office, Mrs. Cherry arrived at my door carrying two large pitchers filled with ice water.

"Drink a large glass every hour. There are two cans of juice in the lounge fridge. They have your name on them, Yates. I want them gone by this time tomorrow." She said it like an army general but she had a broad smile on her face.

That evening at 8:30 there was a knock on my door, then it opened slowly. Sister Leclerc walked in.

"Sister!" I gasped, leaping to my knees in bed.

"Hello, Miss Yates," she said. "No, no, don't get up. I just came to see how you're feeling." Sister was smiling and genuine concern showed on her face.

"Oh, I'm feeling much better, thank you," I said meekly as I leaned against the wall and pulled the covers over my knees, though I thought I should spring to attention.

"You had better stay in bed tomorrow morning, Miss Yates. See how you feel at lunchtime. I'll check on you again tomorrow."

"Yes, Sister. Thank you, Sister."

Sister turned and quietly closed the door, off to see another sick student. A warm feeling came over me. Maybe Sister really did care about us. I began to wonder if the Director of Nurses at the Calgary General, the city hospital, would be visiting her sick students at 8:30 at night? Their director was not a nun and she probably wouldn't even be in the residence at night. My director slept only a few floors away from me. If I really needed her, I knew I could call upon her any time.

Suddenly I realized why Sister had perpetual black circles under her eyes. She alone was responsible for the welfare and conduct of almost 200 very active, often wild, young women. On top of that, she had her daily, rigorous, religious obligations ~ chapel at pre-dawn and last thing at night, plus all the other secretive activities the nuns hustled to all day long.

It was late November and snowing heavily as I flipped up the vinyl blind to signal the end of the rest hour. Lisa Lane, my 17-year-old patient, lay quietly watching me. She had been admitted the evening before with a sore throat and high temperature and though fresh-looking, was quite pale.

At exactly 2:00 p.m., start of visiting hours, her mother entered her room carrying a shopping bag full of schoolbooks. "Lisa called and asked me to bring her books," she said to me, shaking the snow from her coat and paisley scarf. "She insists on studying while she's here."

I took a thermometer from the tray I held and shook it down. I had to get the proper snap of my wrist, a series of brisk snaps to send the mercury down to the bottom of the column. "Under your tongue, Lisa."

Her mother began to unpack the books and pile them onto the bedside locker. Suddenly Lisa sat up and pulled the thermometer from her mouth.

"I have to study, nurse. My Christmas exams are coming up and I want to pass!" She glared at her mother and stuck the thermometer back in her mouth.

Lisa's mother nervously fingered the gold cross at her neck, and said, "I thought Lisa should rest a few days before she started to study, but this is her last year and she wants to do well in her exams. Next year she will be going to university in Edmonton. She wants to be a doctor." Lisa nodded.

"Wow!" I was impressed. We had only two women doctors at The Holy; one a gynecologist and one an anaesthetist, both tougher than any male doctor.

I took the thermometer from Lisa's mouth. The three flat sides could distort the mercury column, making it difficult to locate the silver line of mercury in the glass cylinder, and now it seemed to have disappeared completely in the shiny glint of glass. I slowly turned it again. I couldn't believe what it said ~ 102 degrees.

"You have a high temperature, Lisa," I said. "You must stay quiet and drink a lot of water and juice." I gave her two aspirin to bring down her fever.

During the next four days, the doctors ran a battery of tests and x-rays on Lisa, who became weaker each morning. By Friday she had sores in her mouth to which I applied gentian violet, which turned her mouth, lips and tongue a deep purple. She complained bitterly. "I can't kiss my boyfriend like this. I look so ugly I bet he'll stop coming to visit me."

Monday morning Lisa's test results sent a shock wave not only through St. John's but indeed the whole hospital. Leukemia. Intravenous medication was flown in from the United States. She was moved to a private room near the desk. Everyone was tense. It was a fight to buy time.

Each day as I nursed her, gently bathing her aching body and brushing her long, light brown hair, I tried to encourage her. Though her eyes looked questioningly at me, I respected her parents' wish that she not learn of her illness unless she asked. But she never asked.

"Will I be better by Christmas?" she asked weakly as I applied another coat of gentian violet to her mouth.

"I don't know, Lisa, but hopefully the new medication will make you feel better." Each day I was appalled to see how quickly she was slipping.

On Wednesday, she announced in a weak voice, "I want to see my dog."

I found Dr. Hamilton at the nurse's station flipping through Lisa's chart. "Excuse me," I said timidly, "Lisa is asking to see her dog."

He looked up at me from the papers, his soft eyes listless from fatigue. "Give Lisa whatever she wants," he said in an empty voice.

"Is she going to die, Dr. Hamilton?"

He shrugged. Then he looked up from the chart and his eyes met mine for a moment. He gave a slow, affirmative nod and whispered, "Yes."

I couldn't swallow away the lump that swelled in my throat. My eyes filled with tears. I walked through the open waiting room at the end of the hall where some of

Lisa's relatives sat, waiting. I turned into a tiny bathroom in front of the stairs, closed the door and stared into the mirror on the wall. Looking back was a girl two years older than Lisa, a healthy girl trying very hard to become a nurse. It could be me, I thought. Why Lisa and not me? I burst into tears.

After I splashed water on my swollen, red eyes, I returned to the ward to pass out the breakfast trays. I took a deep breath as I walked into Mrs. Morrison's room with her breakfast tray balanced on my shoulder. My jaw dropped when I saw she was dressed in a flowered print dress and mauve sweater.

I'm going home today," she announced as she sat on the edge of her bed.

"That's fantastic!" I said placing her tray on the table. I was so proud of her.

"You know," she said with a delicate laugh, "my name is Maud, but I'm going to change it to Fantastic, because everyone who comes in here takes a look at me and says fan-tas-tic!"

Not long after I'd taken the breakfast trays away, Lisa's parents returned with her dog, Toby. I put a mask on Lisa's face to protect her from bacteria, bundled her up in bath blankets and wheeled her down to the lobby. Toby was waiting ~ a small, brown-and-white, curly-haired dog that whimpered and tugged at the leash when he saw Lisa. But she was not allowed to touch him.

"Oh, Toby, I miss you!" cried Lisa. "I am going to get better, and I'll be home soon. Soon, Toby."

Her mother cradled Lisa's head against her breast. "Yes, my darling," she whispered as she stroked Lisa's hair. "You will be home soon."

I fought back an overwhelming urge to share her mother's agony. I feel for you, I wanted to tell her. My heart is breaking too. It's not fair, not the least bit fair! But then I remembered Mrs. Whitford's words: "A nurse can be of no help if she breaks down ... she must not get involved ... ever." I had to give Lisa and her mother strength through empathy, not sympathy. I was a nurse, not family. I clenched my teeth and swallowed hard as Lisa pulled her mask down to her chin and blew a kiss to Toby for the last time ... then I pushed her back to her room.

Mrs. Morrison's husband arrived after lunch, even more excited than his wife, and together we packed up Mrs. Morrison's belongings. Mr. Morrison helped with her coat, and I moved the walker in front of her.

"I'm not using that thing," she said indignantly, raising her head in the air. "I said I would walk out of the hospital one day, and walk I will!"

She linked her arm through her husband's, I carried the walker and the three of us proceeded slowly down the hall. The nurses at the station clapped and waved as we passed.

A Crescent Taxi waited at the entrance of the hospital. Mrs. Morrison held a potted yellow chrysanthemum on her lap, and with her husband at her side, she smiled and waved to me as the cab pulled away.

"Take care of yourself," I whispered, and waved until the taxi disappeared around the corner.

Lisa slipped into a coma Thursday. That night, her mother slept in the big armchair that we pulled next to Lisa's bed.

On Friday morning when I passed by Lisa's room on my way to report, her bed was empty. Lisa had died during the night. She had been in the hospital less than two weeks. A small pile of schoolbooks sat on the table, waiting for her father to pick up.

Across the hall, a 78-year-old woman lay in a coma, jaundiced and grotesquely bloated from liver failure. And continued to breathe.

In the lounge after work that day, I asked the girls, "What is life? Poor Lisa didn't have a chance, yet others go on and on. Where is the logic to it?"

"I know," Priestnall said in a flat voice, "it just seems so unfair."

Guenette agreed. "Life is not only unfair, it's also illogical."

"You're damn right," grumbled Niven. "Look at poor old Pops on St. Joe's, suffering day after day." She rolled her eyes. "Somebody up there is not paying attention to what is going on down here."

"Now, Niven," Kaufmann whispered into her coffee cup. "Everything happens for a reason."

Porter had just come out in her pink slippers, her hair in curlers. She was working nights. She spoke in her velvety smooth voice. "That's right, Kaufmann. I believe there's a great master plan and we can't interfere with that. We help those who are sick, but you know disease is a part of life. Some get sick and some die, but life must go on."

Lisa's death haunted me. I couldn't understand it. This beautiful world ~ why should I be well? Lisa was young, not old. What was the purpose of being born, of living, going through the motions, studying, trying, pushing on if we were just going to die at any old time without fulfilling our ambitions?

At home for the weekend, I told my parents about Lisa as we ate dinner. "Where is the sense to life when young people never make it to the good stuff, like a career and kids. Isn't that's what's always ahead ~ the good stuff?" I asked my mother.

"You know, " she said, "just think of how lucky you are to have known such a nice girl, and think of how lucky she was to have had a caring nurse like you."

"But I thought if I tried hard enough, prayed hard enough, she would get better. I couldn't help her, Mom. Her life was so short. It's not fair."

My mother pushed her chair from the table and came to me. She bent over and cradled my shoulders, pressed her cheek to mine. "She was sick, my little girl," she said softly. "You must be realistic. You cannot make a healthy person out of a body that is terribly broken and ill."

"Think of it this way," my father said. "If we knew what happened to us after death, perhaps we'd all be trying very hard to get there. She's at peace now."

An early December thaw had quickly melted the snow. Rivulets rushed down the gutters and gurgled into the sewer beneath the streetlight in front of the hospital entrance. I could hear it at night as I made my rounds on St. John's. I had been jittery about working the night shift, but soon found I liked the quietude of the dimly lit wards, the change of pace, the intimacy of nursing patients through the dark of night, giving them support and helping them back to sleep. It was a challenge and indeed fulfilling.

Each night, all week long, Mrs. Bud's call light was constantly on. She was the same cantankerous patient with diabetes I'd had on my first rotation to St. John's. Every time I answered, I found her standing on the floor, on the stumps of her legs, twisted in bed sheets and intravenous tubing. She would escape from the body restraint I had tied on her and hurdle the bed rails I'd hooked on the sides of her bed. At morning report we were held accountable for our patient's well-being during the night, and no matter how much I would beg and plead with her, she wouldn't stay in bed. I swore she spent the whole day dreaming up ways to terrorize me at night.

As the dawn broke each morning, Leo, the lion at the zoo on St. Georges Island, in the middle of the Bow River, would give his wake-up roar. That was my signal to dive into my morning work, which had to be completed before the day staff arrived. One morning, I had to take the temperatures of all 30 patients on the ward. I shuddered when I arrived at Mrs. Bud's room at four o'clock. Juggling my tray of 30 thermometers and the bulky blood-pressure apparatus, I bumped the heavy door open with my behind and attempted to dash in ~ but the door flew closed, knocking the tray out of my hand. Crash! Slippery droplets of silver mercury skittered across the floor among shards of glass. I desperately pawed through the mess, hoping for at least one unbroken thermometer ... but there was none.

I lifted my eyes helplessly to Mrs. Bud who looked down on me from her usual position on the edge of the bed, two stumps poking through the rails, puffing on her cigarette. And for the first time since I had known her, she looked rather pleased.

I reported my incident to the grad. "Well, these things happen," she said, consolingly. "Sign the breakage list on the wall over there. One line for each thermometer."

I began writing:

       1 thermometer ... D. Yates,
       1 thermometer ... D. Yates....

And I was grateful that student nurses no longer had to pay for breakages. Still exhausted from night rotation, Monday I slept through my 6:00 a.m. alarm.

"Geez, Yates, you slept in," Perry said sleepily, when she stopped at my room on her way to breakfast.

"Better go on without me," I mumbled through a mouthful of toothpaste.

I pulled on my white nylons, taking a moment to make sure the seams were absolutely straight, hooked them to my garter belt and jumped into my stiff uniform that lay across the chair like cut-out doll clothes. It was 7:12. I'd heard of other girls missing prayer and having toast and coffee in the lounge. So I thought, why not?

The windows of the lounge had frosted up overnight. I relaxed with a lovely hot cup of coffee and a piece of toast dripping with honey.

Halfway through my dash through the tunnel, my heart skipped a beat when I heard the faint tinkle of a crucifix. Though the tunnel was dimly lit, I was positive this nun coming toward me was Sister Leclerc, her tiny frame and slight limp from recent knee surgery were unmistakable. My toast and coffee turned to stone in my stomach.

"Good morning, Sister," I said, smiling, hopefully.

"Miss Yates. You were not at prayer this morning."

"No, Sister, I'm sorry. I slept in."

"But you must attend prayer every morning, Miss Yates."

"Yes, Sister."

"This must not happen again."

"No, Sister."

She swished away.

Feeling like a criminal, I checked my watch. Now I really was late. I rushed up to St. John's ward where I would be working days for the next six weeks.

Wednesday when I raised my blinds at six, it was still dark. A December blizzard was in progress. Snow swirled around the hazy lights in the driveway and an inch and a half was piled on my window ledge. A man in a parka with a scarf covering his mouth shovelled snow from the stone steps of the hospital.

When I reported that morning to St. John's, the grad reviewed my new patient's chart with me. Miss Jackson's chart was so large it had to be divided again and again. "She's slowly rotting from her inside out," the grad said.

As I skimmed her old chart, I could see why. Miss Jackson was 32 years old and in a private room near the desk. She had cancer of this and cancer of that and Whipple's surgery, where they took out everything they possibly could and left her with only the bare minimum to keep her alive.

The grad flipped through the pages of her current chart. "Her last setback was cancer of the colon," she said. "She's got a colostomy and needs daily irrigations." The grad looked up. "Ever given an irrigation?"

"No," I said, shaking my head.

"O-o-okay." She tightened her lips and took a deep breath. "Well, I'm awfully busy today. But if you're really stuck come and get me, otherwise do the best you can." She handed me the chart. "Actually, Miss Jackson's been here so long, she can tell you how it's done."

As I prepared to enter Miss Jackson's room, I squared my shoulders and checked my cap to make sure it was straight. I had to look professional, as if I knew what I was doing, give the patient confidence. I opened the door. Miss Jackson was sitting in bed bright-eyed, as if she'd been up all night, waiting for me.

Although she *was* very thin and had deep circles under her blue eyes, she really didn't look as sick as her chart said she was. But she wore a lot of makeup and a gauzy pink nightgown and her jet-black hair was teased into a bouffant with a flip.

I introduced myself.

"So you're my nurse today, Miss Yates," she said with a smile. "You don't have a pin, so you must be a junior." I nodded. My fingers immediately moved to the empty collar at my neck. It would be another two months before I received my intermediate pin.

Miss Jackson gestured to the small record player in the corner and asked me to play Stardust. "It's my favourite," she said. The music began to play. *And now the purple dusk of twilight time / Steals across the meadows of my heart ...*

I gave Miss Jackson breakfast, a bottle of milky fluid that dripped into her stomach, or what was left of it, through a gastric tube in her abdomen. As the fluid slowly dripped in sticky, thick drops, she fussed with her hair with her shocking pink fingernails. *Love is now the stardust of yesterday / The music of the years gone by ...*

I checked the reminder notes I kept in my pocket: Change wound dressings, colostomy irrigation, Demerol injections every three to four hours for pain. As I tidied the stack of fashion magazines on the chair beside her bed, Miss Jackson spoke as if weary and irritated with breaking in another new student. "Keep them in order. Right here where I can reach them. Don't move the chocolates, they go precisely there, beside my creams." I wondered if she knew she was dying. *Sometimes I wonder why I spend the lonely night / Dreaming of a song ...*

I slipped into a large gown, surgical cap, mask and gloves and began the irrigation. It was like an enema, given into the stoma, the bit of intestine surgically brought out through the abdomen and attached to the skin. It looked like two big, shiny lips turned inside out, puckering for a kiss. *The Melody, haunts my reverie / And I am once again with you ...*

When all the fluid was in, I held the bedpan as best I could, to catch the return. But the stoma didn't have a sphincter like the rectum and the return erupted like a volcano, soaking the bed, Miss Jackson's bony body and me. Miss Jackson lay perfectly still as her abdomen gurgled and sputtered and blew out a putrid stench. Her round, dark eyes combed my face for any hint of how I felt. I clenched my teeth, fixed my eyes in an empty stare, tried not to show my repulsion.

What was I doing here? I never imagined that doctors would turn a patient's body inside out like this, and for what? Miss Jackson was going to die anyway, why should she have to suffer like this? It was repugnant, the filth, the smell, her suffering. I had to think of something, something that would take me away, something that would get me through this ordeal. My prayer. ***I shall not shirk any duty no matter how unpleasant.***

Now Miss Jackson lay exposed and vulnerable ~ way beyond pretend. Her eyes revealed her pain, her helplessness, her shame. And when it was over, I could only smile and say, "Well, that wasn't too bad, Miss Jackson. I'll get you all cleaned up now and you'll feel much better."

I opened the small window a crack, "Oh, look," I said. "It's stopped snowing. There's a bit of blue sky and the sun's out." I stood for a few moments gazing down on the glistening rooftops of cosy-looking older homes, stacks sending smoke into the thin morning air, trees heavy with new snow.

"Here." Miss Jackson thrust a bottle of Air Wick at me. "Pull the wick up to the top and set it on the floor under my bed." Her eyes had changed now; sharp again and focused, as if to say, "I'm not defeated, not yet." *When our love was new / And each kiss an inspiration ...*

Next was the lavender-soap-bed-bath followed by her skin care ritual. Her bedside locker overflowed with bottles of body lotion, perfume and creams in big jars, small jars, skinny and squat jars; white and blue, pale yellow and rosy-pink ~ cold cream, night cream, dry skin cream and highlight cream, cover-up cream, circulating cream, pimple cream and peachy-cream with swan's oil. Today she chose Icilma vanishing cream for her face and arms and the sea-green, circulating cream for her legs and back, which I gently massaged into the parchment-like skin stretched over her bones.

"Now the perfume," she said in a regal tone. "The Crepe de Chine." She splashed a bit on her chest, dabbed it behind her ears and on both wrists, then handed the bottle to me. "Sprinkle it down there," she said motioning to her feet.

I sprinkled Crepe de Chine on the sheets like a blessing of the bed.

Miss Jackson took her hand mirror from the drawer and tilted it so she could study the large bedsore on her coccyx. "It's getting larger," she said, matter-of-factly. *But that was long ago / Now my consolation ...*

I slid a small rubber ring under her hips, to keep the pressure off the area. She told me where to put the pillows and small cushions she'd brought from home. "Move them up a bit," she said. "No, down a bit." I had barely touched the cushion under her shoulders when she said in a breathy whisper, "Okay, leave it." But it wasn't long before she asked me to rearrange them all over again.

On Thursday it was *Side By Side*, the baby-pink, and peach wonder cream. *Oh we aint got a barrel of money / Maybe we're ragged and funny ...*

I was in the middle of her colostomy irrigation when Doctor Raymond arrived early. "Quick the Air Wick!" she blurted out in a stage whisper.

I dashed for the bottle as she sloshed Crepe de Chine on her arms and chest, pulled her small, yellow crocheted afghan up to her chin, smoothed her hair and pinched her cheeks ~ just as Doctor Raymond poked his head through the weathered, cream curtains and said, "Morning Clara." *Through all kinds of weather/ What if the sky should fall ...*

Miss Jackson tilted her head coyly to the side and smiled like a model. "I'm so, so sorry for this," she said, with a small wave of her hand across her bed. "I'm not dressed. Can you give me a few minutes, Doctor?"

"Can't. Sorry, Clara. In a big rush today," Dr. Raymond said.

She quickly reached for the box of chocolates perched on top of her brown, crocodile Elizabeth Arden beauty case. "Here, Doctor, a chocolate?"

As Doctor Raymond chose a maraschino cherry, Miss Jackson wrinkled her brow, drew her lips into a thin line and said, "Isn't it early for you to be making rounds, Doctor?"

Doctor Raymond stood at the foot of her bed sucking the liquor out of the chocolate as Miss Jackson complained about her sleepless night and the pain and the bedsore getting larger. He nodded, as if he knew how beautiful she'd once been and how desperately she wanted to look feminine and pretty, even now, though her body had been carved up, riddled with holes, and reduced to skin and bones.

It was almost my third week with Miss Jackson when it suddenly struck me that although I had days off, she was always here, in this small room alone, day after day, week after week, month after month ~ irrigations, baths, perfumes, Air Wick ~ preparing, waiting, lusting for that few minutes with her doctor, when he would burst in and nod and say everything was going well and "Just keep it up, Clara." *Just as long as we're together/ It doesn't matter at all ...*

Dr. Raymond wrote the orders. I kept her clean, eased her pain and suffering, helped her to look pretty. I made her world as pleasant as possible ~ I *nursed* Miss Jackson. *We'll travel the road / Sharing our load ...*

On the third Saturday afternoon, Miss Jackson's sister appeared to deliver her creams. After two minutes, she gathered up Miss Jackson's slippers and said, "I'm taking these. My sister won't be needing them again." *Side By Side.*

On Sunday, *Stardust* again, the robin's-egg blue, Ponds moisturizing cream. *Sometimes I wonder why ...*

Each Sunday I washed Miss Jackson's hair with White Rain shampoo. The orderly removed the back of her bed and I slid a rubber sheet under her shoulders, letting it hang into a pail on the floor. After the shampoo, I rinsed with pitchers of warm water that cascaded down the red, rubber sheet like a frothy waterfall, spilling into the silver pail. Miss Jackson didn't want pin curls or rollers today; she wanted to let her black, natural curly hair dry in the air.

"Dr. Raymond won't be in today," she said with a sigh, as she slipped into her blue bed jacket. It hung loosely on her shoulders, a whisper from her past. *Beside a garden wall / When stars are bright / You are in my arms ...*

Just before lunch, I went in to brush her hair. She had just finished painting a second coat of shocking pink on her long fingernails.

"Let's tie it up today," she said, reaching for the box of chocolates. She lifted the lid and held the box to me. "Take a couple for your dessert."

I twisted her shiny hair into an elastic band and let it tumble down around her doll-like face in soft curls. Miss Jackson reached for the hand mirror, studied her hair from side to side, then placed it back in the drawer of her tray-table. Her porcelain face turned up to me and though sunken and thin, she looked almost glamorous. Her blue eyes were nearly as blue as my mother's, but Miss Jackson's were dull. They had the same resigned look that the eyes of my dog Sally had the day my father took her in the car to put her to sleep. Sally knew, and Miss Jackson knew. Despite that she smiled at me with her knowing blue eyes, tightened the band on her hair and said, "Thank you, Miss Yates. You like the upsweep?"

I smiled. "Love it."

And I thought washing her hair was such a small thing but it was all I could do to make Sunday a special day. *Though I dream in vain / In my heart it will remain My stardust memory / The memory of love's refrain.*

Emergency Ward

Christmas. Almost the end of my first year. White and I had finished our shift. As we made our way to the residence for our monthly evaluation, glittering angels in white with golden hair and gilded wings atop luminous Christmas trees watched over us. The nuns bustled to and from chapel chattering in French, privately sharing their enthusiasm for the joyous season.

"I don't care what they say about my report from St. Joe's," White said as we approached Mrs. Bland's office. Sister Leclerc was away and Mrs. Bland, the Assistant Director of Nursing, would be doing this month's evaluations. "Maybe I did answer that bitch back a couple of times but I liked those old men, and I sure as hell didn't make any mistakes."

My review went quickly. Mrs. Bland tucked a few loose strands of her blond hair into a black bobby pin behind her ear as she read my case study on diabetes, then gave me a toothy grin and said, "I'm pleased with your high mark, Miss Yates." She handed me my pay envelope. I never mentioned my frustration with Mrs. Bud. And Mrs. Bland never mentioned the thermometer catastrophe.

As I waited for White outside the office, I heard Mrs. Bland speaking to her in a most humane manner. "Well, what can they expect of you girls at this point? I think you have done remarkably well considering you've only been on the wards a few months. Don't dwell on this report, Miss White. Put it behind you and work hard on your next rotation."

White was smiling as she pushed through the door clutching her pay envelope, then immediately she burst into tears of relief. "She's such a nice woman, Yates," she sobbed. "She's got a heart."

But her tears had dried by the time we stepped off the elevator on the fourth floor where a holiday window decorating party was in progress.

"Hey, you're just in time to help." Porter, who stood on a chair, hair in pink rollers, waved a paintbrush.

Niven balanced a cup of coffee as she step-nudged across the room and flopped down in a chair. "Just be glad you missed Andresen's history lesson about why Norwegians eat carp at Christmas," she said.

Chris Andresen had her Scandinavian ancestors' peaches-and-cream complexion, fair hair and brilliant blue eyes. She stood steadying Porter's chair.

Suddenly Guenette burst into the lounge. "We have to have an emergency meeting right now. We need a new class president. Prevost quit."

We all gasped.

"Prevost quit?" Andresen said. "Another one?"

"Well, that's just dandy," Niven said. "Now we're down to 23."

"Why?" Perry asked.

Guenette shrugged. "Nobody seems to know, but let's get the show on the road. I nominate Priestnall."

"Yea," we shouted.

And so Penny Priestnall, the dark-haired girl with the pageboy and her mother in a red hat whom I had seen on my first day at The Holy , became our new class president.

Priestnall would make a good president. She walked the straight and narrow and had never come to the York to drink beer with us. She was from Mount Royal, a very affluent neighborhood in Calgary, but never flaunted her wealth. She was more sensible than most of us, she spent her time either studying or cleaning her room ~ the right things for a president to do.

Tanner, Bogarting a cigarette, climbed back up on a chair and began painting Santa's beard. She had more paint on her duster than on the window.

"Geez," Perry said, staring at the windows, "how are we ever going to get the paint off? It's going to take a lot of scraping."

"I think we should all remember the true meaning of Christmas while we're decorating the windows," said Armbruster, a tall gentle girl who looked like Snow White. "Just look at those beautiful angels that Porter's painting. We are truly blessed."

My eyes travelled from the angels to the snowmen, candy canes, and Santa Claus crawling into a chimney, his brown bag brimming with presents. It looked very good.

As we completed junior block, our assignments to the specialty areas of nursing began to trigger panic attacks. Rightly so too, for Robbins and Riley were listed for the operating room and Margaret Ingraham and I were assigned to emergency. Sunday night I tried to sleep. How would I handle the inescapably ghastly sights?

My mind went wild ~ I saw the blood, the mutilation and the pain ~ and I felt so inadequate. I checked the nurses' watch my parents had bought for me before I entered training ~ 1:15. I hadn't slept a wink. The watch glowed soft green in the dark. For a while I watched the second hand sweeping around and around the face, then I turned on my side and listened to the hypnotic ticking which eventually put me to sleep.

Margaret Ingraham was one of the best and most efficient students of my class, a good person to be working with, especially on an important ward like emergency. She had dark hair like mine and deep, brown eyes that caught the reflection of the overhead lights like polished marbles. And she had never been in trouble with Sister.

When Ingraham and I arrived in emergency on that first Monday morning, we looked like two starched dolls standing in the doorway of the main treatment room. I was barely breathing. A young head nurse looked up from some papers she held and motioned for us to enter the room. She had a thin, serious face and soft, dark eyes like a doe, and she wore the winged cap of Holy Cross.

"All right, girls," she said. "It's quiet now, so make the most of this time and familiarize yourself with the layout of the supplies and instruments. When an emergency comes through those doors," she tilted her head toward the entrance to the main room, "you are expected to know where everything is, like this," she snapped her fingers. "In this department, the patients are never kept waiting." She raised her eyebrows. "Nor are the doctors."

Emergency was on the ground floor of the hospital, near the tunnel that led to our residence. The nurses' station was in the corridor, a narrow table was against the wall, a small overnight treatment room was to the right, and an extremely small gynecology room to the left. Across the hall was the main treatment room with six stretcher beds.

I was to work with the RN, Miss Wright, whose hair was pulled tightly off her face and twisted into an awkward knot at the back of her head. She was a Holy grad, close to my age, and never smiled. In fact she practically ignored me as I trotted around after her trying my best to appear efficient. I hoped that she would warm up as the morning progressed.

"Here comes the first one," she said nodding toward the hallway.

I looked down the corridor and saw a young man carrying a baby bundled in a large comforter. His wife clung to his elbow as if steering him while they both looked frantically from side to side until they caught sight of Miss Wright, who waved them toward us.

"In here," said Miss Wright, shepherding us all to the first stretcher. "Now what seems to be the problem?" she asked, unbundling the child.

The baby had a cold with a high fever, the mother told us, wringing her hands. "She was twitching, convulsing, I think. Then her eyes rolled back in her head and she started shaking and turning blue."

Miss Wright turned the baby on her side and inserted a thermometer into her rectum. Her temperature was 103 degrees!

She turned to me and said, "Sponge the baby immediately. We've got to bring the temperature down or she'll convulse again."

The infant screamed and squirmed incessantly and I worried that she might wiggle out of my grasp. Her lips quivered and turned blue as the cool water trickled over her pink body but it drew out the fever and her temperature came down. Then she fell asleep ~ just as the doctor arrived to examine her.

"We'll keep her in a croup tent with cool mist for a day or two," the doctor told her parents. "Never let her temperature go that high again. You must sponge her when it gets above 100 degrees."

I lay Debbie in a small crib and pushed her to Holy Angels, the pediatrics ward on the third floor.

The rest of the day was a madhouse. Surprisingly, Ingraham and I quickly caught on. In no time we were dashing about cleaning wounds and assisting as the doctor sutured. I applied dressings, held broken limbs while the doctor slapped on dripping strips of plaster to immobilize them and calmed screaming children and trembling adults.

By 3:30 I felt as if I had been in emergency for a month. I dragged myself back to the residence. Exhausted, but jubilant, I was eager to telephone my mother to report every detail of my first day in emergency.

Saturday began very quietly, but at 3:20 it seemed as though everyone in Calgary decided to have an accident or begin bleeding or become violently ill at the same time. And they all made a beeline for Holy Cross. Couldn't a few go to Calgary General?

"Yates, get this patient into the gyne room," the grad shouted to me.

I nervously pushed the woman on a stretcher into the tiny room and transferred her onto the gynecological bed, which was awkwardly angled into a tight corner. Her chart said: Mrs. Nicholas, 34 years old, spontaneous, incomplete abortion (miscarriage). I placed the instruments on the silver Mayo stand and was just beginning to lift her feet up into the stirrups when Dr. Gluck arrived. He snapped on the pair of sterile latex gloves, turned and tripped over a metal bucket on wheels I had inadvertently placed behind him.

"Whoops," I blurted out, then wished I hadn't said that.

He stood for a moment, his sterile hands bent upward from the elbows, his face ashen, then he took a deep breath, sat down on the stool in front of the woman and put his upper body between her legs.

While the patient moaned and groaned, he worked silently, pulling out huge clots of blood. My important job was to retrieve these clots and place them in Formalin bottles for pathology to examine for fetal tissue.

I stood watching, fascinated as Dr. Gluck worked mopping up blood with large gauze squares and throwing them into the silver bucket I had repositioned conveniently beside him.

"Light," he said quietly, as if he trusted me to know what I was doing.

I immediately darted to the large light that stood on the floor beside and slightly behind him. It was as tall as I was, and the wide base of the metal stand probably weighed more than I did. I wanted to tilt the light to illuminate the right spot, but the corner was so cramped there was no space to manoeuvre.

"Light!" Dr. Gluck said impatiently, more like a command.

I grabbed the heavy frame circling the large neon light and quickly swung it to the left, but he stood up just as the light wrenched out of my hands and it struck him on the back of his head with a sickening thump.

"Oh, my God," I gasped. "I've killed him!"

I stood rooted to the floor and watched him stumble and stagger around the room, clutching his head. Finally, he came to rest slumped against the far wall.

"I am so sorry," I said in a small voice. "Are you all right?" I thought I should ask, even though he was a doctor.

He didn't answer. It was dreadfully silent for a few moments and I wondered if I should run and get the grad. Then the patient moaned, unaware of the drama taking place beyond her legs. I waited, and thought: I'm going to jail for this. I will be the first nurse to kill a doctor ... and I'm going to jail.

Dr. Gluck slowly took his hand away from his head and thoroughly inspected it.

There was no blood.

"I am so sorry," I repeated, wishing I could think of something more clever to say.

We stood looking at each other for the next few seconds which seemed like a year. Dr. Gluck's face had turned pale and was contorted. I guessed he was in pain and maybe even shock. He drew a deep breath and slowly forced it out. Then finally spoke in a chesty whisper.

"I think I'm okay. Get me a new pair of gloves."

Re-gloved, he resumed his position between the patient's legs. Through clenched teeth, he said, "Move the light, nurse. And for God's sake, be careful!"

Two weeks later I was on the afternoon shift when two ambulance attendants rushed down the hall with a young woman on a stretcher followed by Dr. Sullivan, the gynecologist. When I saw the serious look on his face, a shiver ran down my spine. All the stretchers in the treatment room were occupied.

"Never mind," he said. "I've got an incomplete abortion here: Induced. I want to do a quick pelvic exam and get her to the OR as fast as possible."

As the stretcher passed me, I glanced into the patient's face, something about this young woman made me stop. This was no textbook case, no abstract streetwalker, no note in my scribbler. She looked like a high school girl, a girl like me. Her dark eyes stared directly at me; wide as saucers they held my gaze and spoke to me ~ shame, terror, alone, regret. She had killed her baby. Did she worry about jail or being damned to hell? She looked so pale and limp, so sick. I hoped she hadn't given up.

"Yates, get over here!" the grad snapped.

I dashed ahead of the stretcher and followed the grad into the room. Dr. Sullivan pulled on the sterile gloves and he began to examine the girl, his large fingers probing inside the patient.

As I watched him work I tried to figure this out. This girl had had an abortion, *induced*, caused by something foreign, and it was *incomplete*, which meant she had not passed the entire fetus, or perhaps some of the placenta was still inside her uterus. Whatever it was, her body was desperately trying to rid itself of what was left, and she was bleeding profusely. I suddenly became aware of what profusely meant. The bed linens were soaked, and a large pool of bright-red blood between her legs was beginning to gel. I couldn't believe that so much blood could come out of one person. Then the patient became unconscious. I shook her, "Miss Bowden ... Nancy." But she didn't respond.

"I've got some tissue," the grad said to Dr. Sullivan, as she placed what looked like a large clot into a jar of Formalin. "I'll get it straight to pathology."

The presence of fetal tissue was a sure sign that the fetus had in fact died, and was in the process of being expelled. Then, and only then, would the nuns allow a D&C (dilatation and curettage), a procedure to scrape and clean out the inside of the woman's uterus.

Dr. Sullivan tore off his gloves and threw them on the table. "I'm going to the OR, get her there as soon as you can."

Within minutes the OR orderly arrived with the stretcher and I helped him move the patient to the operating room on the third floor. Sister Champagne stood on the inside of the black line that separated the operating room from the rest of the hospital, dressed in the completely white habit of the nuns working as nurses. Her mask hung around her neck, over her veil. Dr. Sullivan was already in his green OR clothes and had the mask over his face, his unruly, rusty eyebrows drawn together in a frown. Sister held up her hand to stop us before we crossed the line into the operating room.

She spoke to Dr. Sullivan, who towered over her, and although I couldn't hear what she was saying, her voice definitely sounded excited. Dr. Sullivan's blue eyes were intense and he spoke quietly to Sister through the mask he wore. Then he nodded to Sister, pulled on the cloth boots he had been holding and stepped over the black line.

Sister Champagne waved the orderly and me across the line with agitation. As I waited for the orderly to tie his boots, I looked down at the young patient on the stretcher. Her long, dark-blond hair covered her pillow, and she had become so white that she appeared to be melting into the bed sheets.

When I returned to the emergency room, I asked the grad what the girl had done to abort her fetus.

"Gave herself a Coke douche," the grad said, opening a sterile suture set.

I gave a puzzled look. "Coke douche?"

"She shook up an open bottle of Coke with her thumb over the top then let it go up her vagina." It caused her to abort all right, but she had been alone and too much time passed before she got help. "She lost a lot of blood," the grad said gravely. "It's frightening what these girls will do when they're desperate."

Two days later I met Dr. Sullivan in the hall and inquired about his patient.

"Well, we did a D&C. Got her all cleaned out." He shook his head. "She's not doing very well, though. She developed septicemia. I'm afraid she has a long haul ahead of her before she's out of the woods." His bushy red eyebrows slid together in a frown and he shook his head. "She was a very foolish girl. Tragic when these girls get into trouble and feel there is nowhere to turn."

The next day I was sitting in the lounge alone after work when Andresen stepped off the elevator and threw herself down on a chair. Her florid face was now beet red, and as she began unbuttoning her apron, little white spots appeared around her mouth. She looked as if she was about to cry.

"What happened?" I asked.

"I'm on St. Mary's and I got this patient who aborted a few days ago. Well, she got septecemia...."

"Is that Dr. Sullivan's patient?"

"Yeah. You know her?"

"I admitted her."

"Well, she died an hour ago."

"Died?" I felt a thump in my chest. I thought I might throw up. "I don't believe it," I said. "I mean I knew she was sick, but I thought she would get better, fight the infection ... "

Andresen's blue eyes swelled with tears. "The antibiotics just couldn't get on top of it, I guess," she said, then quickly turned to the window.

My heart sank. Gone ... so quickly. Only 17 years old. "Oh, God, that's not fair," I moaned. "That's just not fair."

White and Niven had come in on the last of the conversation. "Christ Almighty!" Niven snapped. "They should get rid of those goddamn back-street butchers once and for all. String them up by the balls! That's what I say."

"But if they don't go to the back-street guys, then what do they do?" Andresen said. "Girls can think up the weirdest things when they're desperate."

White shuddered. "Can you believe it? Losing your life for one stupid mistake."

"So where in God's name are they going to go?" said Niven. "Some doctors give abortions in back rooms on the street just so the girls won't have any problems. And some of those docs end up in the slammer, only because they tried to help. I sure admire their guts, though. Those old guys lay their career on the line for those poor girls."

"And I know of a few kids whose parents kicked them out when they wound up pregnant," Andresen said, still in her Norwegian flush. "They're caught between a rock and a hard place."

"That's for damn sure," said Niven. "How can they keep their baby? Who's going to support them?"

"I think the girls should go to the nuns," I said. "The baby might be another Einstein."

"Hey, big shot," Niven said. "What would your parents do if you got pregnant?"

"Me?" I said. "Well, for starters, my mom would probably have a heart attack and wonder where she went wrong. My dad? I'm not sure. He walks a pretty straight line, you know, and he expects me to do the same."

I was primed for New Year's Eve, 1959, in the emergency room. Hospital legend promised lots of action on full moons and New Year's Eve. Patients in emergency weren't neat and sterile and approachable like they were on the wards. Their insides were spilling out. I was to be working with Tanner who had come to emergency two weeks before and had been worrying ever since about working New Year's Eve. "I hate emergency," she said. "My heart pounds so much, I can't think. Every time someone comes in bleeding, I think I'm going to pee my pants."

"Are you kidding? I love it!" I said and I meant it, and that shocked me a little. I loved the excitement of nursing unstable patients, the thrill of my pounding heart and my shaking hands, the rush of raw fear and uncertainty. I had an appetite for it. I thrived on it. The sicker the patient, the better to test my ability.

On New Year's Eve, the nasty north wind became vengeful. I didn't go to the cafeteria for supper because I knew Tanner and I would have lots of goodies to eat later, at her friends' party.

I was sitting in the lounge with my feet propped on a chair, having a cup of coffee when Riley lumbered in, dragging her suitcase behind her. "We're in for a doozer of a storm," she said, struggling into her coat. "I'm taking a sleep-out at Robbin's.

"What are you guys doing tonight?" I asked.

"Oh, I don't know. We'll think of something." She poked her head out of the elevator, "Don't work too hard."

Squeak, bump the elevator door closed and I was left alone in my uniform wondering why Riley and Robbins were always so secretive.

The New Year's Eve storm brought the city to a halt, even the ambulances. Emergency was empty and the phone hardly rang. Tanner and I sat together on tall stools in the stark white treatment room. Down the hall the grads sat in the dim patients' waiting room on comfy chairs, smoking and gossiping.

Tanner was more keyed-up than usual. "Isn't this just the horse's ass," she said, her unlit cigarette clenched in her teeth. "I get all wound up for New Year's Eve in emergency and now I've got to try to unwind again. God, I can't sit still."

"Relax, Tanner," I said. "It's going to be a long evening. But you'll get the boot if one of the nuns catches you with that cigarette in your mouth."

Tanner giggled and wrinkled her nose. "It's not lit. It keeps me calmer."

During the next hour, Tanner became more and more quiet.

"You okay, Tanner?" I finally asked.

"Sure," she said, sounding much too quiet and serious for Tanner. "Just tired, I guess." She bent over the empty stretcher in front of us and lay her head on her arms. After several minutes she leaned on her elbows and propped her chin in her palms.

"You know how you go along thinking that everything that happens when you're a kid is normal? And then one day you wake up and realize that other kids had these wonderful parents and you have people looking after you that don't give a damn what happens to you." Tanner hadn't been looking at me as she said this but then she turned to me and I nodded.

"Yes, I think I know what you mean ... sort of."

"Well, after all this psychology study and stuff, I can see it all now. My mother never really cared for me. Dottie, my older sister, got all the attention. Mother never even came to my capping ceremony ... did you know that?" I shook my head. "That really hurts, Yates. You know, deep down here," she tapped her chest twice. "And I know she's not going to come to the Mother's Day tea, either."

"Maybe she'll change her mind," I said. "You never know."

"Naw," she said, the distant look back in her eyes. "She's not interested. After my dad died, she married this creepy guy. I was eight. He didn't like me. I can't tell you the pain I suffered because of that man. Mom never said a word. Never gave a damn ... I ... I can't talk about it." She buried her face in her hands and drew a deep breath. "But you know what really kills? My own sister doesn't speak to me anymore. My own sister!"

I sat stunned and silent. Happy-go-lucky Tanner depressed? Tanner was always the one who cheered *us* up when we were down. And Tanner was always so full of energy ~ jumpy, almost nervous. I had never guessed she'd been unhappy.

"Gee, I'm so sorry, Tanner," I said softly.

"Oh, it's getting better now ... now that I have Ralph." She reached down the front of her uniform and pulled out Ralph's signet ring that she wore on a gold chain around her neck. "This is what keeps me sane."

Tanner and I were snowbound. Ralph had been on his way to the residence to pick us up for the party but had become stuck and was somewhere digging his way out. We stopped at the cafeteria, but the food set out for the night nurses was the usual dried up roast beef and stale Christmas cookies left over from the nuns' parties. In the lounge after work, Tanner and I sat staring out at the storm.

Just before midnight, I knocked on Kaufmann's door. "Hey, Kaufmann, come and celebrate with us," I said, trying to sound enthusiastic.

"No, thanks," she mumbled sleepily "I have to work days tomorrow."

"Aw, come on, Kaufmann. It's New Year's Eve!"

"Nooo."

Then I heard her door click as she locked it.

So Tanner and I toasted in 1960 by ourselves with a glass of chocolate milk and a peanut butter sandwich.

For the next ten days, I was in the dressing room on preps ~ a shortened term for preparing a patient for the operating room, or more simply put, shaved. I would be responsible for the preps of the whole hospital.

The February senior class was gearing up for graduation, taking full advantage of the extra freedom given to seniors during their last week in residence. They had written their exams and now smugly strutted through the halls, viewing the rest of us as nonentities. As the seniors boisterously came and went at all hours of the night, I had to rise at an ungodly hour to prep the patients going for major surgery in the morning.

The first evening I began with two minor preps, then I tackled a middle-aged man who was to have knee surgery. He was the most hairy fellow Id ever seen. He looked like a monkey. I had to shave him from hip to heel, then do the 10-minute scrub which would prevent osteomyelitis, an infection of the bone that could be a post-surgery complication. He barely managed a grunt or nod in reply to my efforts to make conversation. The grad on duty in emergency checked the shave and signed the chart to confirm that not one hair remained on the man's leg.

"I had an awful time talking to this patient for ten minutes," I whined as I trotted beside the grad on our way back to emergency. "The women are easy but I can't seem to talk to the men."

"I'll give you a tip," she said. "Make sure you listen to the sports report each day on the radio. All men like to talk about sports."

Just before bed that night, I asked Mrs. Foley, the housemother, for a wake-up call at 4:00 a.m, planning to start my first abdominal prep at 4:30. I scribbled the word "sports" on a piece of paper as a reminder and left it beside my alarm clock, which said 10:00. Then I climbed into bed and promptly fell into a deep sleep.

I dreamed I heard singing far off in the distance. It gradually became closer and louder. Dream shifted to consciousness as I realized it was the graduating class performing their last-night-in-residence ritual, dumping every student out of bed.

I leapt out of bed, locked my door and jumped back in bed to wait out the storm. But the seniors would have a passkey from the housemother. I was up again. I hauled my long, heavy desk away from the wall, heaving and shoving until I had it secured against the door.

Back in bed, I lay like a stone as the seniors marched from floor to floor, room to room, singing their song to the tune of *Get Me to the Church on Time*, from the 1959 Broadway Show, My Fair Lady.

> *We're graduating in the morning*
> *Ding dong the bells are going to chime*
> *Roll back the covers,*
> *Pull out the buggers*
> *But get me to the church on time.*

The seniors didn't have the cockney accent of Julie Andrews, but they did sound as though they had just rolled out of the pub with Eliza Doolittle's father.

I was up grappling with the desk again. I had to return it to its niche at the end of the long closet ~ a last-ditch effort to avert a cold bath.

"Aaaaahhhh." It was White's scream.

Then bang, bang, bang.

"Open up or you are going to be very cold and very wet!"

Silence.

Oh God, I heard them unlock a door. They did have the passkey!

"Come on, guys," shrieked one of the seniors. "Let's get her!"

"No. Oh no ... please." It was Kaufmann's tiny voice, begging for mercy.

But there was no mercy. I heard scuffles and struggling in the corridor. Then an agonizing scream ripped through the barbaric cheers of the seniors: she had been dumped in the tub.

There was no time to push my desk into its niche. I vaulted into bed, closed my eyes and pulled the pillow over my head.

I heard a crash.

My door burst open, giving way to the lawless seniors. The next thing I knew I was on the floor , mattress and all.

Afraid to move, I lay still, not even opening my eyes until I heard the seniors' song echoing from the stairwell as they pressed on, down to the third floor. Cautiously, I picked myself up and peered down the corridor just as Kaufmann shuffled out of the bathroom and down the hall, leaving a trail of water.

White flew into the hall in her babydolls. "Those buggers!" she shouted. Then she noticed the puddle of water. "Ah, did they get poor Kaufmann? Just wait 'til we graduate. Boy, am I ever going to get even!"

Guenette's door was still open. I peered into her room. She was sound asleep on her mattress, still on the floor.

The seniors continued their rampage long into the night. The echo of their song had barely disappeared when my buzzer screeched. I fumbled for the lever without lifting my head from the pillow.

"'llo," I mumbled.

"It's four o'clock," sang Mrs. Foley, her voice full of sunshine. "I believe you are on preps today?"

"Oh. Yes ... thank you," I whispered.

I dragged myself out of bed. Slowly I dressed in my uniform and stuffed my hair up into the surgical cap, which we had to wear on preps. Preparing the surgical area was critical in preventing post-operative infection. Hair, even if clean, is a risk. It's porous and holds bacteria, and it sheds.

I raised my blinds and stared blankly out into the pitch-black night. Bright lamps illuminated the semi-circular driveway of the residence. Beyond, the hospital stood silent, enveloped in a strange stillness, eerie and black, sparsely dotted with feeble lights. It was 4:10. A shiver of intimidation ran through me. I alone was responsible for the preps of all the patients going for surgery today. And as I closed the door of my room, I whispered, *I shall not shirk any duty*.

The chill of the night air filled the tunnel and I pulled my white sweater tightly around me. Although a white sweater had been on our required clothing list, this was the first time I had taken it out of my drawer. We were only allowed to wear our sweater on the night shift. I guessed 11:30 p.m. to 7:30 a.m. was the only time we were supposed to feel cold.

I hurried up to St. Mary's with a plan to start with a woman, rather than risk waking a man who might be grumpy so early in the morning.

I found the treatment room and prepared my small prep tray. On top of this I placed my light ~ a light bulb enclosed in a metal wire cage that threw a halo over the skin and made every hair stand out like the Empire State Building. The skin had to be absolutely bald. No hair. No peach fuzz.

Balancing the tray in my left hand and my flashlight in my right, I made my way down the dark hall. The hall was lined with vases of flowers, which we removed from the patients' rooms each night in the belief that flowers robbed the air of oxygen. Finally, my flashlight beam picked out room 326. Laden with the prep equipment, I gave a swift kick to the door. It was lighter than I expected and it flew open, hitting the chair behind with a fierce bang.

"What the heck are you doing, nurse?" shot a lady from the corner bed.

"I'm sorry," I whispered, groping my way to the fourth bed. I set my tray down on the bedside locker and sent a glass of water crashing to the floor. I mopped it up with the patient's towel. Then, ever so slowly ... inch by inch ... metal rings screeching on the metal rod, I began to pull the curtains round the bed. By now everyone in the room was awake, except my patient, who had been given a sleeping pill the night before and was softly snoring.

"Mrs. Jay," I whispered, gently shaking her shoulder.

"Mmmmm."

"I am sorry to wake you up, but I am here to prep you."

"What time is it?" she mumbled.

"It's 4:35."

"My God, I just got to sleep," she moaned.

After fiddling for a few minutes, I found the electrical socket behind the head of the bed and plugged in my light. Mrs. Jay seemed to have gone back to sleep. Not wishing to disturb her, I gently pulled down the covers to expose her large, soft jelly-like abdomen, the area I had to prep. I dunked the gauze I'd clipped to the end of forceps into the liquid soap and sloshed it energetically over her abdomen, determined to work up a good lather.

"Ooowww!" she screeched, sitting bolt upright in bed, her eyes wide open. "That's damn cold, nurse!" she said, in an unfriendly tone.

"I'm sorry," I whispered, placing my hand on her shoulder until she slowly lay back down, "but I have to soap your skin before I shave you."

After several strained moments, I heard her chuckle. "That's something one of my girls would do. I have three at home, just like you. But honestly, nurse," she whispered, with a wink. "Why don't you try heating the water?"

As I prepared the tray for my next patient, I poured a shot of boiling sterile water from the autoclave into the liquid soap. Mrs. Stribley didn't complain.

Though she was booked for a breast biopsy I had to also shave her neck, arm and back, as well as her breast, because behind each breast biopsy loomed a potential radical mastectomy. The operating room would send the biopsy to pathology where they would immediately perform a "frozen section." If the results were benign, it was simply the end of the operation. But if they found cancer cells, the surgeon would begin the long arduous task of removing the woman's breast, some of the muscles of the chest and all the lymph nodes under her arm.

Mrs. Stribley was silent as I shaved her. I tried to encourage her without giving her false hope in case things did not go well. But I eventually gave up, thinking it was best to leave her to her own thoughts.

The grad quietly checked her prep, smiled and wished her luck, and left. I said encouragingly, "Dr. Knox is a wonderful surgeon. You're in very good hands."

Mrs. Stribley gave a slight nod, her face looking strained and her eyes intense as she watched me prepare to leave.

I squeezed her hand. "Everyone in the operating room will be praying for you, and so will I."

"Thank you," she whispered.

Well into my third prep of the morning, I heard singing coming from the corridor. Excusing myself, I walked to the doorway and stood with the other patients and staff who lined the hall. It was those seniors again, but now they were smartly dressed in their graduate uniforms. The blue-and-white student stripes were gone, replaced by the all-white dress of the graduate nurse, their red senior pin just below the starched collar, matching red and gold cufflinks in their stiff cuffs. A black velvet band, the supreme insignia of a registered nurse, edged each winged cap. This was their finale as student nurses at Holy Cross Hospital. Their day had begun with Father Flanagan and our nuns at an early mass in the elegant chapel, then a graduation breakfast with our instructors and Sister Leclerc, and finally, this farewell march through the hospital singing to the tune *It's a Long Way to Tipperary*.

> *It's a long way to graduation,*
> *It's a long way to go*
> *It's a long way to graduation,*
> *To the sweetest day I know.*
> *Goodbye, Holy Cross*
> *Farewell, Sisters, dear,*
> *It's a long, long way to graduation*
> *But thank God, it's here.*

Could this be the same group of lunatics who had ravaged our residence only hours before? The swearing and complaining, the cavorting and the pranks were gone. Now they were angels. That's what I saw. Beautiful angels of mercy. Proud and dignified in starch and simplicity, they swished by waving their tearful farewell to the head nurses and instructors, to the patients ... and to me. I waved back, determined to be in that march in two years. *So long, it's been good to know you, But it's time I was moving along.*

That evening I stopped at the operating room to pick up my list for the following day. The grad sat at a small table in the office. I asked her about Mrs. Stribley, the eight o'clock case booked for a breast biopsy. "Was it malignant?" I crossed my fingers, both hands.

The grad flipped back the page in the large OR book.

She paused as she ran her finger along the line to read the outcome.

"Yes, here it is." She looked up and smiled. "Just did the biopsy. Everything was okay. It's benign."

"Thank God," I breathed.

PART TWO

Romance

"This is a really important day for you," Sister said with a broad smile as she presented our intermediate pins in the Reception Hall after work. "I hope you will continue to make The Holy Cross proud of you. I know you will find the next two years really interesting."

Of the original 36, 21 of us had made it through the first year.

We smiled and said a lot of "Yes, Sister," and, "Thank you, Sister." Then we rushed upstairs to change for a celebration party at Jean Blackwell's house. Blackwell was one of the few Catholic girls remaining in our class. She was a tall girl from Calgary, whose serious look was only a front for her waggish character. Her dry humour was always at the ready for a quick drollish reply.

Everyone was going to the party except Guenette, who made the mature decision to stay home and study. As I tipped back the brown bottle and swallowed a mouthful of cool, bitter beer, it occurred to me that my parents would never have served alcohol to my friends or me until we were 21. I would have to wait one more year. We jived to the top rock'n'roll hits that blared out from Blackwell's new hi-fi radio and record player ... Elvis, Little Richard, Jerry-Lee Lewis. I had brought Fats Domino's 78 record, *Blueberry Hill*, but Tanner accidentally sat on it.

We even talked timid Kaufmann into coming. She did look pretty in the black slacks I loaned her and Andresen's white sweater. I could tell she enjoyed herself by the way she sat, shyly curled up in a big armchair, giggling at us as she sipped her Coke.

At ten o'clock we arrived back at the residence and automatically gravitated to the lounge to continue our celebration. Twice Mrs. Foley came shuffling out of the elevator, clapping her hands and trying her best to sound authoritative. She would shoo us off to bed, but each time we crept back in our pajamas and babydolls and danced with our flimsy dusters unbuttoned, flying from our shoulders.

"I'm 21 years old," White complained, "and they're STILL telling me what time to go to bed. Twenty-one!" She shouted towards the elevator. "I'll go to bed when I damn well feel like it!"

Kaufmann opened her door a crack and peeked out. We begged her to join us but she shook her head and quietly closed her door with a soft click. The juniors peered out from their doors, probably wondering as I had done a short year ago, how our boisterous group would ever become angelic nurses.

Now rulers supreme of the fourth floor, we were going to make sure the juniors fully understood their subordinate position. How exhilarating it was to flaunt our seniority.

As I crawled into bed and drifted off to sleep, I could still hear the girls laughing in the lounge.

I began my intermediate year back on St. Mary's ward with a short-change shift, which meant I had to begin at 7:30 a.m.and work eight hours, then alternate eight hours off and return at 11:30 p.m. for another eight hours.

On that first morning, one of my patients on the day shift was Mary Mullens, a 23-year-old woman who had suffered a miscarriage, a premature expulsion of a nonviable fetus from the uterus. In medical terminology, a spontaneous abortion. Mary Mullens was pale and her sparse hair hung in wisps around her pinched face. Her listless, dark eyes followed me as I moved about her room. When I told her I would bring her a basin of water, she tightened her lips and turned away from me.

"I know the routine, nurse. Do you know this is my third miscarriage this year?"

"Yes, I know," I said gently. "I'm sorry." But my words sounded so cold, so hard. "One day, perhaps you will be strong enough to have a healthy baby," I said. Even though I knew she had Lupus, I always believed there might be a cure around the corner. I smiled. "Above all, Mrs. Mullens, you must stay positive."

"I can't see it that way," she said twisting the corner of the bedspread around her finger. "I'll never have a baby. Each time I get pregnant, it weakens me ... a little more ... and a little more." She gave a moan. "I'll die if I get pregnant again."

"No one should become pregnant if it might endanger their health," I said. "Have you ever considered birth control?"

She shook her head, speaking barely above a whisper. "Birth control is against the Church."

I stared at her in disbelief. "But we live in a new age," I said. "Pregnancies can easily be prevented. All you have to do is ask your doctor." I could feel my heart pounding. Was I stepping beyond my borders as a nurse by advising my patient about birth control? But Mrs. Mullens might die if she became pregnant again. "I'll give you some names of Protestant doctors, telephone numbers...."

"No." She turned away again. "Dr. Flynn will yell at me. I know he will."

I was in a Catholic hospital with a Catholic patient who had a Catholic doctor, but I had taken an oath: *I will practice my profession faithfully ... devote myself to the welfare of those committed to my care.* Dr. Flynn had also taken an oath. Surely he would give her something for birth control. I pleaded with her, until she finally agreed to ask him. "Will you be here, with me, when I ask?" She said.

"I promise."

St. Mary's was a beehive Monday mornings. Three of my patients had to be in the operating room before 10 a.m. and I helped the orderly move them there. On our way, I had to stop at the desk for the head nurse to inspect my patient. No false eye, false teeth or dental plate was allowed. No clothing, especially underwear. The head nurse checked the skin prep again. Nails had to be free of nail polish so the anaesthetist could check the nail beds for cyanosis, a sign that the patient needed more oxygen. Once the head nurse had signed the report, the orderly and I pushed the patient across the hall and through the large swinging double doors of the operating room. A nurse always had to accompany the patient.

On my way back to St. Mary's, I spied Dr. Flynn striding down the hall to Mrs. Mullens' room. I darted after him. My heart began to throb; she was going to ask him for birth control. I arrived, slightly out of breath, as Dr. Flynn was examining her abdomen.

"Everything's fine," he mumbled gruffly. "You'll be going home tomorrow if your blood count is satisfactory."

He turned and started for the door.

"Dr. Flynn?" Mrs. Mullens said in a thin voice.

I felt as though my knees wouldn't hold me up. Had I put my career in jeopardy?

He stopped and turned. His round puffy face with ruddy cheeks sat on his shoulders as if he had no neck. His body was puffed up, too, but in a lopsided way because of his substantial belly in front and board-flat buttocks in back. In fact, he had to lean slightly backwards to remain balanced.

"I want to ask you something," she stammered. "I ... ah ... I'm afraid I will get pregnant again."

He stood like a stone.

I suddenly felt weak; I leaned against the armchair for support.

Mrs. Mullens twisted the bedspread around and around her finger. "Dr. Flynn ... I don't want to get pregnant again," she blurted out without looking up.

"What is that supposed to mean?" he seethed through his teeth.

She made a nervous attempt to look at him, and whispered, "I want something for birth control."

"What? Birth control?" he roared, then careened across the room and steadied his bulky frame against the foot of her bed. "What are you talking about, woman? You know that's against the Church!" He pulled in his chin and his upper body grew. His neck deepened to a nauseating plum, his wattles bright red. His face and balding head were oddly splotched with blue and white.

Mrs. Mullens seemed to fold into herself; she looked smaller. "But what about me?" She said in a squeaky voice. "I have to think of me, too." She began to sob. "The rhythm method doesn't work for me. I'll die if I get pregnant again."

"I'm surprised at you, woman." Dr. Flynn's voice was forced and raspy. "Very surprised!" He turned like a tank and lumbered towards the door, then wheeled round and faced her. "You know the rules of the Church, woman, and I know the rules of the Church. I will hear no more of this, you hear? No more!" He banged the door behind him and the walls quivered.

I felt as though I was going to burst. Did Catholic doctors have a different code? He had taken an oath, as I had. He had sworn to save lives. He had recited the Hippocratic Oath, *I solemnly pledge myself to consecrate my life to the service of humanity ... The health of my patient will be my first consideration ... I will not permit considerations of religion, nationality, race, party politics or social standing to intervene between my duty and my patient; I will maintain the utmost respect for human life ... I make these promises solemnly, freely, and upon my honour.*

Mrs. Mullens sobbed, quietly. "You see? I knew he would be mad at me."

I fought back the shock and anger that surged through me and I tried my best to comfort her. "A Protestant doctor will gladly give you birth control," I said. "I'll even call one for you."

She raised her face to me and shook her head. "Are you Catholic?"

"No."

"Then I know it's difficult for you to understand. I can't see another doctor. Birth control is against the Church." Mrs. Mullens placed her hand gently on my arm and looked straight into my eyes. "I understand that ... really I do. But if I get pregnant again, nurse, I'll die ... I know I will ... I'll die."

She turned from me and her gaze went out the window. The bright blue sky seemed endless and a dusting of fluffy snow on the rooftops glistened in the sun. It was a glorious day; spring was approaching. Mrs. Mullens raised her hand to wipe a tear that slipped down her pale cheek. She looked terribly fragile and so alone ... I wanted to save her. I had gone out on a limb but I couldn't go any further. It was her life, her decision. Still, I felt terribly helpless.

St. Mary's was a busy ward, especially at night. Each night after report, the grad and I made rounds together, often finding patients awake. I gave pain medication to the post-surgery patients. Some patients were always on the call button, others just lay staring at the ceiling, terrified and trembling in the dark. Those were the ones we had to watch for. Mrs. Whitford's words never left me: *Reassure the patient, don't knock them out with a sleeping pill.* I gave them a back rub, reassurance and a glass of hot milk before I resorted to medication.

During my last week on night duty, Linda Rook, a junior who had just received her cap three weeks earlier, approached me.

"I can't believe it," she said in a nervous twitter, "I have six patients going to the OR this morning."

"Look," I said, handing her a sheet of paper, "here's the list I made you. It's got the time of each injection and pill you have to give your pre-op patients, starting at 5 a.m. I'll be busy all night, I've got four fresh post-ops and four scheduled for the OR in the morning."

All during that night, each time I bumped into Rook she would pull the long list out of her pocket. "I start with Mrs. Brown, right?"

"Just remember to check your list and check the patient's arm band." I'd tell her. "Be very careful and nothing will go wrong."

At 5 a.m., the rush started. The needles, the pills, checking the patients, a bedpan for Mrs. What'shername, an injection. The orderly arrived, left with a patient. No sooner had I turned around then he was back for another. He drummed his fingers impatiently on the stretcher while I drilled the second injection into my patient's buttock. It was hectic and I was nervous, but I kept up the pace and I wondered how poor Rook was doing with her six patients.

At 7:30 the day staff began drifting in. I was writing up my report when Rook rushed over to me, cap askew, some of her hair loose and hanging in strings.

"My God!" Rook cried, her hands covering her face. "I've made a terrible mistake. I've killed all my patients!"

"Okay, Rook, it's okay," I said trying to calm her. "It can't be that bad."

"It is. Oh, it is! I've given all my patients the wrong pre-op medication! I've mixed them all up! All of them!"

My God! I breathed. I felt the colour drain from my face.

She pulled the list I had made for her that morning, from her pocket. "Look!" she said pointing to the top of the list, "this is Mrs...."

"Yates! Your turn for report." The grad had finished her report and was calling me from the kitchen.

I picked up my papers and glanced at Rook. She looked like she was about to run out of the nearest exit and never return. "Go into that corner by yourself," I said, "and systematically check your charts and each patient on the paper and find out what went wrong."

Rook's problem loomed at the back of my mind while I rattled off my report to the day staff. If she left the building, it was probably my fault. Although I was barely an intermediate, I was her senior and I felt responsible for her.

After what seemed an eternity, I finished report and rushed for the door. I almost tripped over Rook who sheepishly stood on the other side.

"It's okay," she whispered. "Sorry about the panic. I thought I'd mixed up the patients, but I didn't." She grinned. "Thanks, Yates." Rook crossed her fingers, and pushed through the door to give her report. I crossed my fingers, too.

One day during Intermediate Block, I received a letter from Lester.

> *Dearest Donna,*
> *It's a long, cold winter out here in this desolate Saskatchewan. All I*
> *do is sit in these lonely barracks and think of you. I miss you every*
> *day. Is there any chance you and some of your nurse friends could*
> *come out to Regina for a visit? I've got a lot of lonely guys waiting.*
>   *A good combination, don't you think – The Holy and*
> *RCMP? Check the train schedules.*
>   *Love, Lester – A lonesome cop – hoping....*

I tucked the letter into my pocket and went up to the lounge and asked White, "How would you like to make a trip to Regina with me?"

"Regina!" She said, incredulously. "You've got to be kidding, Yates, right?"

"No, I'm serious," I said. "Lester's got lots of guys, real Mounties, waiting for us. Just think of it, we'll have a ball!"

"In the middle of winter? Hitching to Regina? Saskatchewan? Oh, not me."

"Come on, White. I hitched with you when you wanted to see your Dad."

"Yeah, but it was spring, Yates. Big difference. Take a look outside, it's way below zero." She brought her hand to her head and took a deep breath, then said,

"Well, okay. But I think you're crackerjack, Yates, correction ~ I think we're both crackerjack to hitch. It's gotta be a few hundred miles?"

"Yeah, something like that," I said, purposely vague.

When I asked Perry, she shuddered. "Are you joking? There's no way I'm going to get out on the highway and thumb my way to Regina. It's the middle of winter!"

Niven wouldn't consider it, either. "Hey, eyeball the weather, you birdbrains! It's not sunny California, here. I think you're both going off the deep end."

So there would be just White and me.

On Saturday morning White and I went for breakfast and filled our pockets with hard-boiled eggs to make sandwiches for our trip. Niven shuffled into the lounge as I was chopping up the rubbery eggs and delightedly told us the weather forecast called for snow and 30 below. I shot a worried look at White who hesitated for a moment, then continued smearing chopped egg on a piece of bread.

"You're both crazy to get out on that highway in the middle of winter," Guenette clucked like a mother hen. "It's noon now, and you have to be back by 11 p.m. tomorrow. What happens if you can't get a ride? Or if a storm comes up and you're in the middle of nowhere? Southern Saskatchewan is awfully risky. You can go for hours and never see a house. If you get stuck without a ride, you'll freeze to death on the highway and nobody will find you for days. How far is Regina anyhow?"

"A little over 400 miles," I mumbled. Guenette stared at me and narrowed her eyes. "Ah, 471 ... I think ... to be exact," I said.

"It's insane!" Guenette continued. "You'll never get back on time. Besides being a stupid idea, it's downright dangerous."

Perry looked like she was about to cry.

"Aw, don't worry about us. We're seasoned hikers," I said, trying to sound confident, though I felt a knot of doubt in my stomach.

White and I packed the sandwiches in a brown bag and walked through the snow to the bus stop in front of the Lotus. We rode up to the north hill and got off at the loop. It was a half-mile walk to the highway, then we began to thumb.

Before long, a farm couple who had been shopping in Calgary pulled up in a Chevy coup. They only took us 25 miles, but we easily got three other rides. At 8 p.m., a salesman let us out on the highway somewhere in the middle of Saskatchewan. He turned south, and we watched his taillights become smaller and smaller until they were only tiny red dots, then they disappeared.

"Hey, look at that," White said pointing to the moon. "Full moon and empty arms." She gave a playful chuckle.

"But not for long. Look out, guys, here we come!" I shouted into the black night.

We began dancing on the highway, singing song after song, *I found my thrill / On Blueberry Hill ...* We bounced back and forth across the dotted line under the cool white moon. We had been there for 40 minutes, when it hit us that not one car had passed. I suddenly realized I was very cold and hungry. There was nothing in sight.

No houses, no trees, only the telephone poles that followed the highway on and on into infinity.

"If nobody comes, we'll freeze to death," I said, and shuddered. My parents thought I was safe at White's for the weekend. They would read about my death in the paper. Two poor student nurses found frozen on a lonely highway somewhere in the middle of Saskatchewan. Now I was sorry I lied.

The air was sharp; it was terribly cold, at least 20 below. My nostrils stuck together when I breathed in and my forehead felt numb. I wondered if my brains were freezing. The sky had an unearthly silver glow I had never seen in Alberta and I realized we were stranded in a foreign part of the country, a place I knew nothing about. Then my eyes began to water from the cold and my lashes became mushy and stuck together.

White and I stood like statues on the snow-spattered ribbon of asphalt which was so cold it squeaked under our feet as we walked. It stretched on and on without a curve, without a hill, without even a bump. Telephone poles lined the two-lane blacktop on one side like giant crosses in a linear graveyard. In the eerie quiet, my heart thumped full speed in my chest. And then I heard something else, a soft murmur ... a weak wail ... the hum of electricity and telephone wires relaying messages, lamenting the cold.

"Better start walking," White said with a worried look.

We began to walk, but soon the chill of the nighttime cold began to seep through our jeans and cloth jackets and cotton babushkas. Fright quickly replaced hunger.

"We can't panic," I suggested through chattering teeth. "No matter what happens, we have to keep our wits."

Suddenly I heard the faint whine of an engine. We stood riveted to the highway. I began to pray. The whine turned into a groan. Our eyes strained into the black emptiness. Two faint lights appeared.

"If this guy looks like he's not going to stop, I'm going to lie across that damn centre line. He'll have to stop," White said.

The lights got larger, closer, and the groan changed to a roar. Through the darkness, we made out several more lights on top of the cab.

"It's a truck!" White shouted jumping up and down. "He'll pick us up, I'm sure." We danced around the highway to make sure the driver saw us. Brakes squealed as he geared down. The pungent odour of cow dung mixed with a blast of diesel exhaust engulfed us as the truck rolled by.

"It's a bloody cattle liner!" White shouted as we sprinted forward.

The truck slowly careened to a halt about 500 feet past us and disappeared into billowing waves of powdery snow tossed up from its large tires.

"Hope his heater's working!" White called over her shoulder as she easily scaled the large front wheels and bounced into the cab. Lacking her experience with farm equipment, my ascent was clumsy, and it took several minutes before I was seated in the cab of the largest truck I had ever seen.

"Where ya goin'?" shouted the driver above the roar of the engine.

"Regina," we shouted back.

"So am I. Orin Penrod's the name. Penrod the roadrod, they call me. Glad ta have ya aboard."

The gears grated. The truck groaned and choked, spewing black exhaust into the clear, cold night air. It lurched, and lurched again. We bounced to the ceiling. Slowly we inched forward, until the pull of the powerful engine prevailed over its massive cargo and we were barrelling down the lonely highway under a large pale moon.

"So what'da you gals do?" Orin shouted.

"We're nurses," White said.

"Student nurses," I added, to let him know we were poor.

Orin pulled down his mouth, nodding as he raised his eyebrows. I knew he was impressed.

"I'll be damned, I says ta myself when I seen you gals on the road," he shouted without taking his eyes off of the highway. "Never seen gals thumbin' it b'fore. Aint you gals sceered?"

"A little," shouted White. "We were sure glad to see you. What are you hauling?"

"Cattle. Beef. Shorthorns."

As we bumped and swayed in the security of the warm cab, the engine whined and the odd cow mooed and we slept.

Near midnight we awoke with a jolt as Orin Penrod began gearing down at a truck stop. I ran inside to telephone Lester while Orin filled the truck with gas. It was midnight.

"Hi, Lester," I said when I finally got through. "I'm near Moose Jaw. White and I are coming in a huge cattle liner."

Lester laughed. "God, you're in a cattleliner?"

"Yeah."

"Well, at least you'll arrive in style. Hang on, gotta tell Bob...." I could hear both of them laughing. Then he was back. "Where you calling from?"

"The Mother Tucker's Truck Stop."

"God," he laughed again. "Look. Bob and I will drive out and meet you. Watch for us. We'll be parked on the right side of the highway."

"How will I know it's you?" I asked.

"Don't worry. You'll know."

The last half hour seemed endless. When Regina cast a white aura into the blackness ahead, we anxiously began to search the dark on the right. Then I saw two headlights facing the highway.

The lights blinked.

We shot by.

A siren screamed behind us and I turned. It was a black car, flashing lights illuminated our cab in staccato red and white.

"Christ! It's them damn cops!" Orin shouted.

88

"Nope, it's our friends," I shouted. "Pull over and let us out." He gave me a puzzled look.

"They're our friends!" I shouted again.

"Cops?"

"Yeah," White and I yelled in unison. "Cops!"

White leapt out of the cab like a deer. I tried to make a dainty descent, but could only manage to galumph my way down the enormous tire and land at Lester's feet like a sack of potatoes.

It was already 1:30 a.m. when we jumped into the RCMP car and the boys announced they had to be back at the barracks by two. We were starving, but nothing was open. "The town's locked up tighter than a drum," Lester said. He drove us to a cheap motel close to the barracks. At 1:55 White and I stood under a weak blue neon sign that flashed B-FFY'S MOT-L, and watched our dates disappear down the street, signalling their goodnight with flashing red lights.

"This isn't exactly what I had in mind," White said, as she pulled on her babydolls.

"Me neither, but you shouldn't complain," I said, jumping into the cold bed. "Your guy is cute."

"Yeah ... not bad," she said half-heartedly.

The next morning Lester phoned. "Bob and I are on horse duty," he said. "Can't leave until we've fed and cleaned all the horses in the barn. Can you picture me bouncing around on a stupid horse in the Musical Ride? It's a joke! Bob doesn't mind looking after horses, he comes from a farm. But I hate horses. I can't ride the damn things, and I hate the smell of them."

I hung up, stunned. I couldn't believe he said that. How could Lester hate horses? I loved them.

As White and I sat on the bed waiting for the boys to arrive, I confessed, "I think we made a mistake coming here."

White leaned towards the mirror nailed to the wall above a cheap-looking table and carefully traced her lips with a small tube of *Almost Natural* lipstick. She slowly turned to me and raised one eyebrow. "I *know* we made a mistake, Yates."

"Are you angry?" I asked, running my finger along a wavy line of the pink chenille bedspread.

"Naw." She turned back to the mirror and smacked her lips together, then stuffed her lipstick into her jeans pocket. "But they sure as hell better buy us something to eat. I'm starving."

When Lester and Bob finally arrived, it was 11:30.

"We have to be back to the barracks for lunch before one," Bob said as we jumped into the RCMP car.

"Well that's just dandy," White said with a crooked smile. "Yates and I haven't eaten since yesterday. I expect you guys to at least feed us before you take us to the highway."

"Sure we will," Lester quickly said. "Feel like a hamburger?"

After we'd eaten, they drove us out to the highway and parked behind a large sign by the side of the road. White seemed to feel better with food in her stomach and giggled at Bob's perfect imitation of Daffy Duck. But soon they were quiet and I could hear Bob's heavy breathing. I drank in the scent of Lester's Old Spice mixed with a faint horsy smell, then his breathing grew heavy too. The RCMP vehicle pitched and rolled beneath the Alpha Dairy billboard that stated, *Our Milk Comes from Contented Cows.*

It was 12:30, time to go. White and I straightened our sweaters and struggled into our coats. Bob gave her one last impressive kiss in the back seat, Hollywood style, then they exchanged addresses and phone numbers and White re-applied her lipstick. Lester opened his door and ran the defrost full blast to clear the fog from the windows.

"Good luck!" Lester said with a wink. "Be sure to write."

Then White and I were alone on the highway. *Dropped*, I thought. Dropped on the highway to fend for ourselves while the boys returned to their horses and shovelling manure and, no doubt, a warm lunch. They would probably put us right out of their minds and move on to some cute Regina girls.

White must have read my thoughts. "So?" she said, as she sat down on her overnight case. "Are you still in love?"

I shrugged. "Lester's a good necker, but I'm beginning to wonder about him. I can't understand why he told us to come all the way out to Regina when he knew he was on horse duty. And I can't believe he doesn't like the smell of horses."

"If you ask me, this trip was a dopey idea." White said. "Come on, Yates, get thumbing, and look desperate. We have to be home in ten hours."

"That won't be hard," I sighed, motioning with my thumb, to a speeding car. "We *are* desperate."

"Have you ever gone all the way, Yates?" White suddenly asked.

I shuddered. "God, I'm scared to go past the necking phase. Three of my friends got pregnant in high school. If I ever got pregnant, that would be the end of my career, I would never be a nurse. I know how my Mom feels. For the rest of her days, she would wonder where she went wrong."

"Ditto," White said. "I've worked too hard to get this far and I'm sure as hell not going to throw it all away for one stupid moment. Hey, look!" She pointed to a car changing lanes. "I think this one's going to stop."

A man and woman pulled over beside us in a new metallic blue Dodge. They were going to Calgary! We jumped into the back seat and thanked them over and over again, then quickly fell asleep.

Near suppertime the couple woke us and bought us each a hamburger. At 9:30 they dropped us off at the residence and we rushed up to the lounge to wait for the others to arrive.

"So you made it back, snow storm and all." Guenette said when she stepped off the elevator and saw us. "You're both absolutely nuts. I hope it was worth it."

"Wouldn't have missed it for the world," laughed White. "And Niven's going to be damn sorry. She passed up the most romantic trip of her life!"

The Secret Life of the Operating Room

March came in like a lion with a blustery storm that dumped several inches of snow on the city. The tunnel was dark and very cold that Friday afternoon when I rushed through after work to check the change list posted outside the classroom. Now that I had completed Intermediate block and was able to work on the specialty wards, I nervously searched for my name. Where would Sister send me next? I stood with a small group from my class and ran my eyes down the list:

Andresen ~ Calgary Children's Hospital

Guenette ~ Pediatrics

Perry ~ Ponoka Mental Hospital

Porter ~ Baker Memorial T.B. Sanatorium

White ~ Calgary Children's Hospital

Yates ~ Operating Room

I saw my name. My wish had come true.

That Sunday evening I sat on White's bed, watching her pack. "Gee, White, I am really going to miss you," I said. "I can't believe you're going to be away for four weeks."

"Don't worry, Yates, you'll be so bloody busy in the OR ... now where did I put that bag of white nylons?"

"You heaved it up on the shelf in your closet," mumbled Niven who was perched on the windowsill eating a banana that Tanner had sneaked out of the diet kitchen.

"Oh, yeah." White retrieved the nylons and went on with her packing. "I have two words of advice for you, Yates. Get used to bloody tonsils, and I mean bloody. And stay the hell away from Dr. Thompson! He's a mean operator, pardon the pun."

The next morning a delighted terror consumed me as I donned a white surgical cap and green cotton OR dress. I pulled the white cloth boots over my shoes and stepped across the black line on the floor that marked the beginning of the operating room. I took a deep satisfying breath of the heavy ether odour that hung in the air.

Bright ceiling lights shone down on a black and white checkerboard floor. Nurses checked the work sheet before scurrying off to their assigned theatre. Orderlies left with empty stretchers and returned with patients. Everyone moved about silently in cloth boots and all the eyes above the masks looked serious. I had stepped into a foreign country, a mysterious specialized underworld where everyone ignored student nurses.

Miss Wilder, the head nurse, was a quiet-spoken, tall and very thin young woman with green-blue eyes. She led our little group of four new students down the hall, pointing out each room. In the theatre across the hall from where I stood, the anaesthetist hovered over his machines, preparing the magic potion that would keep the patient alive and breathing and asleep for as long as the surgeon required. A n orderly moved a patient from a stretcher to the OR table, beneath a huge round lamp suspended from the ceiling. Two nurses in oversized green gowns, wearing surgical gloves and masks, arranged the instruments on a large table beside the back wall. The orderly pushed the stretcher out of the room and closed the double doors of theatre Number Seven.

As we followed Miss Wilder from room to room, her large, cat-like eyes darted everywhere. She would suddenly dash for a suture, move the large light above the operating table or open a bundle of instruments in response to a barely audible grunt uttered from beneath someone's mask.

A white light began to blink silently over one of the theatre doors.

"Number Five coming out!" Shouted Miss Wilder.

Suddenly the theatre doors burst open. An orderly ran past us and into the theatre, pulling on the mask that had been hanging around his neck. He began to help the doctors and nurses slide the patient onto the stretcher. I peered into the room. Empty paper packets and bloodstained gauze that had missed the shiny metal buckets on black wheels, lay strewn over the floor.

"Time you girls had some juice," Miss Wilder said. "We take our break in the utility room. No time to go down to the cafeteria."

The four or us sat on small stools at the counter beneath a large window in the utility room, sipping coffee. I discreetly eyed my reflection in the window. The face was mine, but I couldn't believe it was really me ~ an operating room nurse.

Two cleaning women busily scrubbed blood off the used instruments that sat soaking in large silver basins set all about the room. The autoclave hissed and snorted in one corner as it sterilized the doctors' special instruments, those not included in the standard bundle prepared for each operation. A strange, heavy odour filled the room, a combination of coffee, lemonade, hot steam, and blood.

We had barely sat down when Miss Wilder motioned to us from the doorway. A wisp of black hair poked out from her cloth cap. She had an urgency about her. In fact, everyone in the OR seemed to exhibit a suppressed alarm reaction. We left our coffee and followed her back to theatre Number Five.

"The next case is on the way. This room has to be cleaned as quickly as possible," she said, slightly out of breath as she attempted to tuck the wisp of hair up under her cap. "Jones!" She called to the student nurse piling the dirty instruments into a large silver basin. "Show these girls how to clean a theatre. It's their first day." Then she flew out the door shouting, "Number Seven coming out!"

For the rest of the day we cleaned. "Number Three coming out!" And we scurried in. By the end of our shift, we had cleaned every room, including the cupboards, glass shelves, lights, tables, and stands with alcohol and ether. And before we went home, Miss Wilder gave us a lecture on how to scrub our hands, nails and arms before each operation.

When I went home for supper that night, my mother was more than anxious to hear about my first day in the operating room.

"Oh, there's a lot of blood," I said. "But it didn't take long before I got used to it. The patient was covered with green drapes so I only saw the incision. I cleaned blood off tables and furniture the whole day," I said coolly as I passed the mashed potatoes to my brother. "It's really interesting how they hang all the gauze sponges soaked with blood on a metal rung. Then they count them so they won't leave any in the patient."

"Gee whiz!" My father snapped and pushed his plate away. "Do you two always have to discuss these gory things at the dinner table? Maybe it doesn't bother your mother, but I don't want to hear about it."

"Ditto," my brother said, tightening the corners of his mouth.

My mother and I shared our knowing look and finished our conversation later while we cleaned up the kitchen.

When I returned to the residence, I stepped out of the elevator just in time to hear Robbins tell Andresen, "I don't know why they always suspect that I'm a street walker." She took a cigarette from her mother-of-pearl case and eased it into a shiny black holder, lighting it with her matching mother-of-pearl lighter. That lighter impressed me. All we had were give-away matches from the York. Robbins drew deeply on her cigarette, then slowly released the smoke from her full orange lips as if she was blowing a kiss. She crossed her thick legs and her skirt slowly inched upwards, but Robbins didn't seem to notice, or care.

Andresen eyed her for several minutes then politely said. "You know, Robbins, I think if you combed your hair off of your face and didn't wear your skirts so short, or tight … well … maybe the cops wouldn't pay any attention to you."

But Robbins had a strange detached look in her eyes and she stared out the window in silence.

"How can you be so calm?" I asked. "I would never be able to sit quietly if the police ever questioned me."

Niven leaned back on her elbows against the counter and gave a sardonic chuckle. "If the police report this to Sister, Robbins, you're going to be in deep shit."

Robbins gave a dismissive shrug. "I don't give a damn ~ about Sister or this god-awful hellhole."

"Okay, Johnny, we're going for an airplane ride," said Dr. Rob, the anaesthetist. The gentle giant sat, elbows propped, at the head of the table staring down at his four-year-old patient. He held the mask connected to a machine between his large tender hands.

"Have you ever been on an airplane before? No? Well I am going to hold this mask above your head like this … and we are going to start up the engines, urmm, urmm, just like that. And away we go."

As Dr. Rob spoke, he moved the mask delivering ether a little closer to Johnny's face.

"We're getting higher, Johnny," he continued in a low monotone voice, "and as we get higher, sometimes we get a little dizzy." The mask moved closer to Johnny's face. "When we get dizzy we put on our mask, just like the pilots do, and we take a deep breath. Are you getting dizzy, Johnny? You're doing fine, Johnny, just fine. Here comes the mask, Johnny. Take some deep breaths now."

I opened my little bundle of instruments and had my suture ready on a needle for Dr. Duffy, the surgeon.

The mask was on. Johnny was asleep.

He was so tiny lying there on but one third of the table and I could barely see inside his open mouth. I held a metal tongue retractor against Johnny's little tongue to keep it out of the way, the surgeon grabbed the scissors. Snip.

"Suction, nurse. Suction!"

I fumbled around Johnny's small mouth sucking out the blood that poured from his throat.

Dr. Duffy grabbed the suture from the table, thrust his hand into the mouth and tied two knots. Before I could suction the mouth, he had grabbed the adenoid remover and thrust it in and out of Johnny's little nostrils. He snatched the suction from my hand, stuck it in each nostril, then smacked me in the stomach with it. I took it from him.

"Why in the name of blazes do they always give me these damn students," he snapped. "All they do is get in my way." And he was gone.

"You were fine, nurse," Dr. Rob said in a soothing voice. "Your first day?"

Unable to speak because of the lump that swelled in my throat, I could only manage a weak nod.

Johnny stirred. "Okay, Johnny, time to wake up," Dr. Rob said. He squeezed a few puffs of oxygen from the big bag on the machine, then lifted him gently to the waiting crib and placed him on his side. Johnny began to wake up. I could hear him moaning on his way to the recovery room.

Although I was stunned by the crudeness of the operation, there was no time to lament my first scrub; I had six others to go. And by the end of the day, I was much handier at wielding the suction tube.

By Wednesday, the week began to drag. It was more and more difficult to get out of bed each morning and into the tonsil room. The doctors flew in and flew out full of nervous energy and not all the anaesthetists were as kind as Dr. Rob. Some of them slapped the mask on the frightened, squirming child and held it in place until they went under.

When I entered the tonsil room on Friday, it was terribly hot and stuffy. My first case was with Dr. Schmidt, a doctor from Europe who did very little work at Holy Cross Hospital. As I scrubbed, I read his card propped at the scrub sink in front of me. This informed the scrub nurse of the surgeon's routine, any special instruments and the suture material preferred. But part of the instructions confused me. *Stay suture of 3-0 silk on a straight cutting needle.*

I prepared the instruments according to the card. Dr. Rob put Danny to sleep peacefully. Then suddenly, Dr. Schmidt charged in like an ill wind. Without so much as a good morning to Dr. Rob or me, he picked up the straight cutting needle with the silk thread hanging and thrust the needle through the child's tongue.

"Here," he snapped, handing me the silk thread. "Pull on this and keep the tongue out of the way," then he began cutting out the tonsils.

Horrified! I stared in disbelief. Why not use a tongue depressor like the other surgeons? Then I felt hot ~ and suddenly woozy.

"Suction. Suction!"

My left hand held the black silk suture that ran through the child's tongue, my right hand held the suction tube. I began to feel limp.

"Suction!"

I probed the mouth with the suction tube but my eyes could not focus.

"Suction!"

The patient and his mouth floated further away from me, fading like an ancient, yellow photograph.

"Suction! Pull on that suture. Get the tongue out of the way. God damn you, nurse! *SUCTION!*"

I couldn't see the mouth any more. The tongue, I thought. Let go of the tongue ... suture ... I'm fainting ... I'm going to pull the tongue out. The hissing of the suction swelled to a squealing pitch and surged through my head in undulating waves. Two strong arms grabbed me from behind and dragged me to a nearby chair. It was Dr. Rob.

"I'm taking her out, Hans. I don't want to revive two patients."

Dr. Rob shoved my head down between my knees and summoned Miss Wilder, who took me to the utility room and gave me a glass of lemonade. This was the coddling one received on becoming faint in the operating room.

Shaken and weak, I sat on the little stool, sipping lemonade and watching a plump matronly lady clean bright red blood from straight and curved scissors, scalpel-handles, forceps and other oddly shaped instruments.

"Och, aye," said Mrs. Brown in her broad Scottish accent. "We get many a student in here takin' a wee lemonade after a faint. It's no sin, girl. It happens to the best of 'em. Don't you brood about it now, dearie, ya hear?" She continued cleaning as she talked.

"Some very fine nurses, aye, and doctors too, I might add, sat right here on that very chair and sipped a wee juice after a faint. Give us a look, pet." She bent over and studied my face. I looked up at her like a wounded puppy. She had fine purple veins streaking across her plump cheeks. There was a large bluish-one on her nose, and it looked like it might pop. I felt nauseous.

"Och, you're looking better already, my pet."

Miss Wilder agreed, and sent me back to clean up the tonsil room and prepare for the next case. Dr. Rob was gently placing the child in his crib when I arrived.

"Some things around here are outdated, and definitely barbaric," he mumbled. "We do have tongue retractors now. Must bring this up at the next meeting." He pushed the crib to the door, then turned to me.

"You okay, nurse?"

"Yes, I think so. Thank you."

He winked. "Good."

Later, as we sat in the lounge sipping our coffee, Perry said. "Tonsils are the worst part of the operating room. It's the bloodiest, hottest and most uncivilized room in the hospital. Oh, don't worry, Yates," she giggled when she noticed my worried face. "They won't put you back in tonsils once your week is over. One week is about all anyone can stand."

As I began my third week in the OR, Tanner arrived for her first day. There were four D&C cases booked in Tanner's theatre and she would be the only nurse scrubbed-in.

"I can't think," she moaned. "Everything comes up so darn fast. It scares the pants off me."

"Look," I said. I don't have to be in the orthopedic room for hip surgery until 8:30. I can help you get started."

When we arrived at the theatre, the grad was quietly preparing the instruments needed for the operation, but the anaesthetist, was having problems starting the I.V.

"Miss Tanner, stay with Dr. Stacy until he gets the I.V. going," the grad said, "then go and scrub."

The tall Dr. Stacy looked like a daddy longlegs, hunched over the patient's outstretched arm, taped to a board. "What's the matter with these darn veins," he muttered. "They're all shot to hell. Have your scissors ready, nurse."

Tanner nervously shuffled from one foot to another, her scissors poised, ready for the cut.

"Bingo!" cried Dr. Stacy as he successfully inserted the intravenous needle into the patient's vein. He placed a piece of tape over the needle and waited for Tanner to cut the tape. When Tanner didn't move, he shouted. "Cut, nurse!"

Tanner jolted to attention, then cut ~ the intravenous tubing instead of the tape! Glucose and water poured out through the severed tubing, drenching the patient's arm and Dr. Stacy's shoes.

"Oh, no," he moaned, and little muscles around his eyes began to twitch. "I've read about these things happening, Miss," he said in a breathy whisper. "but I never thought I would live to see the day when it would happen to me."

As Tanner began darting about the room with new intravenous bottles and tubing, I left for the orthopedic theatre to scrub in for a hip operation.

As I scrubbed, they were tightening the large body clamp that would hold the patient securely on his side. Roberta Rowels, a junior from the September '62 class, was working with the circulating grad. Rowels was a wafer-thin bundle of nerves with huge blue eyes. She was petite and delicate and looked more like someone from grade school.

Several hours into the operation, Dr. Murphy came to a crucial point deep in the patient's hip and asked for the light to be changed.

I stood between Dr. Murphy and Mrs. Klassen, his scrub nurse, who motioned to Rowels to change the light. A large lamp enclosed in an upside down metal bowl hung above the patient. It was attached to the end of a horizontal arm suspended from the ceiling, and extended past the patient and the scrub nurse's back table, making it accessible to the circulating nurse. The circulating grad had gone for coffee, which left tiny Rowels, the only nurse in the room not scrubbed in. She rushed to the table, but then hesitated as if confused. The lamp was awkward and heavy and changing the position of the light was a difficult procedure. Rowels would have to hold the end of the handle, push the horizontal arm forward, swing it to the left and then pull it back towards her.

"Light!" shouted Dr. Murphy. "Where the hell is everybody?"

Rowels quickly reached up and gripped the handle. She pushed the horizontal arm forward and swung it to the left, but it hit the end of the track with a loud bump and the light dropped down two feet. The other end shot up ~ with Rowels attached. She was afraid to let go and risk falling on and contaminating the back table, or worse yet, the patient. So she dutifully hung on, dangling in front of me, like a trapeze artist.

My eyes met hers and my mouth dropped open under my mask. The grad and I stood helpless, our sterile hands up, as if victims of a bank robbery.

Just then the circulating nurse returned from her coffee break. She froze in the doorway, her eyes fixed on Rowels, hanging limply from the light.

"Will somebody *please* take that student off the light," Dr. Murphy said quietly, without looking up.

The circulating nurse rushed to Rowels' assistance, then sent her to the utility room for a glass of lemonade.

An hour and a half after the operation, as I helped push the patient to the recovery room I glanced into Tanner's room to see how she was doing. The double doors were open, the place in bedlam. Tanner darted about in a frenzy. A doctor and nurse crawled on their knees on the floor amongst bloody linen and gauze squares. They seemed to be searching for something.

"What happened?" I asked a passing grad.

"Tanner lost the specimen ~ the tissue they collected from the patient."

"That's terrible," I whispered.

"It is," the grad said as she walked away. "It's a damn shame."

I was still staring into the theatre when Miss Wilder rushed by me.

"Go to Room Four and help the circulating grad. Breast biopsy. Doctor Murdoch thinks it might be a radical. Stay until the biopsy result is back."

When I entered Room Four, a strange quiet filled the air. Everyone moved about without speaking. The patient was asleep and the scrub nurse was cleaning her breast with an iodine solution.

Dr. Murdoch sighed deeply as he stepped up to the table and made a tiny incision in the woman's right breast. He cut out a small piece of tissue and dropped it into a specimen jar the scrub nurse held.

"Wait a minute," he said, as the nurse was about to hand the jar to the circulating nurse. "Who's Catholic?"

Nobody spoke.

"Anybody Catholic in this room?" he asked again, his eyes narrowed and his bushy eyebrows slid together in a frown.

Silence. He looked at me and I shook my head.

"Well, hold on here," he said to the scrub nurse. "We've got to get a Catholic in here before this specimen goes down to pathology. You, nurse," he nodded to me. "Get out there and find a Catholic. Anyone as long as they're Catholic."

I dashed into the corridor. It was empty. I ran to the instrument room where a junior sat sipping lemonade.

"Are you Catholic?" I blurted out.

"Why?" she said, with a startled look.

"I need to know!"

She must have realized how desperate I was; she nodded.

"Come on," I motioned. "Dr. Murdoch needs you. He's doing a biopsy." I grabbed her arm and rushed her back to Room Four.

"Here!" I said, shoving the junior in front of me. "She's Catholic."

"Good." Dr. Murdoch pointed to the jar containing the bloody piece of tissue. "I'm sending this biopsy down to pathology and they're going to do a frozen section. In a few minutes, the report is going to come back, benign or malignant. Now, little nurse, I want you to pray it will be benign. Pray as hard as you can."

The junior gave me a quick look of disbelief. Then her eyes darted to everyone in the room. We stared back at her helplessly. She made the sign of the cross and closed her eyes.

The orderly took the little jar to pathology.

Fifteen long minutes passed before Miss Wilder returned brandishing a sheet of paper.

"It's benign!" She said with a lavish smile.

"Knew it!" said Dr. Murdoch. "Thanks, little nurse. You may go now." He gave a sigh of relief, then sutured the tiny incision closed.

Later that afternoon I asked Miss Wilder, "Why did Dr. Murdoch want a Catholic in the room?"

"It's a policy of his. He won't send a biopsy to pathology unless there's a Catholic in the operating theatre. He's Protestant, but he feels very confident of the power of Catholic prayer." Miss Wilder shrugged her shoulders. "Wish it worked all the time."

By lunchtime, I was exhausted. I sat alone in the cafeteria staring numbly at my held-over, dried-up roast beef. In the last four hours I had witnessed the miraculous power of prayer, the execution of a nurse by light fixture, and the frightening series of Tanner's blunders.

"Come on, Tanner, you have to think faster in the operating room," Ingraham said.

Tanner took a bite of her hamburger and said, "It's no use. I go to pieces every time someone asks for something."

It was the beginning of the month and payday again, a miracle, I thought, that they paid us $12.50 for fumbling about in the operating room. But they did, and we celebrated with hamburgers and french fries in the lounge.

As Tanner popped a french fry into her mouth I said, "I'm glad to see Tanner hasn't lost her appetite."

Tanner swallowed. "But I have," she said. "I've no appetite for anything but hamburgers and french fries. I can't bear the thought of going back to the OR"

"We all feel like that," I said sharply. "Tomorrow I've got to scrub for Dr. Thompson." My stomach looped as I said his name.

White gave her coffee cup a quick rinse and stuck it back in the cupboard. "Watch out, he might slice you up instead of the patient."

The Ides of March. I struggled to keep calm as we waited for Dr. Thompson to make his grand entrance. While I helped prepare the instruments, Dr. Gordon put the patient to sleep. Dr. Gordon was not only an anaesthetist, he was Dr. Thompson's tranquilizer. When he was on duty, Dr. Thompson was calm. I had already scrubbed-in with Miss Friend, Dr. Thompson's special nurse, and together we had prepared the back table, filling it with Dr. Thompson's special instruments.

After his 20-minute scrub, Dr. Thompson finally shuffled in as if shackled. The room became quiet as he dried his hands on a sterile towel. I thought he must have used an overdose of blue rinse on his hair, which was poking out from his surgical cap, and between cap and mask, his magnified vague eyes blinked behind black-framed glasses as if he was viewing the theatre for the first time. Though he was not a tall man, his feet were huge. He reminded me of an inflated Snow White dwarf. Definitely not Happy.

Snap ~ snap ~ both gloves were on and Dr. Thompson stepped up to the operating table. I slapped the scalpel forcefully into his open hand, making sure he felt it through his glove, and he made the incision.

The first part went smoothly. Miss Friend helped by giving me the right instrument to hand to Dr. Thompson at the right time. But then at a crucial point deep in the abdomen when Friend was busy re-arranging the back table, Dr. Thompson shot out his hand. I had to give him an instrument, but which one? I glanced into the cavernous belly, but it looked like a sea of red muck. I couldn't recognize anything. I took a guess and slapped a clamp into his hand. He threw it back and it landed on the patient's legs. Another guess ~ ~the scissors. He fired them back with unbelievable force and they hit me in the chest before crashing to the floor. I nervously eyed the scalpel, but if I was wrong.... I gave Friend a swift kick under the table. She glanced into the belly, handed him a curved metal probe then winked at me over her mask.

I looked up for the first time in hours and was surprised to meet Tanner's sparkling blue eyes. She had come to the theatre to replace the circulating grad who had gone for coffee. Tanner looked fresh and alert, ready to run a marathon. She stood beside the rack of bloody sponges, rocking from foot to foot, as always, full of nervous energy. She winked at me over her mask and I returned a weary wave. I suddenly felt tired under the layers of heavy robes. Perspiration trickled down my legs, absorbed by the cloth boots covering my shoes. My back ached and my arches felt flat.

Friend asked Tanner for some sutures and patiently explained where they were, in the large glass cupboard at the end of the room.

God, please don't let her make a mistake, I prayed, as Tanner searched the glass shelves.

Soon she returned to the back table clutching the eight suture packets, each in an outer plastic cover to protect the sterile suture. The circulating nurse was supposed to pull open the tabs of the outer cover, turn it upside down and flip the sterile suture onto the sterile back table without touching the inner sterile packet. But Tanner hesitated. She glanced at the sutures, then at the table and back at the sutures. I tried to warn her. "No, Tanner. No!" I mouthed silently under my mask, frantically shaking my head.

But she didn't see me and threw all eight packets, *unopened*, on the table. With one flick of her hand, she instantly contaminated the whole back table ~ sterile drapes, gloves, sutures, clamps, scissors, retractors, and Dr. Thompson's *special instruments*.

Fortunately, Dr. Thompson didn't notice. He was lost in the gaping belly with miles of shiny, bluish intestine, strewn atop the patient's chest, waiting to be re-inserted into the abdomen. But Miss Friend noticed.

"Miss Tanner, get out of here and get the circulating nurse and Miss Wilder *immediately*," she said in a loud whisper. "We need a new back table. And every last one of Dr. Thompson's special instruments must be re-sterilized. Stat."

Tanner jumped a foot in the air, then darted out through the door.

On Sunday evening we sat in the lounge having our last cup of coffee before bed when Tanner blew in, in a full-blown panic attack. She had just been assigned to night duty in the OR and had begun to buckle under the strain.

"Don't worry, Tanner," I said. "It's easier at night, the doctors are more friendly. You might even go a whole week without an emergency surgery."

"But it's that god-awful last hour that's a bugger," Niven said. "The grad swallows her nasty pills at 6 a.m."

"Here, I made this list for you." I said, handing Tanner the piece of paper I'd prepared. "Everything you need to know about the night shift in the operating room is right here. Each morning at six, you'll have to scrub-in and set up every theatre for the first operation ~ and the grad will push you real hard. You'll have just one hour, Tanner. You have to fly. And I mean fly!"

"I can vouch for that," said Riley, hooking her crooked leg over the chair. She was sitting in the corner studying Robbins' book, *Sex and the Single Girl*, by Helen Gurley Brown. It was the hottest book to hit the market. It was supposed to educate girls on how to catch a man.

Tanner sat wide-eyed and pale, staring into space through a veil of smoke from the cigarette clenched between her teeth. She had a bit of a wild look in her eyes. "I hope they keep me on nights," she kept muttering.

Her prayer was answered. Tanner spent the rest of her time in the operating room on nights, far away from the high tension of days.

April Fool's Day. I stood bolted to the floor in horror. Orthopedics. Amputation. Leg. I'd be circulating on my own with Craig, the orthopedic orderly, who had probably seen more amputations than any grad in the operating room.

As we stood watching the surgeon cut through the muscle to reach the bone, Craig leaned over and whispered through his mask, "Just leave everything to me, Miss Yates."

Then he began to spread newspaper on the floor. "I'm going to wrap the leg in this then I'll take it away to pathology," he said. I felt greatly relieved. I took a deep breath and smiled at him under my mask. But then I froze when Craig said,

"Orderlies aren't allowed to take the leg from the surgeon, Miss Yates. You will have to do that, that's the rule."

I gasped. "Me?" He nodded. "Oh, no, I can't."

But I had no choice. The saw began to buzz, a low drone at first, signalling the final stage. My moist hands shook unbelievably and my head throbbed. I tried to imagine I was in a carpentry shop, making furniture, sawing wood. But it was no use, I couldn't concentrate. The incessant whir cut through my brain, and when I was unable to listen another minute, I pressed my hands to my ears and took refuge in the autoclave room.

The screech carried on ... and on ... I thought it would never end. Then I felt a tap on my shoulder. It was Craig. He waved me over to the operating room table. Everything had stopped. The surgeons, the nurses, the anaesthetist all seemed frozen in time.

Silence. Silence that throbbed in my head and pounded against my eardrums as I approached the table. I felt like I was under water, unable to surface for air ... drowning.

The surgeon turned to me. The leg lay cradled in a drape, which he held up by two silver clamps. The leg looked so large, so foreign dangling there in the air, just the leg ... all by itself.

I quickly drew a breath and stepped back.

The surgeon pressed it towards me.

As I reached for the clamps, my hands shook terribly. My fingers closed around the clamps but the leg was so heavy the clamps slipped out of my grasp and the leg fell to the floor with an eerie thud.

"Good God, nurse!" shot the surgeon. "What were you expecting, a pound of feathers?"

I cringed and glanced at the anaesthetist. Our eyes met and he raised his eyebrows, as if to say, I know the leg is heavy, but you shouldn't have dropped it.

The next morning during breakfast I was telling Priestnall about how heavy the leg was when Riley rushed frantically up to our table and cried, "Robbins is gone! I went to pick her up for breakfast but her room is empty. They kicked her out!"

"Sister is coming!" shouted the senior student.

There was no time to discuss the matter further. We stood for prayer.

I shall not shirk any duty however unpleasant rang in my ears as I walked past Sister, who never smiled anymore, and back to the operating room, to orthopedics.

Later that day our fears were confirmed. Robbins had been expelled. Rumour had it that she'd invited several friends, mostly males, to a party in the beau rooms. Unlike the Calgary General's beau rooms that had walls of wood, ours had walls of glass. I don't know how, but Robbins managed to sneak the boys in the front door while the housemother was making her rounds. She might have pulled the whole thing off had not Sister Leclerc awakened in the middle of the night with a burning desire to pray in the chapel. So voluptuous Robbins with her short skirts and Veronica Lake hairdo became history.

Dr. Decosta was a good-looking Italian who was working at Holy Cross to replace the regular cardiac surgeon who was away. He performed open-heart surgery, bypass surgery and lung surgery. Today it was open-heart surgery. All the drama I had been seeking was about to begin. Dr. Decosta's jet-black eyes and tanned complexion provided a striking contrast to his white mask and surgical cap. Dr. Decosta was Dr. Handsome and he knew it.

The scrub team consisted of two staff doctors, an intern and Mrs. Laval, the cardiac scrub nurse. Although I longed for a look inside a patient's chest cavity, I was only a student nurse, and in Room Five, student nurses could not be part of the scrub team. The excitement was electrifying as I helped position the patient on the table.

Miss Styles, the circulating grad, had come in early to prepare the room, and the incision was made at precisely 8 a.m. So began the task of the surgeons, cutting and entering the chest, connecting the patient to the heart-lung machine, and performing the bypass surgery. The team stood atop footstools to provide an unrestricted view into the cavernous chest cavity. I assisted Miss Styles, opening package after package of sterile gauze sponges and sutures onto the back table, all of which were counted by the scrub nurse and Miss Styles. The surgeons soaked up the blood with the gauze squares, then threw them into metal buckets on the floor, hit and miss. Miss Styles and I picked up the bloody squares with long-handled forceps and hung them one by one on a metal rack that held 50 sponges: five rows of ten hooks.

A scrub and circulating nurse would count them again, wrap and label them in packages of 25, which were recounted at the end of the operation.

Miss Styles whispered to me that she was going for coffee. "Things have slowed down, and you should be all right for ten minutes."

I sat down on a three-legged stool beside the rack of sponges that dripped blood onto a narrow metal pan at the bottom of the rack. As the blood hit the pan, it pinged in a Three Blind Mice rhythm. The scrub team stood on their platform, dwarfing the patient, working in silence. But the room was alive with vital sounds. *Zzzitt* of electricity on metal as the surgeons cauterized the small bleeding vessels; the hissing and snorting suction, sucking out blood and fluid that collected in the cavity; long gasps of the heart-lung machine ... swish, inhale ... pause ... swoosh, exhale.

The patient's heart had been stopped, and now lay still, deep in the yawning chest while the team attached new arteries where old clogged ones had been. The surgeons re-routed the entire blood supply of the patient to the heart-lung machine, which did the work of the motionless heart. The machine created rhythmical bleeps as it took in the blood from the patient, filled it with oxygen and pumped it back into the patient. The humming and hissing, bleeps and gasps, punctuated by the calm voices of the surgeons as they moved their arms in and out of the great cavity reassured everyone that all was well, so far.

The anaesthetist motioned to me. I jumped up and dutifully ran to his side.

"What is the blood count of the sponges?"

I glanced at the blackboard for the sponge count and weight of the sponges. Using simple mathematics, I calculated the patient's blood loss. It was 400 cc's.

"Get another two units of blood."

I asked a passing nurse to give the message to Miss Styles. In a few minutes she returned with the bottles of blood.

From his domain at the head of the table, the anaesthetist carefully calculated and replaced the fluid and blood loss. He moved amid metal poles draped with a collection of bottles of blood and intravenous solutions at various stages of emptying, columns of cylinders containing potent gases that kept the patient at a desired level of unconsciousness, and the beating, sibilant heart-lung machine.

"Okay, that's it," said Dr. Decosta interrupting the rhythms of the room. The crucial moment had arrived for the patient to come off the heart-lung machine. "We're ready to convert."

The pace picked up and so did the anxiety. The patient's own heart had to beat again. For patients who had exercised and eaten sensibly, the odds were in their favour. If, however, the patient had been sedentary, ate heavy foods and did not exercise, the heart, which is a muscle, would be soft and weak and have difficulty starting up.

"He's fibrillating!" shouted one of the assisting surgeons.

"Mama mia," breathed Dr. Decosta then commanded, "Defibrillator!"

I couldn't see it but I pictured the impotent heart quivering like a bowl of jelly, unable to produce a strong, effective contraction to circulate the blood to the brain and body.

"Give me the electrodes," Dr. Decosta said, though I detected a slight waver in his voice.

Laval handed him two small metal paddles, connected by a wire to a large electric box. Miss Styles, in charge of the box near the table set the voltage on 250.

Dr. Decosta placed one electrode on each side of the patient's heart. "Everyone back," he said in a clear voice.

The scrub team and the anaesthetist moved away from the table to avoid the danger of being shocked along with the patient.

A click ~ thump ~ the patient gave a convulsive jerk. Silence. The needle of the electrocardiograph still recorded a squiggly line. The heart did not respond. In an ineffective attempt to keep beating, the heart called on its auxiliary nodes which were inefficient, weak impulses. Only the sinus node, the heart's pacemaker, a small mass of cardiac fibers in the posterior atrium, could generate an electric impulse strong enough to stimulate the heart to beat at regular intervals.

"Again!" shot Dr. Decosta. "Stand back."

Click, thump, jerk ... nothing. The heart shuddered, erratically. It seemed to have forgotten how to beat properly.

If the heart refused to beat normally, the last eight hours would have been nothing more than a valiant and academic exercise.

"Shove it to 800." Dr. Decosta shouted to Miss Styles. "Come on, baby, come on." He muttered to the limp heart as he tried to coax it to grasp the surge of life-energy he offered. The electric current had to neutralize the ineffective nodes that continued to fire at random and allow the sinus node to take over. Beads of sweat began to dot Dr. Decosta's forehead.

Laval made the sign of the cross.

Click. Thump. Jolt.

Bleep ... bleep ... bleep. The cardiograph was recording a correct heartbeat.

"I've got a pulse here," said the anaesthetist. "A good strong pulse." He looked up at Dr. Decosta and his eyes smiled over his mask.

"Any leaks?" asked one of the surgeons.

"Dry as a bone." Dr. Decosta said, as he checked each anastomosis, the point where the new artery was connected to the patient's artery. The treacherous transfer from the heart-lung machine to the patient's heart was successful.

"Let's get out of here," said Dr. Decosta. "I'm closing."

Miss Styles and I counted all the sponges, needles and scalpel blades with the scrub nurse.

"Sponge and needle count?" Dr. Decosta asked.

"Correct," Miss Styles said, with a nod.

They wheeled the patient out of the operating room with tubes protruding from his chest. The anaesthetist, still wearing his mask, continued to pump oxygen from a portable oxygen tank through the intubation tube in the patient's mouth. A nurse on each side of the stretcher held the precious chest bottles in place, and the entourage disappeared round the corner to the recovery room. The intravenous bottles clink-clanked from the I.V. poles as the assistant surgeons scurried behind to catch up.

Dr. Decosta watched for a few moments from outside the theatre door, then pulled off his scrub gown and gloves, and with a flamboyant flair tossed them back in the room on the floor. His mask hung from his neck. Then he turned and with a confident stride, walked towards the recovery room.

My last day in the OR: The Urology Room. Although I looked forward to the informal atmosphere, urology had a reputation of being unbearably embarrassing for student nurses. Urine flowed freely, as did the jokes by the urologists, who were reputed to be a different breed of surgeon. White's advice was simple and pointed. "Make sure you wear a mask, because those urologists are such damn practical jokers, they'll embarrass you to death. At least with the mask you can hide your face."

So primed, I reported to the urology room on Friday morning, my mask firmly in place. The bright spring sun poured through the large windows and though the room was sparkling clean, a heavy odour of urine hung in the air. The patient lay on a stretcher, watching me. He'd had a spinal anaesthetic and was unable to feel or move from the waist down, but otherwise was wide-awake.

George, the orderly, strained as he lifted the patient's limp, heavy legs up into the stirrups. Dr. Slater bounced in wearing rubber waders, a rubber apron and no mask. His OR cap sat in a crumple atop his fuzzy red hair, and I wondered why he bothered to wear it at all. The room was located outside the line of the operating room, and not considered sterile like the other theatres.

"Good morning, nursey." He chirped. "Welcome to our outer sanctum, where we have fun, fun, fun! Isn't that right, Georgie?" he said winking to the orderly.

"Right." George nodded, as he connected rubber tubing from the water tap to a long, shiny, silver instrument.

"Good morning, Mr. Robinson." Dr. Slater said cheerily to the patient.

"Morning." Mr. Robinson mumbled as best as he could without his false teeth.

"Mr. Robinson is having a bit of trouble with his prostate. Know what a prostate is, nursey?"

"Yes," I uttered, barely above a whisper.

"Good. The nurse knows about prostates, Georgie."

George nodded.

"I suppose you know all about the male anatomy, too, nursey," the doctor said, as he waved the long, shiny instrument back and forth in the air.

"I ... ah ... ah ... " I stammered, wondering if this was a trick question.

"Speak up, nursey, I can't hear you."

"Yes, ah, we have taken anatomy in the classroom. Is that what you mean?"

"Good. You see, Georgie?" He bellowed in a voice like a foghorn. "Nursey is an expert at male anatomy."

Mr. Robinson chewed nervously on his gums. His eyes darted from Dr. Slater to George to me.

"Okay, nursey, we are going to ream this prostate out." Dr. Slater shoved the tube down Mr. Robinson's urethra and cut out the over-grown prostate that was choking it. Water from the tap ran in clear, flushed out the area and sputtered out blood red. It splashed all over Dr. Slater's yellow-brown waders and gurgled down the round drain in the floor.

"There! That is all there is to it, nursey." Dr. Slater said, pulling out the pipe that dripped bloody water.

George did all of the assisting. My small job was to have the instruments sterilized for each operation. It was sort of a little like tonsils, in and out, eight patients a day, but here, thankfully, I didn't have to assist during surgery.

Mr. Peters was our last patient, a 28-year-old man with a questionable bladder tumour.

"Oh, boy, would you look at all the nice healthy tissue in this bladder," sang Dr. Slater as he looked through the glass opening at the end of the metal instrument inserted into the patient's urethra. "No sign of a tumour here." He worked the tube in and out and around in tiny circles. I felt uncomfortable staring at Mr. Peters' private parts, which were on full display. I wished that he had been old like Mr. Robinson. It wasn't as embarrassing to look at the older men. I turned to the window and pretended to be interested in the partial view of the parking lot.

"Come over here, nursey." Dr. Slater said with an impish grin. "See what a nice bladder Mr. Peters has."

I walked reluctantly over to Dr. Slater, who held the end of the long instrument inserted in the patient's penis.

Dr. Slater winked at Mr. Peters. "Nursey is very knowledgeable about the male apparatus." He turned to me. "Here, nursey, bend down and take a *good* look."

I bent over and looked through the glass lens. The instrument was equipped with a tiny microscope and light. I saw something bluish-red and shiny that was the lining of the bladder and my nose was millimeters from Mr. Peters' penis. He tried to show indifference by twirling his thumbs and staring at the ceiling. He even tried to whistle, but because he'd been given an injection to dry-up the secretions in his mouth, Mr. Peters could only utter peculiar little breathy noises.

I felt a prickling in my face as it heated to a high flush. How I longed to be swept down the drain with the gurgling water. I bit my lip and tried not to look Mr. Peters in the eye, and whispered a thankful prayer for the mask that covered my face.

When I returned to the residence at 3:30, still feeling humiliated from my day in urology, the lounge was empty. It was Friday; my mother would be working late. So I walked to the Hudson Bay Company store where she worked.

The air was brisk but the sun felt warm on my back. It was a glorious spring afternoon. A day which made you feel glad to be alive, to count your blessings, and I did feel *truly blessed*, as Armbruster would say. Blessed with a cushy childhood, loving parents who were no pushovers, but wanted the best for their children, and most of all, a stable family life.

Mom went to work when I was 11 years old. She worked first at the Hudson Bay, where they chose her for the notions department because she was such a whiz of a seamstress, then at *Betty and Bobby,* a children's clothing store two blocks from our home. I liked that better, because she was always home for our lunch. I could run to the store anytime to ask her questions; "Sandy and I are going to Dell's Dairy for a chocolate noodle sundae ... I did the dishes. May I have a quarter? What should I make for supper?" Now she worked in the watch repair, nestled in a little niche on the mezzanine of the Hudson Bay store. There she learned basic watch repair skills, and became especially proficient at engraving.

I always liked being with my mother. I liked to surprise her by showing up for her coffee break in the afternoon. We would have a sandwich in the cafeteria or a frosty malted milk on a stool at the milk bar and laugh at silly things, and always talk over my day in the hospital.

Today it was a frosted malted milk and urology stories. "This guy had a tube in his penis, Mom. I felt so embarrassed, for him and for me."

"Well, you're a nurse, dear," she said, sipping her malted milk. "You're expected to deal with these situations, just as if there's nothing wrong."

"But that surgeon made me put my nose right there, Mom. Right *there!*"

My mother gave a soft chuckle. "I remember being terribly shy when I was young, but I got over it." Her finger traced a drop of water as it tumbled down the frosty glass. "Funny how life ~ embarrassing things like this ~ seems to get easier as we get older."

"But he was a young guy. And good looking, too! It's not as bad, somehow, when the men are old. I mean it's still awfully embarrassing, but I don't think the old guys mind as much as the young ones do."

"Eventually you'll get used to these situations, dear. One day you will suddenly find that you're not embarrassed any more."

"Oh, how I wish! At least now I have the consolation of intermediate block coming up. I'll be in class for the next few weeks and won't have to worry about male patients and cruel doctors that delight in embarrassing me."

Mom finished the last of her malted milk, then daintily dabbed the corners of her mouth with a paper napkin. "Well, time to get back to work." She stood up, slid her purse over her arm, then slipped a dollar bill into the pocket of my jeans. "Go have your hair done tomorrow, my treat. That will make you feel better."

Mom and I walked arm in arm back to the watch repair. I looked forward to having my hair washed and styled at the beauty parlour next to the Tivoli Theatre. They only charged a dollar to nursing students if we made an appointment with the student hair stylist. I felt much better already.

"Thanks for the malted and the treat, Mom," I said, clutching the bill. "I'll call you tonight."

Mom slipped behind the watch repair counter and waved. Just as she said, "Good bye, dear," the ticking, oscillating wall behind her announced five o'clock in a medley of chimes and cuckoos.

My Life as a Diet Kitchen Criminal

In the classroom, I was panting to get back to the wards and nursing patients again. But when I saw my name next to Diet Kitchen, I felt a bitter wave of disappointment.

"Don't feel bad, Yates," Porter said in her soothing voice as we all talked about our new rotation in the lounge after supper. "At least you'll have a cool summer, way down there in the basement."

Peggy Wolkoff would be working with me for the next four weeks. Wolkoff had almost as much energy as Tanner. And while Tanner looked like June Allyson, Wolkoff looked like Keely Smith ~ black hair, short bangs and two kiss curls at each cheek.

Monday morning, Wolkoff and I covered our heads with surgical white cloth caps, like the ones worn in the operating room, and stepped through the swinging metal doors into a humungeous kitchen. I could smell each vegetable cooking ~ tomatoes, celery, carrots, cabbage. Standing in the kitchen was like being inside of a large soup pot. The odour oozed out of the kitchen and hovered about the ground floor of the hospital like a transparent fog.

We found the diet kitchen in the left corner, separated from the main kitchen by a four-foot yellow tiled wall. Here, the special diets were prepared for the hospital. Miss Bowman, the dietitian, Queen of the Castle, ruled supreme. And the large kitchen did remind me of a castle: the high ceiling, with wooden butcher blocks strategically placed around the room, and quaint old pots and pans hanging from hooks in the ceiling. Men wore high chef's hats, the women had their hair tucked up inside caps like mine. Wrapped in white aprons from neck to knees, they moved from one enormous, heavy pot to another, all steaming on gas stoves. Food was lying everywhere waiting to be prepared.

Miss Bowman took us back to a refrigerator the size of a large room with walls stacked with more juice, milk, cheese and other perishables than I had ever seen in a grocery store. A thick, metal door in the back wall opened into an extremely cold room where skinned animals, with no heads or feet, hung from huge metal hooks in the ceiling. Rumour had it that a student nurse almost froze to death once when the door slammed shut behind her.

Wolkoff and I carried bottles of orange juice back to the diet kitchen where Miss Bowman showed us how to measure the morning juice for the diabetic patients. I had to weigh the glass on a small scale then pour the exact measurement of juice into the glass. The amount was important because the doctor calculated the patient's insulin injection according to their food intake.

Every morning of our four weeks, Wolkoff and I arrived at six to prepare breakfast for all the special diets. We would cook the porridge, toast, bacon, and eggs ~ boiled, poached, or scrambled. We juggled bowls, plates, oatmeal, butter and jam, and carefully placed the glass of orange juice, which we had measured the previous afternoon, onto the food cart. The cart had to be loaded and ready to leave the kitchen by 8 a.m.

During the month that Wolkoff and I were in the diet kitchen, we practiced our cheers for inter-hospital week, the athletic competition between Calgary General and Holy Cross nurses. Two days before the competition was to begin, Miss Bowman sent us to work with Cookie, the chef in charge of the main kitchen. I taught Wolkoff the cheers. As we stood at a butcher block chopping cabbage for Cookie's soup, we chanted:

Klickity, klackity
Klickity, klunk.
We're the team that's got the spunk
We've got the drive, we've got the spirit
We've got the team, so let's cheer it.
H-O-L-Y, H-O-L-Y, H-O-L-Y, HOLY!

"*Touché!*" I said, raising my long chopping knife and assuming the fencing stance. Wolkoff obliged with "*En garde!*" And we clinked and clanked about in front of the butcher block until Miss Bowman raised her head above the yellow-tiled separation and cleared her throat. Immediately we turned our backs to her and resumed our chopping, quietly.

My mother often urged me to bring the girls home for dinner. She knew most of them very well by now, especially the out-of-town girls. That night after work, Blackwell, Andresen and I caught the bus to my parents' house. After supper, we sat at the breakfast nook making cheerleaders' pompoms. Mom was at the stove, cooking a batch of chocolate fudge for us to take back to the residence. As I cut strips of red crepe paper, Blackwell's eyes began to flash playfully, as they usually did when she was about to tease one of us. "Hey Yates," she said. "How come you've never sneaked any food out of the diet kitchen for us?"

"I guess I'm a chicken," I said with a shrug. "Bowman and her assistant are always around checking us and I don't want to get into any trouble."

"But everyone does it," Blackwell said snidely. "It's a Holy ritual. Come on, get with it."

As we prepared to leave with my father who would drive us back to the residence, Mom handed me the pan of fudge and leaned over to whisper in my ear. "Do be careful, dear," she said. "Don't do anything foolish that you might regret."

I knew that it was a Holy tradition for students to take food, they had been doing it for the last 40 years. Cans of fruit or fresh fruit, sometimes cheese. I heard that someone once took six steaks that were meant for the nuns.

When we got back to the residence, Niven began to nag. "I don't know what you're afraid of," she chided. "Everyone snitches things when they're working in the DK. You go home for goodies, Yates, so you don't know what it's like to be deprived. But what about the rest of us who are stuck here day after day with nothing but that hospital crap to eat? I sneaked out good stuff when I worked in the DK. Now it's your turn." She reached for her third piece of fudge, held it up and said, "Your Mom makes good fudge."

The next day was sunny and very hot. At the end of our shift, Wolkoff and I opened the door to the refrigerator and walked in, sending a blast of cool condensation out into the main kitchen. I was sweating in my heavy uniform and the freezing temperature of the refrigerator felt wonderfully refreshing as I began pulling cans of fruit from the shelf.

"I'll take peaches," Wolkoff said, shoving four cans between her bosom and starched bib.

I grabbed two cans of pears and slid them under my bib, then we quickly walked through the diet kitchen toward the door.

"Miss Yates! Miss Wolkoff!"

Miss Bowman. Oh God, she must have noticed our bulging bosoms. We stopped and turned. I tried to smile natural but my face felt tight. I knew she could tell I was guilty.

"Going to the inter-hospital ball game?" she said from her corner desk.
"Yes," we said.

"Give those girls at the General a good run for their money. The Holy always comes through in baseball. Good luck, and see you in the morning." She smiled and went back to her papers.

"That's it," I said to Wolkoff as we hurried through the tunnel. "This is the last time I am ever going to do this. It's not worth it. I feel like a thief. Just think of what would happen if we got caught."

As we stepped off the elevator and into the lounge, the girls noticed our oversized busts and began to cheer. Wolkoff slapped four cans of Bing peaches down on the counter.

"I've got pears," I said proudly as I pulled out my stash. But I gasped when Niven snapped, "Don't tell me you brought crappy peas."

"Well, I took them so fast, I thought they were pears," I said.

"You're such a chicken liver, Yates," Niven said, gruffly. "You're going to have to do this again tomorrow. Don't think that we're going to let you get away with pukey peas."

"Not me." I said, shaking my head, defiantly. "I'm not going to do it. I would rather die first."

The next day, as Wolkoff and I were sliding cans of fruit under our bibs, Wolkoff said, "Look at it this way, Yates, we don't go for supper much any more so these measly cans of fruit aren't worth a whole meal that we would eat in the cafeteria. Either way, they have to feed us, so the hospital's ahead of the game, don't you think?" She lifted her apron and slid a pound of Velveeta cheese under the top of her nylons, leaving the empty box on the shelf.

We began our cautious walk out of the diet kitchen.

"Miss Yates!" Miss Bowman called. I stopped. My face flushed. "You're walking funny, Miss Yates."

"It's the ball game ... well ... I didn't play, but I was a cheerleader. I'm so stiff today I can hardly walk." I gave a thin smile.

"I'm glad The Holy won. Good old Alma Mater!" she waved her hand above her head. "Too bad about the swimming team. Oh well, better luck next year." She thrust some papers at me. "Take these up to St. John's."

I took the papers, gave a weak nod, then hurried to catch up to Wolkoff, who was half way to the tunnel.

"I'm not going to wait for you," she said. "You'll be okay, just hang on to those cans. See you in the lounge." And she disappeared into the tunnel.

After delivering the papers, I was awkwardly rushing down the hall when I saw a nun approaching me on her way to chapel. It was Sister Rocheleau, the afternoon supervisor. She was followed closely by White, carrying a load of sterile gauze packets for the operating room, piled up to her chin. Suddenly White tripped; two rolls of gauze popped out and rolled down the hall. She bent over and picked one up but her toe nudged the second and it wobbled forward. Still bent, she shuffled awkwardly after it, snatched it up, but as she tried to rise, she stepped on the hem of her apron, which launched the whole lot of packets and sent them skittering across the floor.

One rolled over to me. I bent down to pick it up but a can of mushroom soup slipped from my bib and wobbled right up to Sister Rocheleau's feet. She stood motionless, watching me pick it up. "Good afternoon, Sister," I said, the can of soup in one hand, a roll of gauze in the other.

Sister shook her head, brought her hand up to cover her smile and swished off to the chapel, mumbling, *"Mon Dieu."*

Later, as we sat eating our spoils, I said to Niven, "You'd better enjoy those pears, because I'm never going to do that again, for you or anybody else."

"Gee that's too bad," she snickered. "I was going to order mandarin oranges tomorrow."

Wolkoff and I planned the special meal menus for the patients on the ward: diabetic diets, ulcer diets, high-caloric or calorie-restricted diets, and diets for patients with gastric problems.

"Now make sure you vary the meals and pay particular attention to the colour and texture of the foods," Miss Bowman said dryly.

And each day before the end of our shift, we ordered the special-diet-food for the following day from the main kitchen.

On Tuesday morning, when I opened the waxed paper package of bacon, I was surprised to see it was more than we needed for our patients. I looked, questioningly at Wolkoff, who glanced around, secretively, and whispered. "I ordered double. We're going to have bacon for breakfast."

"Yikes, Wolkoff! What if we get caught?"

"Listen, I can't stand to watch all this good food go marching out of the kitchen for the nuns and the interns, when all we get is dry roast beef and stale leftovers. Remember that big juicy turkey Cookie cooked for the nuns yesterday? Well how come we never, ever see turkey from one Christmas to the other?" She turned and continued stirring the porridge. "You've got to have a little imagination, Yates, or you'll die in this hell hole."

When the back of the food cart disappeared through the double doors of the kitchen, Wolkoff made two bacon sandwiches while I stood on the lookout at the end of the counter. We each wrapped a sandwich in a paper napkin and shoved it under our bibs, then told Miss Bowman we were going for breakfast.

We sat brazenly at the first table in the cafeteria. It was after nine, who would be having breakfast at this late hour? I unwrapped my sandwich, all toasted to a lovely brown, the crisp bacon smothered in ketchup, the first bacon I'd had since entering The Holy. I took a long, lovely whiff, a big bite, and glanced up. Miss Bowman and her side-kick-assistant were coming towards me, each with a bowl of cornflakes on their tray. I froze. Wolkoff had her back to the door and was heartily devouring her sandwich.

Miss Bowman stopped at our table and said coolly, "Enjoy the bacon, girls. It's the last you'll ever get from the diet kitchen." She joined her assistant at the back of the cafeteria and I could see them both snickering.

For several seconds I held the bacon in my mouth, cheeks packed chipmunk full. I wasn't sure if I should eat it or throw it out. Wolkoff's blue eyes flashed mischievously and she began to giggle. "That was too close for comfort," she whispered, with a full mouth.

I couldn't swallow. I spit it out in my napkin and watched Wolkoff wolf her sandwich down. On my way out of the cafeteria, I tossed the remains of my sandwich into the garbage can.

Wolkoff's cheeks puffed up into a wide grin, her mouth opened and she gave her delightfully contagious belly laugh. "Aw, don't be so sensitive, Yates," she said, with a quick nudge of her elbow. "I'll bet Bowman used to do the same thing when she was a student."

Each afternoon, when Wolkoff and I planned the special diet menu for the following day, we thoughtfully chose rare and delicious food for our VIP patients.

"Mrs. Snidely's lost her appetite," Wolkoff mused over her list. "I believe she loves ham."

"Oh, good choice," I said. "Haven't seen ham all year. I'll give some to Mr. Cutter, too. Better order plenty. Lets see ... what else do you like, Wolkoff?"

On my last day, my grand finale in the Diet Kitchen, I was loading the diabetic breakfasts onto the food cart when Miss Bowman rushed over and asked, "Have you got a tray of juice there?"

I immediately yanked the full tray of diabetic orange juice, which I had painstakingly measured the day before, out of the trolley. But the tray was shorter than I expected and it tipped upside down. Every glass of orange juice hit the tiled floor in unison. The explosion reverberated through the diet kitchen like a mighty cannon at 7:55 a.m. Astonished cooks and helpers dashed over to our corner. I stood as if turned to stone, the empty tray dangling from my hand, the shattered glass glistening in a river of sticky orange juice at my feet.

How would I ever measure all those juices before eight o'clock?

Miss Bowman gaped at me for several moments, and then she closed her mouth and swallowed. "Better get busy, lady," she said, trying to sound composed.

I dashed to the fridge, lined up the glasses on my tray like an assembly line and slopped the juice into them, hit and miss. I had no time for the tedious measuring. But for the rest of the morning I nervously prayed that none of the diabetic patients would have a reaction.

Later, during lunch in the cafeteria when I told Perry my clumsy mistake, she just laughed and said, "Geez, Yates. You must be the only one still weighing those juice glasses. Everybody eyeballs them."

If by-the-book Perry could do that, I knew I had nothing to fear.

Silent Unity

My first tour of night duty required I report at 11:30. This allowed me the luxury of sleeping in Monday morning.

While everyone else was either working or sleeping, I sat snuggled in my pajamas and duster in the quiet lounge savouring my solitude and hot coffee. Then after cleaning my room, I walked through the hot streets to the Hudson Bay to visit my mother.

"Men again," I said swallowing the frosty malt. "I'm going to be on St. Joseph's." I pulled my lips into a tight, thin line.

"Oh, Donna, you'll be fine," she said. "You have experience now. You're not worried about men, you're worried about death."

"But they're all old, Mom, and they'll probably die on me during the night."

She smiled and patted my knee. "I think it would be better if it did happen. It would be over and done with and you would see that it isn't that bad. Death is a part of life."

"Yeah, that's what they all say."

"It's true." She smiled. "Now I hope you will get some rest before you go to work tonight, dear. I'll worry about you all night if I think you haven't had any sleep before you go on duty."

She stood up and slid her purse over her arm and said, "Now don't worry. You'll be fine. But promise me you'll go to bed when you get back to the residence."

"Promise, Mom. I'll call you in the morning when I get off duty."

That night, uniformed and crisp, I joined White, Perry and Simm at 10:30 as they sat in the shadowy fringe in the lounge drinking their last cup of coffee before bed. The only source of light came from the hall in front of the elevator, which cast a soft glow on the floor.

The girls fed me tidbits of information they thought might come in handy during my rotation. White said, "I had a death my first night on St. Joe's and three more that same week. In fact by the time I finished my rotation, I was on bloody first name basis with the undertaker."

"Same thing happened to me," Simm said in a low voice. "You have to expect it, Yates. There are a lot of old men on that ward." She motioned towards the hospital and her huge engagement diamond glinted in the dark.

"You're making me nervous," I said. "I've never had a patient die while I was at work. My patients always went on my day off or before I got to work, or after I left, and that's the God's truth."

"Hey, let us in on your secret," White giggled. "I could use a little of that luck."

I slipped the comb of my cap into my hair. "Whatever it is I hope my luck holds tonight. I've got my fingers crossed."

I was relieved to find I would be working with Miss Stokes, a grad from Medicine Hat, who was sympathetic to students. Flashlights in hand, we made rounds together, and I was grateful to find everyone quiet and comfortable. No sooner had I returned to the desk to check my medication list, than a light turned on in 209.

I entered the room with my flashlight pointed down and at my chest, as I had been taught. The light reflected off of my white bib and illuminated the patient in a soft glow. The man lay in the corner bed beside the window, the only patient in the room. The other bed had been removed ~ a service the hospital rendered very ill patients.

"I'm having a sweat," he said in a raspy voice.

I pulled the string behind his bed and turned on the light. He was curled up in a small ball, soaked to the skin. His face was flushed and his large brown eyes were wide open in a hazy stare. I registered a small shock when I saw his young, unwrinkled face.

I quickly checked my notes: Mark Birch, 24 years old, had been in the hospital for one month with Hodgkin's disease.

I took his temperature, 103 degrees. The mercury was almost at the top of the thermometer. I gave him two aspirin, sponged him, and changed his pajamas and sheets. Then I gave him a back rub. It would increase circulation and prevent decubiti (bedsores), and would hopefully relax him. He was painfully thin and frail and his neck grotesquely swollen from enlarged lymph glands.

I noticed some textbooks and scribblers on the table. "Are you studying?" I asked. But he turned his head to the wall and didn't answer. "Are you in pain?" I would get him an injection.... "Or would you like some hot milk?" He shook his head to my questions, so I tucked the covers around him and told him to ring if he needed anything.

"I don't think he likes me," I said to Miss Stokes as I sat down at the desk. "I can't get him to talk."

"Mark is studying to become an accountant," she said. "Poor guy was supposed to take his exams the very same week he was admitted. He's pretty sick, you know."

I wanted to ask her just how sick, but I didn't think I could bear to hear her answer.

Each night, Mark Birch's symptoms struck like clockwork. His first sweat came around 12:30 in the morning, followed by a needle for his pain at 2:00, and another sweat about 5:00.

Thursday night was different. When I arrived, he had an intravenous running. His condition had deteriorated during the day and Dr. Hamilton had ordered blood plasma. I changed Mark's bed and pajamas, gave him two aspirin, and a back rub. But he was suffering from more pain than usual. He settled for a short time, then his light blinked on again. He told me he was in pain. It was too early for another injection, so I asked him if he would like some hot milk.

"Maybe."

I went around the corner to the little kitchen, heated up the milk and gave it to him. Thirty minutes later, his light was on again. I gave him a back rub.

"You asked me the other night what I was studying," he said in a weak voice as I worked the alcohol into his back. "I'm taking my exams to become a CA."

"That's wonderful."

"If I ever take them," he mumbled.

"I'm sure you will. The plasma will help you get stronger," I quickly added.

He turned over and I tucked the covers round his wasted body. He had a kind, handsome face, the face of a young man, yet his body was fading away. His wide eyes followed me round the room. I turned out the light.

Before I got back to the desk, his light lit up again. I returned to his room. He looked distressed.

"Please leave the night light on in the corner," he said.

But he still could not sleep, and soon he wanted another injection. I called Mrs. Noseworthy, the night supervisor. She had the authority to make decisions for the doctors during the night, and seldom had to wake them for an order.

"My, my, my," she said shaking her head as I handed her Mr. Birch's chart. "This poor young man is very sick. Having more pain, is he?"

I nodded. "His medication isn't holding him. I gave him his last injection at one. He's had hot milk and a back rub, but nothing has helped."

"Well," she said, flipping the pages of the chart. "Why don't we repeat the injection and give this poor boy a little peace. He doesn't have much to look forward to."

"Is he ... " I hesitated, "terminal?"

"I am afraid so." She nodded, sadly. "Outside of a miracle, I am afraid there's nothing else Dr. Hamilton can do for him."

My heart sank. Why him? I asked myself as I prepared his injection. Old people died on St. Joe's, not young men beginning their lives.

Mrs. Noseworthy was still sitting with Miss Stokes at the nurse's station when I passed with Mark's injection. "The poor boy is very scared," Mrs. Noseworthy said. "And I don't blame him. I would be too. It wouldn't hurt if you sat with him for a while, Miss Yates. Maybe he needs someone to talk to. Miss Stokes will cover your patients. It's not too busy tonight."

I gave Mark the injection and rubbed his back again, hoping the needle would take effect quickly and put him to sleep. Mrs. Noseworthy was right, I thought. He did look frightened.

"Are you sleepy?" I asked as he turned over on his back.

"No, I can't sleep."

I sat on the chair next to his bed and for the next twenty minutes we had an exciting talk about jazz, his great passion. After several quiet moments, he said, almost apologetically, "I don't think I will ever write my exams."

Here it comes, I thought. I tried to remember what I was supposed to say when a patient wanted to talk about dying.

"Why do you say that?" I ventured.

"Because I don't think I will get better." He paused. There was a knowing look in his steady eyes.

I had to respond. Had to say something, anything to encourage him. But his words hung in the air like a wall that divided us. I was healthy, taking up a profession, living my life. He was sick, in the hospital, and though I didn't want to admit it, perhaps even dying. I could think of nothing to say.

He broke the silence, speaking in a low voice. "Dr. Hamilton has tried everything, you know, and I'm not getting any better. In fact, I am getting worse. Look at me ... I'm half the size I used to be...I can't even walk to the chair any more."

Mrs. Whitford's voice came to me, "If the patient knows he is dying, then we must let him talk about his fears. If we insist he is going to get better, then the patient will never really trust us. Patients know how they feel. They know if you are not being truthful."

"Are you afraid to die?" I asked timidly. This was the question Mrs. Whitford said we must ask.

"No." He paused. "No, I'm not afraid." He gave a nervous laugh. "But I sure would like to live."

"Would you like to see a minister or priest?" I suggested. Another question we were supposed to ask.

"My minister comes often," he said. "Thanks, anyway."

My brain whirled. A knot tightened in my stomach. How could I leave this man thinking he was going to die? I had to do something to keep him alive. After all there were miracles. I had to give him hope ~ I had to!

"I'm sure something will come up," I said, desperately wanting to believe that was true. "You're young. There could easily be a cure around the corner. Never give up," I urged.

I came off duty in utter despair and ran to the lounge for comfort, but today, of all days, no one was there. I dashed for the phone.

"He can't die, Mom," I cried. "He's too young. There must be something we can do. Where are all the miracles that used to happen thousands of years ago? Why did they stop?"

"They didn't stop, dear," she answered. "Look at what doctors can do today. Look at the medicines we have. There are still miracles. Just pray for one."

"Remember that little booklet Auntie Violet sent me? You know, the Daily Word? Those people pray in a Silent Room. They pray for anyone. Maybe they would pray for my patient ... what do you think?"

My mother hesitated, "Well ... I suppose it couldn't hurt."

I rushed to my room and tore through my drawers until I found the little booklet Auntie Violet had given me. On the first page, it said:

There is no need you can have which is so trivial, no pain you can experience which is so great that prayer cannot soothe it. Prayer is the heart of Silent Unity that serves people of all faiths. You can write or call us about any need, day or night, and we will pray with you. There is never a charge, and all prayer requests are treated with reverence and confidentiality.

I wrote a letter asking them to pray for my patient. The next morning I sent the letter with a money order for five dollars, all I had left from my monthly pay.

Mark Birch's condition continued to deteriorate and he lost his appetite. I suggested that his family bring him in a milkshake every day. The extra calories and nourishment would do him a world of good. But Mark's father had died some years before and his mother was incapacitated with multiple sclerosis. His sister worked full time and looked after his mother at home. She tried to visit him at least three or four times each week. Because I worked nights, I'd never met her.

For days I thought about taking Mark a milkshake. A strict rule, however, absolutely forbade us from visiting patients while off duty. We had to obtain written permission from Sister Leclerc to visit relatives and friends in the hospital, even our own mothers. But I was determined to do whatever it took to make this man better. I made up my mind to visit Mark. I would take him a chocolate milkshake from the Dairy Queen. If I did bump into Sister, she might think I was collecting information for my next case study. If she found out the truth, then I was ready to face the consequences.

It was an unusually hot June afternoon when I dressed in my blue blouse and white skirt and walked to the Dairy Queen. Carrying the milkshake, I marched right through the front door of the hospital. My heart pounded ferociously. Sister always took the elevator, so I rushed up the stairs, balancing the milkshake. When I reached the second floor, I saw a group of nuns moving down the hall toward me. I panicked and dashed into an empty room and hid behind the curtains until they passed. Then I snuck down the hall to Mark's room. I knew he was pleased with the milkshake because he drank all of it.

And so this became my routine: waking at 4 p.m., a trip to the Dairy Queen for a milkshake, then sneaking it in to the hospital and up to Mark Birch's room. His attitude improved, he gained a little weight, and I continued to look after him each night on St. Joseph's. But his sweats and his pain continued. By the end of the week, I had an answer from Silent Unity.

> *Dear Miss Yates,*
> *We received your request for our prayers for your patient. Our volunteers are praying for him at this moment, and we trust God will bring comfort and strength to him. Thank you for your donation. It will be used to ensure that Silent Unity will continue to pray 24 hours a day for all who need God's help throughout the world. God Bless you and your patient.*
>
> > *Silent Unity.*

When I arrived on St. Joe's that night, the evening nurse gave an encouraging report about Mr. Birch. A new medication had arrived from California, and Dr. Hamilton added two new words to his critical report. *Guarded optimism.*

"Thank you, God," I whispered.

Friday, I jumped out of bed at 3 p.m. after only three hours sleep. It was my day off, and I didn't want to waste it sleeping. Sunlight flooded the lounge as I sat in my yellow duster sipping a cup of coffee, trying to clear my foggy head.

White walked into the lounge tugging at her bib and apron. "Saw the change list, Yates," she said. "You're scheduled for Ponoka."

"Ponoka!" I cried. A shiver ran through my body. Ponoka Mental Hospital was 100 miles away.

"Monday." White said pouring herself a glass of milk. "You and Standish."

Mark Birch. Who would take him milkshakes? Visit him? Reassure him in the middle of the night? If Sister knew about my visits to Mark, she never mentioned it. But her timing was flawless.

Separation Anxiety

Later that night, at home after supper, as I helped my mother wash the dishes, I said, "I hate to leave him, Mom. He will get depressed and I think he'll die."

"I know how much effort you've put into your patient, dear, but there *are* other nurses. He will be looked after. You can't become involved with your patients like this."

"But he's so young, Mom. It isn't right that he is so sick."

"Of course it's tragic for such a young man to be that sick. But you're going to have to care for many patients, Donna, and must go on with your education."

I knew that determined look in my mother's eyes. I had to go to Ponoka. "It's all part of being a nurse, dear, there are rewards and there are heartaches. I'm sure you will see many heartbreaking situations. But that's how life is. It can be cruel at times." She put her arm around my waist and gave me a squeeze. "I know you'll do the right thing." She looked up at me and brushed the hair from my face. "You're getting too thin, Donna."

Although I pretended to be normal, going about my activities as usual, I had lost five pounds. Deep down I realized that I was falling deeper into a hole.

Puffs of cottony clouds floated across the royal blue Alberta sky. Today it was all that was boasted from the signs along the highway: Look Up. The Bluest Sky In The World Is Above You.

The Rocky Mountains to the west stood like cut-out pictures pasted on the horizon, massive, silent peaks covered with snow. Though 75 miles away, today they seemed to converge with Calgary. The rolling foothills then gradually melted into flat prairie as Edith Standish and I drove towards Ponoka.

Standish had short black hair and a constant twinkle in her blue eyes. She was an easy person to be with, never moody, and had a wonderful sense of humour.

And if that wasn't enough, her brother gave her his car to use while she was in Ponoka. No matter what happened, Standish had the ability to remain calm. And she certainly was cautious. We crawled along the highway, barely approaching the speed limit. But I didn't mind. It beat bumping along in the Greyhound.

We finally pulled into the driveway of Ponoka Mental Hospital, parked the car, and reported to the administration office. A matronly housemother walked us to the nurses' residence. "You'll be sharing the residence with student nurses from other hospitals in Alberta," she said.

Ponoka Mental Hospital was a community in itself. It sat on a large working farm a mile and a half east of the small town of Ponoka. Acres of beautifully manicured grounds with breathtaking flowerbeds surrounded the buildings. Behind the campus stood silos containing food and grain for the many animals on the farm. The hospital's farm had a large barn for dairy cows, and several smaller outbuildings that housed chickens and pigs. Grazing cattle were brown and white dots in the green fields still lush from the spring rain. The air was fresh-smelling country air. There were no houses beyond the hospital complex, just healthy green fields instead of the mid-summer dry, buff look of the Calgary foothills.

Though the hospital and the small town of Ponoka sat in the middle of farmlands, I felt far removed from the wide-open space and tumbleweed ranch country that surrounded Calgary. I missed the cowboys, their colourful Stetsons and fancy shirts with pearl snaps on chest pockets and cuffs, dusty boots and jangling spurs. I missed the Indians in beaded, fringed doeskin and long hair, moccasins and proud faces. I missed Calgary, where country life was woven into the rich fibre of city streets. Ponoka had no Stetsons or shining spurs. Here farmers dressed in plain dark shirts and wide-brimmed felt hats and the hospital doctors, and patients out on a pass, wore fedoras and city clothes.

Ponoka hospital was almost self-sufficient. Patients at various stages of recovery formed the workforce. The hospital also maintained a large kitchen, laundry and sewing room along with many gardens, all partially staffed by patients. Each department employed several outside workers to supervise. They didn't wear uniforms and I found it impossible to tell the employees from the patients. But we student nurses had to wear our uniforms to identify us as the fledglings we were.

On the outside Ponoka Mental Hospital was a sanctuary of serenity.

My first day inside was a shock. After our morning lectures, we followed the instructor to our respective wards in one of the several pavilions. We stopped at the entrance to my ward, Pavilion C. The instructor pulled a large ring full of keys, from her pocket. Choosing a long, thick one, she unlocked the door, then drew it shut behind us. The door connected with a hollow clunk that echoed eerily. My heart began to race as we marched down a wide hall. The wooden floor, buffed to a high lustre, reflected slices of bright sunshine entering through barred windows.

We passed a patient polishing the windows with intensity. Another mimicked Jesus Christ, pacing up and down and reciting parables, arms outstretched in a saintly fashion. A man with his hair combed like Napoleon had his hand tucked in his shirt and was giving an ardent speech about war. None of the patients took any notice of us.

We came to another door. Again the click of the nurse's key, the loud resonant clank as it locked behind us. The corridor was empty, only the eerie sound of our footsteps echoing in the empty halls and I began to wonder about my safety.

Finally we climbed a narrow flight of stairs. My ward was on the other side of the locked door at the top. I followed my instructor through the door and stepped into a crowd of middle-aged women, most in flowered, cotton dresses. Empty faces, empty eyes, messy hair ~ human beings who mechanically moved back and forth and milled around in aimless circles.

I was introduced to the head nurse who told me to try and mix with the patients. "Get to know them," she said.

As I stood wondering just how I was going to mix with these patients, I heard someone call, "Yoo-hoo!"

A tall woman, slightly on the heavy side, rushed towards me, her black hair fixed in a tidy bun at the back of her head. She smiled and waved as she approached. She was dressed differently from the other women, she looked like a moving kaleidoscope: long black skirt swinging, red and white low-cut blouse and heavy makeup to match. Her dangling earrings and rows of colourful necklaces jingle-jangled in time with her bosom. Everything about her was in motion. She looked like a gypsy, or maybe a Hungarian countess. I soon learned that she preferred the latter, as she walked and talked with an air of aristocracy. She insisted on giving me a tour. I followed her, trotting around the ward like a puppy as she introduced me to the other patients, who paid no attention to either of us.

"Come with me into the lounge!" she announced, then swooped down the hall carrying an unlit cigarette in her hand, nodding royally to all she passed.

Once inside the patients' lounge, the countess walked over to the wall, pushed a red button beside the cigarette lighter that sat in the middle of a flat tin plate, leaned forward and lit her cigarette from the red-hot element in the wall. Patients were not allowed to handle matches. She paused, her right hand braced against on her hip and with an affected flair, blew out a puff of smoke.

"Allow me to introduce myself," she said authoritatively. "My name is Cynthia Brown." Her red lips spread into a broad smile, revealing her large, white teeth. I liked her. Compared to the other patients, she seemed almost normal. I had seen people on the street behaving just like her and I wondered why she was on this chronic ward, or for that matter, in this hospital at all.

I glanced around the lounge at the other patients rocking back and forth. Some were talking to imaginary voices in the air, listening for a reply, obviously hallucinating. It was just as my textbook had explained. I was spellbound.

"Come meet Margie!" Cynthia said.

We walked over to a woman sitting by the window engrossed in a jigsaw puzzle that lay in pieces on a table in front of her.

"Margie, it gives me pleasure to introduce you to Miss Yates, our new student nurse from Calgary." Cynthia spoke as if announcing royalty at a ball.

Margie looked up with sad blank eyes, then fumbled with her puzzle.

Mrs. Wilson, the head nurse, appeared in the doorway of the lounge and called to me. She suggested that I read as many charts as I could before the end of my shift.

"By the way," she said. "Cynthia Brown exhibits manic personality behaviour. She's grandiose and very manipulative. Be careful she doesn't have you running in circles."

I read Cynthia Brown's chart first, it was a heavy thick one. A long history of grandiose behaviour had devastated her life and her relationship with her husband. Cynthia suffered from megalomania, delusional fantasies of wealth and power manifested in bouts of buying mania. She spent every cent she could get her hands on and ran up exorbitant bills in store after store, extending the limits of their credit. The grandiose spells were cyclical at first, but then became so frequent that Mr.

Brown feared bankruptcy. He had the doctors intervene. A panel of psychiatrists reviewed Cynthia's case and forcibly admitted her to Ponoka for treatment. That was six years ago.

Margie's chart revealed a history of manic-depressive illness. In her mania phase, she would burn herself out, unable even to sleep for days on end. Then her depression would take over and render her immobile. She was now taking tranquilizers, which kept the hyperactivity at bay, and helped her regain some of the 30 pounds lost during her depressive phase. Her husband and three teenage children came to visit her every week.

As I read her chart I suddenly realized I had always taken my mother's health for granted. Margie's children had grown up without knowing their mother's love, and Margie had been denied the joy of watching her children grow and mature, all because something had gone wrong in her brain, or in her mind.

Nobody seemed to know what or where, and nobody seemed to know how to fix it. The doctors could only subdue her symptoms, conceal them. Margie had been in the hospital eight years. Eight years of swinging from manic pole to depressive pole. Eight years of suppression. She now suffered from dementia, which my *Webster's Dictionary* said, was a progressive, organic mental disorder characterized by chronic personality disintegration, confusion, disorientation, stupor, deterioration of intellectual capacity and function, and impairment of control of memory, judgment, and impulses.

Through the glass walls of the nurses' station, I watched the patients with their expressionless faces pacing the hall as I read their charts. Ten minutes later, I glanced up. The corridor was empty. I crept to the door of the office and peered down the hall. The patients had congregated in front of a closed door. They shifted from foot to foot seemingly oblivious of each other. Suddenly a short, plump motherly-looking woman in a light blue, cotton dress pushed through the crowd, holding a ring of keys above her head.

"Okay, ladies. Excuse me, please," she said. As soon as she unlocked the door, the patients stampeded into the small kitchen and grabbed bread, jam and peanut butter.

"If I didn't know better," the little woman said as she walked towards me, "I would think they are starving to death."

I looked at her and raised my eyebrows, quizzically.

"It's the drugs, you know. Makes them ravenous. That, and the fact they have nothing else to think about in here." She shrugged, and fixed the ring of keys to a large safety pin inside the pocket of her dress. Her steady brown eyes studied me through gold-rimmed glasses. "I see you're the new student."

I nodded.

"Maybe you can think of something creative for our patients. Plan a project to try and keep them occupied. God knows they need something to do. I'll help you with whatever you decide to do, I'm in charge of the activities." Then she smiled. "Welcome. My name is Millie."

"Hi," I said. "I'm Miss Yates."

"If you need anything, just let me know. I've been working here ten years. Know the patients better than any of the nurses, or doctors for that matter. I'm the one that makes sure all the patients get washed and dressed each morning. The student nurse works with me so we'll get to know each other tomorrow."

During the next few days I read chart after chart. Many of the women suffered from depression. Many were suicidal or homicidal, or both. Pavilion C was a restricted, locked ward for their protection, and for ours.

Their daily medication did control, or at least minimize, the extremes of their behaviour, and most of the time it granted them quietude. But peace came with a high price. The drugs caused many to develop coarse features and facial hair. Millie and I had to shave the women every morning with an electric razor.

Soon I discovered the patients had a peculiar, offensive body odour from the medication and some had open sores on the palms of their hands from the penny roll, a complication from their medication that forced them to rub their thumb incessantly in a circle around their palm. The medication also tampered with their brains, often reducing their senses to a bare minimum. But they were quiet, and they were safe, and that was important. It was better than if they walked the streets alone, forgetting to take their medication, unable to care for themselves. Most had been in the hospital from 4 to 20 years, swinging between mania and depression.

At times they became catatonic, like Doreen who lay curled up on her bed as though sleeping. Yet there was something surreal about her. I hesitated in front of her bed, unsure of how to approach her. What does one say to a patient whose mind has apparently left our world, yet her body continues to live?

"Doreen is very ill right now," Millie said quietly. "She can hear us, but she's too sick to move."

The next morning a patient came to talk to our class. Mr. Sear had been in the hospital for 15 years with manic-depressive illness. He explained very eloquently how he felt during both phases of his illness. His catatonic phase had lasted for a considerable length of time, he said, and he had curled up as if in a cocoon. He became unable to control his actions or thoughts. He retreated, unaware that he had severed his connection with the real world. At one point, he said, the medical experts questioned that he would ever recover. But he did recover, and gave a detailed account of the nightmare he had endured for years. He said he had the ability to hear what relatives and staff said to him, yet he was unable to respond. When he did recover, he was able to remember who was kind, and who was not, and he could name those who moved him gently, and those who abused him. Now he was on a mission to enlighten nurses and staff.

"My manic phase was as painful as my catatonic phase," he said calmly. "My mind and my body were never quiet. I was in constant motion. It was physically impossible for me to be still. I paced the halls, cleaned windows, walls and floors, and when I finished I started all over again. I worked and moved and talked to the point of exhaustion, yet I could not stop. My mind was as active as my body. I wrote letters all night, to the Prime Minister, to the President of the United States, the Queen of England. I felt that I alone was capable of solving the problems of the world.

"The voices never left me. They played over and over in my head. I was unable to shake them loose. I listened to them and talked to them day and night. Voices that told me where to go, what to do, whether to trust someone or not. They told me what to eat, or not to eat. At times they told me the food had been poisoned, or that someone was going to kill me. These voices sounded as if they came over a radio. Their perceptions were falsely distorted, yet I had a compelling sense of their reality. One day they told me that I should kill a particular person before that person killed me. And *that's* when I was admitted to Ponoka."

"Who were these people that wanted to kill you?" asked one of the students.

"Anyone. Could be a doctor, a nurse, a floor cleaner. Simply anyone."

Before his illness, Mr. Sear held a responsible job as a teacher. Although the doctors now considered him well enough to be discharged, he chose to remain within the physical and emotional security of the hospital. He was now teaching at the high school in the town of Ponoka, and he spoke to each class of student nurses at the hospital. Mr. Sear was living testimony to the fact that there is always hope in the face of illness.

On Friday night after work at the end of my first week in Ponoka, Standish and I had the weekend off and made the 90 minute drive back to Calgary. I was more than anxious to see my parents ~ and Mark Birch.

As I dressed to visit Mark, I brushed away the thought that I was dressing for a date yet chose a pretty pink blouse and the stylish beige skirt Mom had made me. I leaned into the mirror and applied a coat of Mom's deep pink lipstick then took the bus to the Dairy Queen. Now I carried two milkshakes into the hospital. I ran up the stairs throwing a quick glance toward the chapel. Why should I be worried about Sister Leclerc's wrath? It was such a small price to pay for Mark's life.

In Mark's tiny closet of a room, we sipped cool milkshakes as we discussed hot jazz. Outside the window, cars swished down Second Street and a dog barked incessantly across the street. Suddenly the bells of St. Mary's Church, a few blocks away, struck a joyful clamour, announcing another wedded couple.

"I have a record I'd like you to have," Mark said. His voice had become even more raspy from the increased swelling and pressure of the lymph glands on both sides of his neck. "It's called *The Hawk in Hi Fi*. This guy, Coleman Hawkins, plays good jazz. I'll ask my sister to bring it in. I'll have it for you next week."

His eyes danced when he talked about jazz and I wondered, were those eyes for me? I loved the way he smiled now. The lonely, worried man I saw my first night on St. Joe's was gone. He had improved to the point of being able to walk to the chair, though he still needed help. But he was getting better. Guenette was working nights on St. Joe's now and I was elated when she told me that the doctors felt that the new medication was working.

124

Sunday afternoon I said good-bye to Mark. "See you next week," I said. "I'm sure I'll have the weekend off."

"I hope so." He smiled his big, beautiful smile. "I look forward to these milkshakes." He winked, and I felt my heart quicken.

I skipped down the marble stairs, ecstatic that the medication was working and the prayers were working.

Back in Ponoka Monday morning, I made up my mind to be creative with the patients in Pavilion C. I'd have the ladies bake cookies. We had a small kitchen downstairs. The head nurse agreed with me and I couldn't help but feel I accumulated a few Brownie points for my originality. But none of the patients wanted to join me. None, that is, except Cynthia, who jumped at the chance.

Off we went downstairs, Cynthia full of enthusiasm (not unusual for Cynthia) and I with a cookbook under my arm. Millie had stocked the kitchen with all the ingredients we would need for chocolate chip cookies.

"We are going to bake brownies," Cynthia announced as I opened the cookbook to Grandma's Old-fashioned Chocolate Chip Cookies.

"Brownies might be too complicated," I suggested, "and besides, I don't think we have all of the ingredients." But Cynthia began slinging pots and pans around the kitchen, and she melted down the chocolate chips to substitute for bars of chocolate.

"We will make a double batch," she announced with authority. "We must have enough to go around to all the ladies."

When the first double batch was in the oven, Cynthia began measuring a second round.

"We have enough brownies ... don't you think?" I said lamely as Cynthia began her third double batch.

"Oh heavens, Miss Yates, you don't realize how the ladies will love these. Why, there's barely a taste for everyone," she said, dismissing my concern with an affected wave of her arm. "And don't forget, the nurses will want some too."

The brownie machine was in motion. I had no way of stopping it. When we finally finished, and only because it was three o'clock, almost time for me to go off duty, we had six double batches of brownies.

The head nurse sent a message with Millie that I was to see her immediately.

"This," she said, waving her arms over the sea of brownies, "is exactly what should *not* have happened! Do you realize that Cynthia has a problem with excessive behaviour?"

"Yes," I mumbled.

"Miss Yates, you have played right into Cynthia's illness. All these brownies are a result of excessive, grandiose behaviour."

"I'm sorry," I offered. "But I had trouble reasoning with her, and I didn't want to hurt her."

"You must realize that all of the patients in this hospital are ill, even though some may appear normal. You, as a professional must try to curb the symptoms of the patients. Try to help them, Miss Yates. Don't feed into their problems. Cynthia is very persuasive, and manipulative, but you must be firm. That does not mean severe, Miss Yates. Just firm. You also must remind Cynthia to stay within the boundaries of normal behaviour. Cynthia is here because she is mentally ill, Miss Yates. You must remember that."

Millie re-stocked our kitchen and Cynthia and I continued to bake cookies.

By the end of the week I was encouraged ~ two other patients had joined us. Though I tried to interest them in baking, once seated in the kitchen they continued their rocking and hallucinating. But it was a change for them and it gave Cynthia and me something to do.

Privileged to have two weekends off in a row, on Friday at five, Standish and I jumped in her brother's car and drove back to Calgary.

After a quick trip to the Dairy Queen, I ran straight up to St. Joe's. I knew the nurses on the ward wouldn't tell Sister about my visits to Mark. I hoped they would not notice how excited I was when I was with him and how we'd glance at each other secretly, sipping our thick milkshakes.

Mark greeted me with his beautiful smile and gave me the record, *The Hawk in Hi Fi.* "I will always cherish it, Mark," I whispered. "Thank you."

Mark was in good spirits, though he had lost weight since last weekend. He looked weaker.

Late Sunday afternoon I went back to see Mark. We drank our milkshakes and discussed Elvis's new hit recording, *Wooden Heart,* which was playing on Mark's little transistor radio. Mark said he liked the song, and was going to buy the record when he got home. I thought I would buy one too, to remind me of Mark. *Can't see you, I love you, Please don't break my heart in two. That's not hard to do, 'Cause I don't have a wooden heart ...*

At five o'clock I said, "I have to leave now. Standish is waiting for me."

Reluctantly, I said, "Good-bye, Mark. I hope I have next weekend off. If I do, I'll be back to visit. Please keep getting stronger." I reached for his empty milkshake container. He looked up, his dark, soft eyes caught and held mine. He reached over and gently took my hand. My heart began to race again. I could feel my face warming to a bashful pink. I stood still, afraid to move, afraid to breathe. Then there was a magic moment when the world stopped and my body tingled and I wondered if he felt it too. His hand felt warm ~ no, hot. He was burning up. No. Maybe the room was too warm. He must have sensed my concern.

"I'm fine," he said with a chuckle. "In fact I'm wonderful." His gentle eyes held mine still, and he squeezed my hand. "Thanks for everything," he whispered. "I hope I see you next week."

"Me too," I said shyly. "I hope I can get another weekend off." *There's no strings upon this love of mine / It was always you from the start / Treat me nice / Treat me good / Treat me like you really should / 'Cause I'm not made of wood ...*

I walked to the door and turned around to wave good-bye. He looked like a tiny man in a very large bed.

Mark waved back, a broad smile on his shrunken face. He looked flushed, and I thought he was about to have another sweat.

"Thanks for everything," he said again in his raspy voice. *And if you say good-bye / Then I know that I would cry / Maybe I would die / 'Cause I don't have a wooden heart.*

Back in Ponoka after work the next day at 6:30, my mother called. Mark was dead.

"I can't believe that, Mom," I finally blurted out. "I saw him yesterday. He was fine when I left him. He was going to get better." My voice quavered. I tried to take a deep breath, but it came in short gasps. My mind flashed back to Mark ~ his flushed face, his raspy voice, and his smile, oh, God, his beautiful smile.

"I'm sorry, dear."

There was always something when my mother said "I'm sorry, dear" that would make me cry and this time was no exception.

"When is the funeral?" I sobbed. How could I possibly be talking about Mark's funeral?

"The paper says it is on Friday at one thirty."

"Mom, will you go to the funeral for me?"

She hesitated, but only for a moment. "Yes, of course, dear. Your father and I will go. "There was a pause. I was barely aware of my mother speaking to me. "I know you are upset, Donna ... death is a part of life ... a circle that must be completed ... God ... has other plans for Mr. Birch ... Just remember him as the wonderful man that he was."

As I walked through the campus to the residence, I was surprised to find the world still alive, the colourful flowers, the birds flitting from tree to tree, and singing. Oh, God, the birds were still singing. Nothing had changed. But Mark was gone forever.

When I returned to the residence, Standish was sitting in her jeans having a cup of coffee. She had spent the day in the fields, digging fence posts with her patients.

"Isn't that just the pits? Pardon the pun." She chuckled.

"Well, digging fence posts would be better than baking cookies every day with my ladies."

"Yeah? I'll change places with you."

"Hey, maybe our ladies could make your men a lunch. We could bring it to the field and have a picnic together."

"Good heavens, they would never let us do that," Standish said.

"But everyone keeps telling us to get the patients to interact. My ladies might interact with your men because they sure don't want to interact with me."

The next day, to our surprise, our head nurses gave their permission for us to have a picnic. Millie and the male assistant working with Standish's group would have to be present.

Millie was delighted. She ordered the food from the main kitchen and Cynthia and I baked cookies. It was difficult to keep a rein on Cynthia, but I had learned something about controlling excessive behaviour. Together, Cynthia and I set a limit on the number of cookies ~ *before* we began to bake.

When I awoke on Friday morning, my heart sank. It was the day of Mark Birch's funeral and the day of the picnic. How would I ever get through it?

Millie had arranged to use the farm pick-up truck to transport our group of seven ladies, and all the food, out to the field where Standish's men were digging holes for fence posts. Millie took Cynthia in front with her and that left six of us to sit behind on the floor of the truck, holding the food. Cynthia guarded the cookies on her lap and I hoped that the chocolate chips would not melt from the heat of her body.

"Watch that food," Millie said, as she struggled up onto the running board and climbed into the large cab of the dusty navy blue truck. "Nobody is allowed to eat until we have our picnic. Is that clear?"

She might as well have been talking to the moon, for the only one to respond was Cynthia. She clutched the plate of cookies even tighter, and gave a crisp military nod of approval. "Right," she said without a blink, and continued to stare out the front window.

Millie started the ancient truck, which leaned too much to the left, and revved the engine several times. As the pistons reluctantly kicked in, we all jiggled up and down. I hoped that Standish's field was not too far away. As we sat waiting for the engine to warm up, I realized that this was the first time in months, maybe years, that my women were going to leave the hospital. Finally they had the sun on their cheeks and the wind in their hair. And they looked pretty, too. Millie and I had set their hair in pin curls yesterday and made sure each put on a fresh dress this morning.

Suddenly we felt a jolt, a lurch and we were off, bumping over the dusty prairie; the dutiful women bringing food and drink to the working men. I felt like a goalie in the heat of a hockey game as I tried to save the food and lemonade from bumping right out of the open tailgate of the truck. I sat in the truck bed in my starched, white uniform constantly tugging my skirt down as we bumped along on our behinds for 20 minutes. Millie and Cynthia alternately bounced up and down in the front as if they were on a vicious merry-go-round. Millie increased her speed, but my women never changed expression. Just shook like bowls of Jell-O, staring into space as if they were still sitting in the hospital lounge.

Suddenly, Millie applied the brakes and we skidded to a halt in a cloud of dust. Standish, her men and the male assistant were waiting under the shade of several large trees, surrounded by an expanse of red and white clover. I was shocked that Standish's men looked exactly like my women. Their strange gait, and vacant, distant eyes ~ fixed on a drama only they could see.

But I did notice the men's eyes sharpen as we helped our ladies out of the truck. Then a strange feeling came over me when I realized these men had not been in the company of women, other than nurses, for many, many years.

"We'd better watch them carefully," I whispered to Standish, as we spread a tablecloth on the grass under the trees, then placed two large blankets on each side for everyone to sit on. Three of my ladies sat down, apparently unaware of the men, and Cynthia discreetly arranged their skirts.

I kept my eye on Standish's men while Millie and I arranged the picnic lunch on the tablecloth. Something about the way the men were leisurely leaning against the trees and watching the ladies struck a cautious chord in my body. One chewed lazily on a piece of grass, a knowing smirk on his face.

I was relieved when the patients dug into the picnic lunch and devoured the food with their usual gusto. The men's focus had returned to their private stage, once again oblivious of the women. They were really behaving very normally, I thought, and felt sorry I had read something in the men's behaviour that was probably not there. I had been too critical, I told myself. From now on I would put more trust in these patients. I began to relax.

Cynthia strutted around like a mother hen. "Don't eat so fast," she nattered. "No, you can't have any more, you're going to be sick!" She guarded the cookies until everyone was finished eating, and then passed them out as if they were the host at Communion.

The food was consumed in a matter of minutes, so we asked everyone to rest under the trees while Standish and I tidied up. I wanted to make their outing last as long as possible. After all, my women finally had their feet on green grass and were breathing the fresh summer air, heavy with the sweet fragrance of clover. I noticed that one of the men had moved over to sit beside one of my women, and I was touched to see that they were finally interacting. Though they didn't appear to be talking, I was glad he had chosen the lady who was most ill. I wished I had done a better job of shaving her chin this morning, but perhaps this man could improve her mental condition. Make her feel human again.

I gave the tablecloth two or three brisk shakes, and as I turned, I was surprised to see my lady in the blue dress had gone over to the men's side of the blanket, and was sitting, albeit in a somewhat unbecoming position, with one of the men. The patients were definitely interacting, just what the head nurse wanted. I smiled. Everything had gone so perfectly. Perhaps we might make this outing a weekly occurrence.

Suddenly, I heard a commotion behind me. Turning around, I realized that something had gone terribly wrong. At first it looked like a fight, but then I realized our patients had finally come alive, a little too alive. The men ran for the women. The women ran for the men. There were grunts and groans, bodies twisting, entwining. I gasped, and for several moments stood riveted to the spot, unable to move. They must have had some sort of secret signal, for everything began so fast. My God, I thought, Standish and I are the only nurses here. We're responsible for this picnic!

I heard a *riiipppp* as two of Standish's men tugged at the dress of one of my patients. Millie shouted for help. She had grabbed the lady in the blue dress, and was valiantly struggling to keep her from Standish's man. Then my heart stopped when I saw two running hand in hand down the railroad tracks.

"Stop them. Quick! Stop them!" I yelled to the male assistant as I frantically pointed toward the two runaways. He took off in hot pursuit like a chase scene in a silent movie.

Another couple tugged at each other and slipped to the ground. I couldn't be sure if the man pulled my patient down, or she pulled him. Then from the corner of my eye I saw Standish struggling to hold back her lonely male patient who had not yet found a woman. But the man in the baggy overalls had found his woman and had her under the blanket, wrapped up in a world of their own.

In a panic, I jumped in with both feet to help Standish and Millie. We began tackling the patients, pulling them apart and then shoving the women into the truck. The assistant returned with the two escapees, and it took all three of us to pull the lovebirds out from under the blanket. All the while, Cynthia stood in the middle of the commotion getting butted from end to end, shouting futile commands.

Finally it was over. My cap lay trampled in the dirt, the buttons gone from the waistband of my apron. Cynthia's hair had come undone. I almost laughed when I saw her face smeared with bright red lipstick and skinny black ropes of hair dangling around her face: Then I almost cried. Because for the first time since I had known Cynthia, she looked down, beaten, confused. Cynthia's crucial control had vanished and her small, secure world had unravelled. I gently circled my arm round Cynthia's waist and helped her back to the truck.

We were a sorry looking bunch when we limped back into the hospital. Millie gave the report to the head nurse, who, immediately called me to her office.

"It's true, Miss Yates, that the patients are mentally ill," she said. "But you should not have thought that they would behave like robots. They are human. Sick, yes, but they have human needs and emotions."

After work on Sunday, I had just settled down with a book in a futile attempt to put Mark out of my mind when the housemother called. I had visitors.

I dashed to the reception desk to find Mom and Dad waiting for me.

"I knew this would be a difficult weekend for you, dear," Mom said as I clung to her. "We just thought we would take a Sunday drive up and surprise you."

Mom, Dad and I drove to a small park on the edge of town and sat at the picnic table eating cold turkey and potato salad that Mom had packed in an ice cooler. I was yearning to hear about the funeral.

"There were so many young people at the funeral," Mom said. "That's what I found difficult, so many young people. And my, that young man's mother is very sick. She was in a wheelchair, and didn't go to the cemetery. That poor woman lost her husband and now her child and she's so sick.

"The chapel was crowded, dear, overflowing, actually." Mom shook her head. "And his sister cried all through the ceremony. So many young people."

"I'm so glad you went, Mom."

"I'm happy I was able to go for you, dear," she said gently. "He looked like he was a very kind man. My, he was handsome."

Mom leaned towards me and took my hands in hers. "Did I tell you that they played *In the Garden?* It's my favourite hymn. It's gospel, you know." As though I hadn't heard her playing that song a thousand times after her father died. "A woman from Mark Birch's church sang and her face was wet with tears when she finished."

"Well, I'm going to pack up the car while you two talk," my father said. Mom began to sing softly to me in her sweet voice.

> *I come to the garden alone,*
> *While the dew is still on the roses;*
> *And the voice I hear,*
> *Falling on my ear;*
> *The Son of God discloses ...*

Mom pulled me close, as she had so many times when I was a child and stroked my hair. I pressed closer to her; I needed her. Needed to be held. Needed to be understood.

> *And He walks with me,*
> *And He talks with me,*
> *And He tells me I am His own,*
> *And the joy we share as we tarry there,*
> *None other has ever known.*

Nobody could understand me like my mother. Nobody.

"He must have suffered terribly," my mother whispered, as she brushed her lips to my hair. "God has a way of working things out for the best."

After a while we slowly drove back to the residence, and then the dreaded time came when I had to say good-bye.

"Take care, my little girl," my mother said holding me close. "It helps to go to the garden from time to time, to talk with God. I know how sad you feel now, but not *all* of your patients will live, dear. And you must not lose part of yourself every time a patient dies. There comes a point when their lives are in God's hands."

My eyes began to burn. "I know, but it's very hard." I paused for a moment, and swallowed. "He was only 24, Mom."

Just before they left, my father wrapped his arm around my shoulders. "Don't dwell on this patient, Donna. Remember that life must go on. Let the dead bury the dead."

No Choice

After the disastrous picnic, Mrs. Wilson would not allow me to bake any more cookies with Cynthia. So I tried to find ways to interact with some of the other patients. I sat in the solarium and rocked back and forth with my uncommunicative patients. I willed them to transfer their innermost thoughts and fears to me. I could help them. I would run and tell the head nurse that I had made a breakthrough! But we sat in silence, my patients and I, and we rocked.

I gazed into their stagnant eyes. I care about you, I want to help you I tried to tell them. But they were locked in a vacuum. Prisoners.

Why them and not me? Was it their families or lack of family, some disturbing emotional experience, or abuse? Or was it in their genes? What lay behind these empty eyes? What were they thinking? The key lay in communication. The patients had to talk. Give us a clue. But in Pavilion C, getting the patients to talk was an impossible task.

One day when I returned to the ward after lunch, the head nurse called to me: "Get over to Pavilion A immediately. I want you to observe a patient who is in crisis. She's about to have emergency shock treatment."

I arrived at the pavilion, the guard directed me to the second floor. Once there I heard a woman screaming. I rushed down the hall to the room. Two orderlies and a doctor were trying to lift the patient up onto a stretcher.

"Help ... help. They're going to kill me. Help!" The patient shouted, as she fought with all her strength to free herself.

I stood with the small group of student nurses also called to observe the procedure. The woman was unbelievably distressed, desperately fighting for her life. This is real, I said to myself, not a movie. These are real people.

As the patient passed me, her arm shot out from under the sheet and grabbed my arm. She pleaded at the top of her voice.

"Help me. Please help me. They're going to kill me!"

I stepped back. She held on with raw, frantic strength, begging me to help her. I was confused. I thought I should help, but I didn't know what to do. Her sunken eyes flashed from their dark pits and held my gaze. I gasped and pulled back, trying to free my arm. The orderly pried her fingers loose. Then they charged down the hall and into an operating room.

"Nooo. Nooo. Don't take me in that room! They're going to kill me in that room. Help!" The screaming and struggling increased to a hysterical pitch.

Two more orderlies appeared. Each took an arm and a leg and strapped them to the stretcher. They placed straps across her forehead, her knees, her abdomen, her chest. She could not escape. Her screams changed to whimpers, begging, pleading.

"I will do anything you say, anything. Please don't kill me."

Dr. Peats, black hair, black-rimmed glasses, white lab coat, was waiting. He bent over her and placed an electrode on each side of her head.

"No! Nooo!" The screams exploded again, wild, blood-curdling, desperate.

Thump. Zap. The patient jerked in convulsions for several seconds, then lay silent, peaceful, asleep.

An orderly pushed her back to her room. While our group stood silently by her bed waiting for her to wake up, I studied her face. She was now calm and relaxed and had a strangely innocent look. Five minutes ago this patient had been hysterical, suicidal, and perhaps even homicidal. I wondered what had happened in her brain. I wondered if she would be calm when she woke up.

Dr. Peats then appeared in the doorway and ambled over to the patient's bed. "I'm sorry you girls had to see shock therapy like this for your first time," he said softly. "But this was an emergency. The patient suffers from delusions of persecution, a psychotic process that plays in her brain like a recording stuck in a groove. If allowed to continue she might hurt herself, or somebody else. The electric shock should remove whatever triggered her reaction."

We stood silent, stunned. He told us that it was normal for the patient to experience a brief loss of short-term memory. That whatever was causing her problem may or may not return, but at least now they would be able to get her into a program of therapy. "And with time, and therapy, I believe this patient has an excellent chance for recovery." He smiled. "Any questions?"

We shook our heads.

The patient moaned, took a deep breath, and opened her eyes. She gazed at us around her bed.

"Where am I?" she said, looking confused, but not upset.

"You're in Ponoka Mental Hospital," the doctor said, "You've had shock therapy, but you're doing fine."

The woman sat up and gazed around the large room as if seeing it for the first time. There were five other beds. Those occupants, unperturbed, were familiar with the aftermath of shock therapy, they had experienced it, some more than once.

An eerie quiet hung in the room, the calm after a storm. A feeling that said everything is over, yet it was just beginning, and where would it end? It said something had changed, and I hoped the change would be for the better.

"I can't remember where I put my cigarettes," the woman said.

"In here," said the RN, opening the locker drawer and handing her a package of Matinees.

The woman remembered her name and almost everything else, except where she had put her cigarettes and slippers. She seemed to have forgotten her paranoia, which hopefully, with time and therapy, would never return.

I ambled back through the campus toward the residence, wondering if I could ever forget the fear and panic I saw on that woman's face as they placed the electrodes on her head, or the way they strapped her down and held her against her will. And I wondered if she had understood that an electric current was going to rip through her brain.

Other patients told me they knew what was happening, they had been there before, two or three times, maybe more. I wondered if they could feel their muscles exploding and contracting, their joints being propelled front to back, thrust into positions joints were never meant to be in. I wondered if they could feel their backs thrown into an arch almost to the point of breaking. And I wondered if they knew they might never be the same again.

But what else could the doctors do? The alternative was a padded cell to wait out the storm. Wait until the delusions burned themselves out, or destroyed the patient.

Wednesday was my second to last day in Ponoka. Our group of student nurses followed the head nurse to the pavilion that housed the criminally insane. A guard unlocked the door and led us into maximum security. It was too risky for medical staff to carry keys in this area. We followed the supervisor of maximum security into the conference room decorated with beautiful oil paintings. The door slammed shut and locked behind us. My body stiffened. Trapped.

We sat at the conference table as the supervisor spoke to us about the patient we were about to visit. "Tom Brice murdered an RCMP officer 18 years ago in the Northwest Territories, and was tried in Edmonton for first-degree murder."

The supervisor paced nervously as he talked. He had a distracting twitch in his right eye and kept twirling the ends of his handlebar moustache. "Tom had a very smart lawyer who got him off on grounds of insanity. They sentenced him to a mental hospital for the rest of his life. When Tom arrived, he showed no signs of mental illness. But he's been in maximum security ever since his trial, one room with a cot and only the bare necessities. Three guards always have to be with him whenever he leaves that room for exercise, or to use the bathroom."

The supervisor's eye took off in a twitching fit. Then he continued. "When we found that Tom was a gifted artist, we encouraged his talent." He motioned around the room. "Tom did all these paintings you see on the walls.

"Several years ago Tom began showing signs of abnormal behaviour. He became distant, unable to converse in the intelligent manner of his earlier years. He began to harm his body. First scratches, then cuts, and it progressed. When he pulled out two of his fingernails, we were forced to remove his painting supplies. He is allowed an hour each day to paint, of course under close supervision. We've had patients who gouged their eyes out with paintbrushes. They will use any sharp object they can to harm themselves. Unfortunately, Tom has now regressed to the point where he can no longer paint at all. His room has been stripped clean, except for a mattress at night, and one chair."

"Will he ever be allowed out of the hospital?" asked one of the students.

"The law states that a criminally insane patient might be allowed to go free at the Queen's consent, but that has never happened. So, humph, Mr. Brice's chance for freedom is virtually nil. Any more questions?"

None. "Fine," he said. "Then let's all go upstairs to see Mr. Brice."

I was almost afraid to breathe. Stories of an occasional guard being attacked and even injured were whispered in secrecy, but I had never heard of any students being hurt here. Surely they wouldn't put us in harm's way.

Standish was in the first group. She glanced at me and made a baleful face as she walked out the door. When my turn came, I followed the supervisor up the narrow stairs to the second floor. Men guarding the doors unlocked them to let us through, then banged them shut and locked them again. We walked down a short, narrow hallway where all of the doors had a barred square opening at eye level. We stopped at the last door on the left.

"This is Tom." The guard whispered.

I peered through the bars, making sure I kept a safe distance. A thin man of medium height with long, brown stringy hair was standing with his back to me. He stared out a small window also guarded by steel bars. A blue and yellow plaid shirt was carelessly tucked into his loose-fitting beige pants, rolled halfway to his knees, and he wore sandals but no socks. A wooden chair stood in one corner of the small empty room, a bare mattress lay on the floor. Tom walked over to the chair, stood for a moment as if in a daze, then picked it up and slowly carried it back to the window.

"Hello, Tom," said the guard in a soft, calm voice. "Some student nurses are here to visit you."

Tom put down the chair, turned and slowly approached us. His thin fingers gripped the steel bars. His gaunt, expressionless face had a chiselled look with sharp, high cheekbones, thin lips and square jaw. His languid eyes sat in sunken sockets like two small lumps of coal. They moved from the guard, to me, to the other two students but he didn't react. After several intense moments he turned, shuffled back to the rear window and retreated into his own turbid world.

The next day when I said good-bye to Mrs. Wilson, the head nurse, I felt no remorse about leaving Ponoka. I was terribly homesick, my four weeks had seemed like four years. I wanted to go back to The Holy.

"If you ever want to work in psychiatry, you have a job here," Mrs. Wilson said. "We're very pleased with the way you interacted with the patients. You were very innovative, Miss Yates. Sometimes a little too innovative." She chuckled. "The patients liked you, though, and they will miss you."

As Standish and I drove back towards Calgary I felt free, almost back to normal.

"Would you ever want to be a psychiatric nurse?" Standish asked.

"Not on your life," I sighed. "I prefer the fast pace of the general hospital."

Standish took a deep breath and let out a groan. "If I had one more week of fence-post digging, Yates, I swear I would die. I'm sure my back will never be the same."

As we drove south past Red Deer the prairie grass turned brown and dry and small foothills began to spring up. When I saw the snow-covered Rockies on the western horizon, my heart lifted. Almost home.

The next day after work, our class reunited in the lounge. Class of February, '62 had been living together for 18 months, we were family now. Many of us had been out on affiliations and it was now a rare occurrence for us to be in the residence together

It was 4:30 when Sister Leclerc called us down to the Reception Hall to mark our halfway milestone

"I am really happy for all of you today," Sister said. "And I have a little gift for your class. You have all been good girls." Surprisingly, Sister was all smiles and genuinely pleased as she handed us her gift, a large ashtray for our lounge.

Priestnall thanked her on behalf of our class. I smiled at Sister and she returned a stiff nod. Though Sister still frightened me, I felt more familiar with nuns now. I had made it through the emergency room, the operating room and the mental hospital! I was beginning to feel like a real nurse.

Then we dashed upstairs to celebrate, ordering hamburgers and french fries from the Lotus.

Priestnall threw her greasy hamburger bag in the garbage, then turned to Niven and said, "You'd better stop that whistling on the ward, Niven. Sister, told me she was going to take disciplinary measures if your whistling continues. They could expel you, you know."

"Oh, yeah?" Niven said as she stood ramrod straight and faced the hospital, hands braced on her hips. "Well la-di-da, Sister. Go ahead and expel me for being hap-hap-happy on the wards."

"Perry," Priestnall said. "You're going on affiliation to Ponoka with Niven. Watch her."

"Oh, Christ," Perry said. "How do you think I'm going to get Niven to listen to me?"

The hall door suddenly burst open and Riley pushed through dragging her suitcase to the elevator. We all turned. I realized that she hadn't been at Sister's presentation. And she hadn't come to our celebration, either.

"Bye, guys," she said as coolly as if she was going off to work the night shift.

"Where the hell are you going?" shot Priestnall. "It's eleven o'clock!"

"I have a system," Riley said. "I go through the tunnel, through emerg, take the stairs up to the main entrance and voila ~ out the door. I've been doing this for the last six months and it works every time. See you tomorrow, you poor working stiffs." She limped into the elevator. "I'll be back at six. It's as easy as pie, I simply come in the same way I go out."

How could Riley just walk out of the residence as if she were going to work nights? "Riley, you're nuts!" I called after her. "You're going to get caught."

"Have no fear." Riley gave a theatrical wave as the elevator door squeaked closed.

Niven, hands still on her hips, stared incredulously after Riley. "One of these days she's going to get a large charge from Sister."

"Yeah," White said. "Dis-charge."

I was back on St. John's for a week, my favourite ward. I had missed looking after patients who were physically ill, missed the routine of bathing, rubbing backs and making them comfortable. That was my time to talk to the patients and observe them, a crucial physical and mental evaluation. Even carrying the bedpan had become a necessary habit that I almost missed.

One of my new patients was Sandra Bower, an angelic-looking 18-year-old girl with creamy white skin, and the most gorgeous flaming-red, long hair I had ever seen. The year before she had given birth to a baby, but because she was an unwed mother, she gave it up for adoption. That was when the doctor found the lump in her right shoulder and there was no choice but to remove her arm. Unfortunately, the cancer spread to her lungs, and now they suspected, to her spine. This was her third admission in the past six months.

Sandra was sleeping when her mother arrived at visiting hour, two o'clock. Mrs. Bower was standing by her daughter's bed studying her pale face, when Sandra opened her deep blue eyes and smiled. She looked so young, I thought, too young to be this sick.

"Hi, Sweetie," her mother said. "I brought you some cookies, peanut butter." She turned to me, "That's her favourite, nurse."

"My favourite, too," I said.

Mrs. Bower pointed to the box. "Don't forget to come and get a couple before you go for your coffee break."

For the rest of the morning, Mrs. Bower sat holding Sandra's hand and stroking her hair while they talked and giggled over private jokes. They reminded me of my mother and me.

My other young patient, Roxanne Crisp, was also 18. She too had become pregnant a year before and given her baby up for adoption. The head nurse told me that Roxanne's mother, older than most mothers of teenagers, was ashamed of her daughter and had not allowed Roxanne to leave the house during the entire length of her pregnancy. She denied her daughter the care of a doctor, even when Roxanne's blood pressure became elevated. She went on to develop toxemia in her third trimester. At first Roxanne's legs swelled, then her whole body blew up. Then she couldn't walk, became nauseous and began vomiting, but her mother did not relent.

When Roxanne finally lumbered into the hospital at the end of her pregnancy looking like an overblown balloon, the medical staff was shocked. They gave her medication to bring her blood pressure under control, but she began to have convulsions. They moved her to a quiet, darkened room where she remained on bed rest and carefully monitored until her baby was born. The baby was normal, but Roxanne had suffered irreversible damage to her kidneys. The baby left for the Crèche the same day that Roxanne went home with her mother.

Roxanne's health continued to deteriorate and now her kidneys barely functioned at all. The doctor brought her into the hospital for peritoneal dialysis, a fairly new procedure that we all hoped would keep her alive. Although experiments with peritoneal dialysis began in the 1920s, it carried a high risk of peritonitis. With the recent development of Teflon and silastic, which produced antimicrobial and antifungal catheters, and advances in sterilization, it was now possible to have safe access to the peritoneum and aseptic, sterile solutions.

Roxanne's father had died some years earlier and her mother was her only visitor. A chubby, stoic-looking woman with a powdered white face and greying hair, she seldom spoke. Each day she would perch like a stone-faced sphinx in the chair at the foot of her daughter's bed, knees clamped together, small black purse, worn around the edges, on her lap.

Roxanne said very little though I often went to her room to change the bottles of dialysate fluid that ran through a plastic tube inserted into her abdomen. The peritoneal membrane enclosing the digestive organs allows waste products or toxins normally filtered out by the kidneys to pass from the blood into the dialysate, which drained from her abdomen, through a tube into a bottle on the floor.

I always hesitated before going into the room when her mother was there. A feeling of shame and disgust hung in the air like a decomposing memory, or perhaps her mother's victorious revenge. How different from Sandra's room, which was filled with her mother's love and sympathy for her dying child.

Roxanne lay quietly in bed, bloated with fluid retention, pasty-grey from the build-up of toxins in her blood, at the mercy of her mother, who in the name of her own honour had cast aside her daughter's life as worthless. Roxanne's listless eyes followed me as I bathed her, cared for her and changed the bottles of dialysate that kept her alive. She never complained. She suffered in silence.

After a week of dialysis, the doctor sent Roxanne home for a few weeks' reprieve. But the toxins would gradually increase and she would become sick again and have to return to the hospital. This was her life ~ merely existing from dialysis to dialysis -- Roxanne and her heartless mother.

St. John's ward had six private rooms at the end of the hall, three on each side of the corridor. These patients were either very sick or hospitalized for their annual check-up and not sick at all. Patients paid dearly for these rooms and, in return, were looked after only by registered nurses, or in a pinch ... a senior student nurse. We junior and intermediate students sailed in and out of their rooms to deliver meal trays and at times assisted the RN with nursing care.

A private room near the desk was kept for very sick, usually terminal, patients. Sometimes, intermediate students were allowed to nurse these patients under the supervision of either a senior nurse or an RN.

One day the call-light went on in the private room near the desk. The grad covering the room had gone for coffee and I answered the light. An emaciated woman lay under an oxygen tent. As I got closer, I gasped when I realized the patient was Mary Mullens, my former patient from St. Mary's who had lupus.

"Mrs. Mullens!" I said walking over to her bed. "I didn't know you were back in the hospital."

A faint smile crossed her lips and she struggled to find an opening under the plastic tent. I slid my arm into the tiny space and squeezed her hand.

She spoke barely above a whisper. "I'm so glad to see you, Miss Yates. I was thinking about you ... how you tried to help me when I was on St. Mary's ... you know, with birth control." She took a laboured breath. "I became pregnant again a few months ago ... had another miscarriage. Look how sick I am now. I can't breathe."

I tried to encourage her, but she gave a tiny gasp and turned to the window. I followed her gaze. There wasn't a cloud in the southern Alberta blue sky and airy trees flaunted their extravagant foliage in the summer breeze.

"I've had the last rites," she whispered as if to the trees.

I felt a jolt in my chest, a ringing in my ears. She must be wrong. She couldn't be dying from something that could be prevented. She's a young woman. She could have a happy life with her husband ~ just the two of them. I suddenly became aware of two nuns who sat at the foot of her bed, fingering their rosaries.

Mrs. Mullens quickly whispered introductions. They were her own sisters who lived in Saskatchewan. The two glanced up, barely acknowledged me with a nod and went back to their prayers.

"I know you don't understand our religion," Mrs. Mullens said, in a painfully slow, coarse whisper. "But I followed the Church laws ... I did my best." She winced, then tried to smile. "I need another painkiller."

I told her I would ask her nurse to bring it right away. I turned to leave but she held onto my hand, her eyes clung to mine with a sad, questioning look.

"I know I did the right thing, Miss Yates ... but I'm scared," she breathed. "I want to be brave."

I swallowed hard. "You are *very brave*, Mrs. Mullens," I tried to sound normal though my throat felt as if it had been squeezed shut. "Your family must be proud of you." I blinked quickly in an attempt to ease the burning in my eyes. "I'll be back a little later to visit, I promise."

I left her room, but her eyes haunted me. I was not sure if she really did believe that she had done the right thing. Mary Mullens had made the ultimate sacrifice for her religion, her life for a pregnancy ~ a brief spark that could never ignite.

Before I went off duty, I returned to Mary's room to say good-bye. She was sleeping. Her two sisters still praying. Her husband was at her side. He glanced up and walked over to me.

"Please tell Mrs. Mullens I'm going home now," I whispered. "But I'll see her tomorrow."

"I'll tell her," he said. "She was very glad to see you, Miss Yates. She's so sick, you know."

"I know. I'm so sorry."

Mr. Mullens covered his face with his hands and began to weep. "It's all my fault," he sobbed. "It's all my fault."

"No, don't blame yourself," I said. "The blame does not lie with you."

He slowly turned and walked to the window.

I quietly closed the door.

The next morning, the night nurse reported that Mary Mullens had died in her sleep at 4:30 p.m., one hour after I left her. The all-too-familiar lump grew in my throat. I barely made it through report, then I rushed to the little bathroom at the end of the hall, where I had wept for Lisa and Mr. McPherson and so many others, and I wept again. Wept for the woman who desperately wanted to live, for the woman who should have lived.

After work, Guenette walked into the lounge looking quite serious, and announced, "Kaufmann's mother died. Kaufmann took it really hard. I drove her to the bus. She's gone home for a week."

Poor Kaufmann would be an orphan now. Her only relative was a sister, a nun who lived in a convent in Regina.

"Aw, I feel so sorry for Kaufmann," Niven said slowly. "We really should spend more time with her. Christ, do you know I didn't even realize she wasn't around?"

"I don't think any of us did," Porter said, sadly. "She's like a little mouse that tries not to be seen."

Guenette collected one dollar from all of us and gave it to Father Flanagan to say a mass for Kaufmann's mother. And Sister, on behalf of the School, also asked Father to say a mass.

At mid-morning on my last day on St. John's, Cooper, a new junior on the ward, rushed up to me in a panic. "Sandra Bower has just died," she said. "Will you help me get her ready? It's my first time. I'm so nervous." Cooper bit her lip and looked like she was about to cry. "I can't do it alone. And I can't ask the senior, she's a real crab."

Death! I stood rooted to the spot.

Cooper continued. "Her family should be here any minute. Please help me, Yates!"

How could I tell her I had never touched a dead body? That I was more frightened than she? But I was the intermediate. I had to do it. So I took a deep breath, and said, "Get the morgue pack." My voice sounded strangely calm to my own ears.

Cooper returned and stepped into the room. How brave she was to go in there alone. I dashed to the desk for the procedure manual and tore through the pages until I found, *Preparing the Body for the Morgue*. My breathing changed to short, shallow gasps as I read. Then I imagined Sandra alive. She was a sweet girl. I liked her. Why should I be afraid of seeing her dead? Suddenly a thought came to me, I didn't have to actually *touch* the body. I could just stand there and tell Cooper what to do. After all, *I* was the intermediate.

My knees suddenly felt weak. I wanted to run away, but instead I forced myself, step by step, down the hall, until I reached the door of the silent room. My fingers closed around the vertical brass handle. I entered.

Sandra looked like Sleeping Beauty waiting for the kiss of her prince. Cooper stood near the bed, benumbed.

"I gave her a bath, and closed her eyes," she said, almost unaware of me. "I think that's all I can do until her mother comes." Cooper's wide eyes remained fixed on Sandra.

I fidgeted for a moment. I had to say something, I had to be the strong one here. "Life is difficult, Cooper," I said softly. "Some people seem to get all the bad luck." Then I straightened Cooper's cap and patted her shoulder. "I don't think we ever get used to watching someone's life slip away forever. Especially someone so young."

Cooper left to attend her other patients. My eyes slowly lowered to the bed, to the remnants of Sandra's once beautiful body. Her long hair swirled around her shoulders in soft curls and lay at rest on her pillow. Gorgeous red hair that had once framed her pretty face, now only a reminder of her vibrant youth. Almost nothing had changed but everything had changed. She was a skeleton of adolescence. How quickly Death had seized the moment. Death was never beautiful. This death was not beautiful.

"Good-bye, Sandra," I whispered. "There will be no Prince Charming to awaken you." I stared at the empty sleeve of her gown that had fallen limply into the cavity meant for her arm. What might she have done with her life if things had been different? She might have had a career ~ a teacher, or perhaps a nurse. She would have enjoyed private lunches with her mother, crazy trips with girlfriends. She would have had a future to plan.

As I lay in bed that night, my mind was on Sandra. Not only Sandra, but images of sick and dying people that floated around my room. Each time I closed my eyes, I felt the ghostly image of a corpse I had seen on St. Joseph's when I was a junior. I could almost reach out and touch his sharp, waxy face, wide eyes staring blindly at the ceiling, his mouth slightly ajar with teeth too large that now didn't seem to fit. I remembered placing my hand in front of his mouth, the air was still ... not a trace of a breath. His twiggy limbs were bluish-white, and that sharp smell of death that always comes ... slowly, silently, surely ... I could smell it now, in my room, on my hands.

Was I losing my grasp of the real world? I could not look at the hospital any more without wondering who was dying. My world was filled with illness and death and I couldn't stand it any more. I threw the covers back and went into the hall and softly knocked on Perry's door.

"Hey, Perry," I whispered, as I opened her door. "Are you sleeping?"

"Yates? No ... well yes ... well, it doesn't matter," she said sleepily. "Come on in." She leaned on her elbow and blinked into the light that pushed through the door as I entered.

I could always count on Perry in a time of crisis. She listened patiently as I poured out my fears, nodding, sympathetically, knowingly.

"Sometimes I feel the same way, Yates," she said. "But you know we *are* nurses, and we're in a hospital where there are very sick people. You have to expect that some of them will die. We don't want them to die ... but they will. People can't live forever, you know, no matter how hard we try." She yawned and gave a little giggle.

I looked at my watch. We had been talking for two hours.

"You need a break ... get away from it all for a while." She stifled another yawn. "Guaranteed you will feel better when you get to the San. It's a whole different way of nursing. I know you'll like it." She cocked her head to the side, and smiled. "It's in the country and it's quiet, and nobody died while I was there. I liked it."

"Thanks, Perry," I said as I got up and walked to the door.

"Hey, are you okay?" She lifted the cover. "Do you want to sleep here tonight? There's not much room, you'll have to perch on the edge, but you're welcome to stay if you want."

I gave a weary wave. "No, I'm fine now," I smiled. "Thanks. Good-night."

On Sunday morning I asked Allan to drive me to the cemetery so I could put some flowers on Mark Birch's grave.

"I wouldn't do that if I were you," Allan said. "I don't think you should get stuck on any of your patients who die. It's not healthy, you know."

But I was determined to see the grave. It would be just this one time.

I picked a bouquet of honeysuckle, sweet peas and baby's breath from Mom and Dad's garden, Allan drove me to the cemetery. The gatekeeper gave me directions without even having to look in his book.

"I remember that poor family," he said, puffing on a yellowy-brown pipe. "Sad, very sad."

I asked Allan to wait for me at the gate; I wanted to walk by myself.

Mark's grave was on the side of a hill beside his father. His father's stone was large and black. Mark's was smaller and grey-white. When I read his name on the stone, a heaviness came over me, a feeling I never had before. I couldn't believe that Mark was gone for good. I thought of his little body, his big brown eyes, and his wonderful smile. A knot grew in the pit of my stomach. Would I ever get over this feeling?

The western valley, called the Gateway to the Rockies that led to Cochrane and on to the mountains, was before us, Mark and me. A soft breeze brushed my face as I knelt down and placed the glass jam jar of flowers beneath the grey stone.

"You have a beautiful spot facing the mountains, Mark," I whispered. "I'm so glad I knew you."

I felt grateful I had the weekend off before I began my affiliation. My parents knew how to comfort me and hold me on course. They listened to me, made me laugh and encouraged me. And they expected me to graduate. They knew I would learn to hold my own.

I rushed down the back steps of our house and into the Chevy where Mom and Dad sat waiting to drive me to the Baker Memorial Tuberculosis Sanatorium. We left the city and drove over the old metal bridge that traversed the swift-flowing Bow River. Unlike the gentle Elbow River near Holy Cross, the clear sparkling, innocent-looking blue-grey water of the deceptive Bow carried a strong, swift undercurrent that claimed the lives of several boaters and swimmers each year.

We followed the Bow for 45 minutes until we came to the Sanatorium, which was a group of several buildings that sat on the riverbank amongst large shade trees. It was a beautiful serene area, which looked more like a resort than a hospital. Behind the long administration building were several pavilions that housed male and female patients and one for children. All had an airy, screened-in porch on each floor.

I kissed my parents good-bye, and promised to call them when I got settled. Then I registered in the office. A matronly receptionist behind the desk checked my name off the short list of new student nurses. Her steel-grey hair was combed in an upsweep, which made her angular body look even more long and narrow. She handed me a map of the campus and told me to follow her.

We marched along the narrow sidewalk lined with colourful snapdragons and pansies. She was several paces in front, taking great strides with her granddaddy long legs, as I scampered behind her, toting my small suitcase. It was a short walk to the nurses' residence, an old building with small dingy rooms and wooden floors that squeaked and groaned under our feet as we walked down the hall. I was sharing a room with Ronnie (Veronica). Ronnie Roam was a serious-looking girl from the Calgary General Hospital, who spoke very little and kept her nose in her book all evening.

The next morning, after a hearty breakfast of bacon and eggs, which we had never been served at The Holy, we met in the lounge of the main pavilion. Mrs. Card, the nurse in charge of student education, gave us a lecture on nursing the patient with tuberculosis. She was a chubby woman with sandy hair that exploded in tight curls over her head. She had shiny tangerine-tinted lips.

We all sat in a circle and sipped coffee as she told us that recovery from tuberculosis was a slow process. Patients were here for many years. That morning, we learned that tuberculosis could strike the lung, the bone, the spinal cord, or even the brain. If a culture of the affected area contained the TB bacillus, the patient was *positive* for active tuberculosis. As long as the test was positive, the patient could transmit the disease to others and therefore had to be hospitalized, isolated from society to prevent the spread of the disease.

Mrs. Card told us that although chemotherapy was successful and patients became negative, many patients did not respond to the combination of drugs. For those patients, the cure was rest, complete rest, many months or even years. She said that with time, a sac would form around the tuberculosis bacillus and the patient would become negative, free of *active tuberculosis*. The tuberculosis bacillus would remain in the body, but would no longer be active.

"Tuberculosis of the lung is an extremely contagious disease that is spread in the sputum of the infected person," Miss Card said. "When that person coughs, the bacillus is scattered into the air, and when inhaled by another, they, too, become infected with the TB bacillus. That is why we must wear a mask when nursing these patients." She looked around our small circle of six girls. "Does that make sense?"

We nodded. Ronnie was sitting across from me and began to fidget.

"You must instruct the patients to spit their sputum into sputum boxes and not swallow it," Mrs. Card said. "And shaking the linen stirs up the bacillus, sends it into the air, making it more of a danger to inhale. We gently unfold the linen."

I quickly glanced around our circle; the other girls appeared as nervous as I felt about nursing these patients. Those nasty little bacilli were lurking everywhere.

"We must take every precaution to protect ourselves," Mrs. Card continued. "Tuberculosis knows no boundaries. This disease attacks anyone at any age, at any station of life. While it is more prevalent in overcrowded areas with poor ventilation and malnutrition, I must stress that TB is not limited to the poor. Our patients include doctors, nurses, lawyers, and business people." Mrs. Card raised her hand. "Now before you become too worried about working here, I must add that TB rarely strikes those who are healthy. Therefore, you absolutely must ...

"*One*, be sure you get enough rest, at least eight hours each night. *Two*, eat properly. We have good food and lots of it. We ask you to have a snack between your meals. *Three*, make sure you get lots of fresh air. Take a long walk outside every day and sleep with your window open. And for goodness sake, if you are not feeling well or break up with your boyfriend or have any other reason to feel down, please come and talk to us. We want to keep you girls healthy and working. We don't want you to end up on the other side of the fence as a patient. Questions?"

She looked round our circle. We sat in silence. The TB bacillus had just punched us in the stomach.

Then I remembered the three tiny injections given in a triangle at the top of my right thigh when I entered training ~ the BCGs ~ bacillus Calmette-Guérin vaccine, or attenuated human tubercle bacilli, named after two French bacteriologists. All nurses and doctors received this vaccine. My reaction had been severe. The little triangle festered and drained for almost two months, sticking to my underclothes and the bed sheets. But now I was grateful for all I suffered. I felt that I had a bit of an edge.

Mrs. Card took us to the staff lounge for our snack. I couldn't believe the food ~ bread, jam, doughnuts, sweet buns, cheese, peanut butter. An absolute banquet compared to the food at my hospital, and this was only coffee break! As we sat stuffing ourselves with a mountain of high-caloric food, Mrs. Card continued her lecture. She told us that a bed bath was to take no less than 30 minutes.

"Thirty minutes?" said the girl next to me. "Thirty minutes just for a bed bath?"

"Exactly," said Mrs. Card. "You must change the bath water every five to ten minutes to keep it nice and warm throughout the bath. The patient must be kept in a very relaxed state at all times. Complete rest means no activity whatsoever ~ physical, emotional, mental, or otherwise."

We looked confused. Or otherwise?

"In other words," she said self-consciously rolling and unrolling her papers. "You are not allowed to rub the backs of male patients, just in case it may arouse their ... well ... emotions."

I tried to keep a straight face. Ronnie brought up her hand and covered her open mouth.

"Do you mean that the male patients here might attack us?" asked the blond girl sitting beside me.

"Oh goodness no," chuckled Mrs. Card. "What I mean is that these patients must never use any unnecessary energy, emotional energy as well as physical. We must concentrate on encouraging the sac in the lung, to wall off the bacillus so that the TB doesn't spread. If the patient is excited, or physically exerted in any way ... well ... this could inhibit the healing process."

We all stared at Mrs. Card. I estimated that I had rubbed the backs of at least 100 male patients so far and wondered if I had ever excited any of them. And if I did, would I know?

When I stepped into the male pavilion with Mrs. Card the next morning, I felt I was walking into a combat zone. It was going to be me against the tuberculosis bacillus. Armed with my little triangle, a gown over my uniform, gloves and a mask, I walked down the hall with a large silver basin full of hot water, about to bathe my male patient. I had slept well and my stomach was full of doughnuts, definitely a plus.

Mr. Gerling, my patient, was a thin man with wisps of brown hair stretched across the top of his otherwise bald head. A nervous shiver ran through my body when I noticed the dull, grey look of his skin and the deep, dark circles under his troubled eyes. When I began his bath, I prayed that whatever might arouse this patient would not happen while I was bathing him. I couldn't imagine what secret method the doctors could possibly have for detecting these things.

Mr. Gerling made a valiant attempt to keep the conversation going while I dragged his bath out with the slowest motion that I could muster. But having spent the past 18 months perfecting a complete bed bath in five minutes or less, I found this a trying exercise. I also seemed to spend more time running down the hall to change the bath water than I did washing his skin.

But the half-hour finally ended and as I was ever so slowly tucking Mr. Gerling into a clean bed, the head nurse suddenly whisked me away to help the cleaning ladies wash and shine the silver washbasins. After that, I helped them place all of the blankets, pillows and rubber sheets on the veranda to air in the noonday sun. I found out that sunshine kills the TB bacillus. My new tasks certainly did not require much skill but I did enjoy chatting with the cleaning ladies, especially Marion. She strongly reminded me of my grandma Yates. Marion's Scottish burr stimulated my olfactory buds. I could almost smell Grandma's roast chicken wafting from her tiny apartment. Marion told me a story about the doctor who found the cure for TB.

"Not very long ago," she said, settling down into one of the wicker chairs, "a doctor contracted TB." She spoke as if she was telling a story to children.

"His doctor told him that there was nothing to do but to get his things in order and wait to die," Marion continued. "'Well,' said the doctor with TB, 'before I die I'll do what I love to do the most. I'm going camping in the mountains.' Which he did. And guess what? He didn't die! Fresh air, rest and good food cured his disease." She smiled and patted my arm. "Time for lunch, dearie. Make sure you eat well."

Mr. Gerling was scheduled for pneumothorax surgery. That meant pumping air into the pleural cavity to surgically collapse the affected lung, then packing the empty space with small Ping-Pong balls to prevent the spontaneous collapse of the good lung. This surgery was dreadfully disfiguring; the chest developed a sunken, caved-in look, and the shoulder on the affected side dropped much lower. But for patients who developed a resistance to the drugs, this was their only hope of becoming negative, their only way out of the hospital.

The following day, I wheeled Mr. Gerling to the surgical pavilion. "You're coming back to our ward, so I'll see you in a week," I said, as I settled him in his new bed.

"And I will be one step closer to being home with my wife and kids," he said, flashing a wide smile. This brought on a fit of coughing, which ended as it always did, with a long throaty hack and a wad of sputum. He flipped the lid of his waxed-cardboard sputum box and deposited a thick greenish-yellow blob of bloody phlegm in the box. It was his third box today and already half full.

"I'll sure be glad to get rid of this damn thing," he said, sliding the box on his bedside locker. Then he collapsed back on the pillow and sighed deeply. "I'm just plain fed up with this."

I squeezed his hand. "Good luck. The surgery will make you a healthy man."

"Hope so," he smiled. "Thanks, nurse. See you in a week."

The days were long and tedious, for I did very little nursing, except measure the sputum in the dreaded cardboard boxes. Each day I gave my patients their half-hour bath and assisted with arts and crafts.

One day as I stood at the foot of my Native patient's bed, I asked, "How is your painting coming, Johnny Little Bear?"

"Real good," he said, his round face smiling from ear to ear. Today his shiny black hair hung loosely down his back. Yesterday, it had been in two neat braids. He held up his canvas for me to see ~ a half-finished painting of the Rocky Mountains.

"It's beautiful," I said with a smile and a nod.

Without answering, he gently slid the painting into his bedside locker drawer. I could feel his loneliness and his hopelessness. I wanted him to trust me.

"How long have you been in the hospital?" I asked.

"One year," he said without looking up. "I don't see my family. None of them have a car to bring them all the way out here for a visit.

"Are you married? Do you have children?" I asked.

"A wife," he said, "and a daughter. One in the women's building and my little girl in the children's pavilion. I see them once a year ... Christmas time when they take us to the cafeteria for Christmas dinner."

"Here?" I asked, shocked. "They're here and you only see them once a year?"

He nodded, almost ashamed.

Johnny and his family were part of a group of sick and desolate North American Indians. The tuberculosis bacillus, a disease unknown to their ancestors, was rampant in their community. Alberta law forced them to leave their reservation and be under house arrest in the hospital for months or even years.

"Do you ever go home on a pass? Your sputum is negative, Mr. Little Bear. You're entitled to a day-pass."

He shook his head again. "Like I said before, have nobody to take me. Besides, it's too far. Can't go to Cardston and back in one day even if I did. And I can't run for cover either. Look at poor Freddy Cloud. He ran back to the reserve. 'Course his sputum was positive, so the RCMP brought him back here, twice. He's back in that room down at the end of the hall like a prisoner. Got a police officer sittin' there with him so's he can't leave again."

As soon as I got off work I ran for the phone and called my mother. "I want to bring a patient home for supper on Sunday, Mom. Johnny is allowed out on a pass. His sputum is negative so there's no danger of TB. At least we can give him a few hours of pleasure. A change of scenery will be good for him."

She hesitated, then said, "I don't think your father will allow it, dear. He's been awfully worried about you catching TB. I don't think he would want you to bring a patient *home*."

"But Mom there's no danger. You can convince Daddy. Please try."

Mom called back on Thursday evening with good news. My father would allow me to bring Johnny home for supper. "Are you sure there's no danger for us?" she added.

"Of course not. They wouldn't let him out if there was." I was ecstatic. "I knew you would say yes, Mom. Thanks."

Friday after work, my father picked me up from the San and took me home; it was my weekend off. Sunday he drove me back to pick up Johnny, who had a pass from five until ten o'clock.

My parents loved Johnny. He was full of tales about the reserve and the horses he rode there. Mom and I loved horses. How I envied him.

Monday morning, Johnny was all smiles when I entered his room. He waved me over to his bed.

"This here's my friend Frank Singer," he said pointing to the new patient in the bed beside him. "He's an old friend from back home. They moved him over from the other pavilion last night. It'll kind a perk him up to be with me. Haven't seen him in a dog's age. Been away makin' lots of money at them rodeos."

"Hello, Mr. Singer," I said through my mask, which by now had become second nature to me. "What's this about rodeos?"

Mr. Singer glanced briefly at me, then away. The all too familiar look of loneliness filled his dark eyes.

"Frank's got a heavy heart," said Johnny. "Hard for him to be cooped up in this here place."

"What do you do at the rodeos Mr. Singer?" I asked again.

"He's on the circuit." Johnny said proudly. "Travels all over Canada and the United States. Why Frank here was the bull ridin' champion at the Stampede, twice! Rides saddle broncs, too." He looked at Frank and Frank nodded.

"Do you ever ride bucking horses?" I asked.

He was silent for a moment, then turned his big brown eyes to me and slowly nodded. "Yeah, at times."

"Riding in rodeos must be exciting," I said. "Something I've always wanted to do myself."

A smile spread across his face. "It's a rough life out there ridin' those bulls and horses. Tough, too. Get all banged up like I am," he spoke softly, almost in a hypnotic tone.

"Did you ever break any bones?" I asked.

He laughed gently, his eyes narrowed and the little creases that had formed against the weather deepened. "Most every bone in my body, at some time."

Mr. Singer had a classic native look. Deep-set black eyes, high cheekbones, a reddish tinge to his cheeks ~ an out-doorsy look. And absolutely perfect lips. He looked as though he would be tall, if he stood up, and his slim, bronze body was quite handsome, in a rugged sense. As we spoke, he whittled a piece of wood with his pocket knife, delicately carving an image that resembled a horse. He cut off a sliver the size of a toothpick and began chewing on one end as if it were a wisp of hay. I asked him what he was making.

"Oh, just foolin' around with some wood."

"Looks like it could be a horse."

"Could be." He smiled, and for a moment his eyes brightened.

"He won prizes at the Stampede for his wood carvin's," Johnny said with his big smile. "He's got the gift of an artist."

The following Sunday afternoon, and every Sunday for the rest of my rotation at the Sanatorium, Johnny Little Bear and Frank Singer came to our house for supper.

Although neighbours glared at us for inviting TB patients into our neighbourhood, my mother and Grandma Yates, who always came for Sunday dinner, stood confidently with me in the doorway to greet our guests as they arrived. They strode up the walk ~ Frank in his plaid shirt, jeans and cowboy boots, with a bright red scarf tied around his neck, his beautiful black, silky hair blowing in the breeze, Johnny in pigtails, brown dress pants, white shirt and a bow tie.

At dinner, the potatoes, roast beef and Yorkshire pudding were passed from hand to hand without hesitation and by the third week, Frank was more relaxed.

"Did you go to school on the reserve?" My dad asked.

"I went to the Mission School," Frank said.

"What was that like?" Allan asked.

"Well we had a man teacher and I must tell you he was mean. He taught boys from grade eight on down. He taught anything that came along, like us fugitives from the kindergarten, which we had outgrown." Frank paused and smiled before he put a forkful of potatoes in his mouth.

"Well, me and Long, another kid, were about the dumbest pair of young warriors that ever set moccasins in the classroom. We kept the teacher's arm in good exercise by getting the strap from him nearly every day. Like the one day I was thinkin' about Victoria B.C. when the teacher asks Long, 'Where is God?'

"And after he asked Long three or four times and not getting an answer and getting his strap out from the desk drawer and then he was in front of us and Long was nudging me for an answer. So I whispered, B.C. and Long said out loud and real slow, 'God is in B.C.' Well, I believe Long would have come out of this one a little cheaper if he had went and sneaked up to a sleeping Grizzly Bear and kicked him in the seat ~ and Long bein' older and stronger ~ well, I didn't come out so good neither. Next day I had to introduce myself to the teacher 'cause he thought I was a new pupil."

Frank and Johnny laughed and we smiled to be obliging, but it was a very sad story.

Later as we did the dishes, my grandma Yates laughed at the neighbours' fear of TB. "There's no need for you to worry," she said in her broad Scottish accent. "TB does ne run in ourr family."

"But Grandma," I said with concern as I dried the meat platter. "TB doesn't run in *anyone's* family. TB is very *catching*. One person can get it from another by breathing the same air. It has nothing to do with running in families, except that families tend to catch it from each other."

"Ach, go way wi ye, girrl," she chuckled, as if I was kidding her. Then continued in her burr. "When I was a wee girl in Glasgow many people died of that consumption. It was called consumption in those days. From the time I was a wee girl, maybe three or four years old, I would go into our neighbours' homes to help. My mother made meals for them. We bathed them and took their washing home. I always went wi' her. Whole families died because consumption ran in their family. But did ne run in our family. Not one Craig died of TB." She smiled and put her arm around me. "Ach aye, you come from strong stock, Donna. D'ne worrry about TB. The Craigs and the Yates are strong people. Aye, always were."

On Wednesday I worked a split shift, which gave me the afternoon off from one to four. It was cool and sunny, a beautiful day for a walk along the Bow River. The leaves were beginning to change to their fall colours, and the river looked as blue as the sky. A little squirrel scampered across the dry leaves, his cheeks stuffed with food for the winter ahead. Oh, the wonder of nature and how grateful I felt to be a part of it. My heart ached for Johnny and Frank cooped up in the hospital, having to view nature, so precious to them, through glass.

I returned to work in time to give out the dinner trays and then began to prepare the patients for sleep. Johnny called me over to his bed.

"Me and Frank are going to miss you when you go," he said. "We want to give you something. It's sort of an honour we bestow on you."

"We don't often give white people Indian names," Frank said. "But we have an Indian name for you." He glanced at Johnny. Johnny nodded. Then Frank said in a slow, soft voice, "We name you *Yellow Bird*."

I was taken aback for a moment. "Thank you," I finally managed to say. "This is truly an honour. Yellow Bird is a beautiful name ... I'm very touched. Does it mean something?"

"Well, it suits you. You're free, you fly, and you sing," Johnny said. "You lighten a heart."

I was deeply moved; I knew Johnny and Frank had accepted me as their friend.

On Friday, my last day at the San, I had the pleasure of discharging Mr. Gerling. He had made a remarkable recovery after his surgery and his sputum was now negative. He hadn't seen his children for two years and was ecstatic about finally being able to return home. His wife enthusiastically flitted about as I pushed her husband to the front entrance and helped him into their waiting car.

"Get lots of rest, and eat properly," I said when he was comfortably seated.

"Don't worry, nurse," his wife said, wagging her finger at her beaming husband. "I am going to take good care of him. You know, I think this is the happiest day of my life. Dave hasn't been home for years and our children are so excited they didn't sleep a wink last night. Neither did I," she added with a nervous laugh.

I waved good-bye as they disappeared out the front gate and crossed my fingers that the sac in his lungs wouldn't open up again.

As I walked back to the ward, a feeling of excitement came over me. I was going back to The Holy, back home. I suddenly felt lonesome for my classmates. I also looked forward to tossing my mask in the garbage once and for all. It had begun to wear a sore on the top of my nose.

When I said good-bye to my two Native friends they were quiet and withdrawn.

"I made you somethin'," Johnny said. He held up his completed painting of the Rocky Mountains. "Take it. I want you to have it."

"I made you something, too," Frank said in his gentle voice. "Here." He gave me a picture album made of heavy, shiny red plastic. He'd painted red roses on the cover with the words *Yellow Bird* in his Native language, the edges laced with white, soft leather.

"I know you like to go for walks along the river," he said softly. "This is sort of like, well, a reminder of us. Go on, open it."

I opened the cover, and on the first page was written:

To my good friend, Yellow Bird
From your friend, Frank Singer.

"These are both so beautiful," I said feeling a lump grow in my throat. "I will always cherish them ... I'll never forget you guys. When I get some time off I'll come back and visit." I knew I wouldn't get many weekends off, but I told them that when I did, I would still like them to come for supper.

Several weeks later, I called the nurse on the ward at the San and asked for permission to take Johnny and Frank out for supper on Sunday. She told me that Johnny Little Bear had signed himself out of the hospital and gone back to the reserve. And Frank Singer had returned to Wyoming. "I'm sorry, they're gone," the nurse said. "They weren't well enough, really, but their sputum was negative and we couldn't hold them."

Suffer the Little Children

I had just fallen asleep when a ruckus from the lounge awoke me. Although I was dead tired, my curiosity overcame my desire for sleep and I crawled out of bed, threw my raggedy yellow duster over my pajamas and shuffled out to the lounge. White, Perry, Andresen, and Simm hovered over Tanner like mother hens.

"Come and see what Tanner's got," said Andresen excitedly.

Tanner, with her extravagant grin and a lit cigarette clenched in her teeth, leapt out of her chair like a gazelle and danced over to me waving her hand about in a teasing way.

"Oh my God!" I said, grabbing her hand. "I don't believe it. Tanner you're engaged!"

The elevator door squeaked open and I heard the tinkle of Mrs. Foley's earrings as she stepped out.

"Girls, girls," she said, clapping her hands as she shuffled towards us. "I can hear you all the way downstairs. Get to bed right now."

"Look!" Simm said. "Tanner's engaged!" she thrust Tanner's hand towards Mrs. Foley.

Tanner's face disappeared into Mrs. Foley's sizable bosom as the housemother gave her a bear hug.

"All my best, dear, many years of happiness," Mrs. Foley said. "When are you getting married?"

"When Ralph is finished university, probably in a year and a half."

"We're just making coffee," Perry said, with a nervous shrug. "Is that okay?"

"All right, all right, but do be quiet, and don't be long. If Sister finds out, I'll be in a tight spot. And close those drapes, it's not lady-like to run around in your pajamas like that. My, my, you girls are going to be tired tomorrow."

The next morning I arrived for my first day on Pediatrics and walked into an entirely different world. A miniature world with impossibly small beds and linen, tiny intravenous bottles, syringes and needles ~ and patients. A stir rippled through the awakening ward. Unfamiliar sounds swirled down empty corridors ~ the moans and whimpers and wails of forlorn children.

As I entered my assigned room, five pink, pleated faces wet with tears shrieked at me. One little toddler sat in the middle of his crib, teddy bear face-down at his feet. "Mommy. Mommy," he blubbered, puffy eyed. Another lay blissfully asleep under a croup tent.

I went to the one with the teddy bear and held out my hands. He lifted his chubby little arms and I picked him up. His hot, wet body snuggled against mine and he made a soft hiccoughing sound. I wasn't his mother, but for now, I would do. The little girl by the window woke up, opened her mouth and began to scream. Balancing the other child on my hip, I rushed over and patted her back, but consolation was not what she wanted. She was sick, and hungry. She wanted her mother.

The senior student, Cramer, called to me from the doorway. "Yates, what are you doing?"

"They're all crying!" I said lamely.

"Put that kid down and get going! Breakfast will be here soon."

I pried the child from my body and set him back in his crib, which triggered another screaming attack. By this time there was such wailing in the room that I could not hear Cramer talking. I moved toward her, but gave a loud gasp when I glanced back and saw the child I had just deposited in his crib, standing like King Kong, ferociously rattling the bars ~ and turning purple.

"Leave him, you'll get used to this," Cramer said with a tight smile. "Get your OR bathed and ready. The orderly will be here to pick him up soon and you've got a lot of kids to feed."

Somehow with Cramer's help I made it through the desperate morning. Bobby sucked his thumb all the way to the operating room, clutching his teddy bear. Soon his cries gave way to the silence of inescapable submission.

Bobby pulled through with flying colours and the next day, spent the afternoon pedaling a miniature tricycle up and down the hall, oblivious to the fact that he'd had surgery the day before. Very different from the post-op adult patients who clutched their abdomens and clung to the wall as they shuffled up and down the hall after their surgeries.

Angela, my ten-year-old big girl patient, had severely burned her abdomen and thighs while making candy and was in a room by herself on protective isolation. A veteran on pediatrics, she had been in the hospital for several weeks. Before anyone entered, they had to don a mask, a large gown, latex gloves, and cloth boots to prevent bacteria from entering the room on their clothing.

As I bathed Angela's slim body, we talked about her three sisters and two brothers. "All brats," she said with a mischievous giggle.

"And in what order do you come?"

"Right in the middle. I'm fairdemiddlin." She gave a wide grin.

I smiled as I inspected the grafts on her abdomen and noted that they were healing well.

"Want some chocolates?" she chirped, as I took off my gown, and prepared to leave the room. I shook my head. "Piece of coffee cake?"

"Nope."

"Licorice?"

"N-O. Angela, you are going to make me F-A-T. I'll be back in an hour." I stripped off the layer of protective clothing and waved as I left the room.

During the course of the next few weeks, Angela would have two more skin graft operations. The plastic surgeon would shave a thin piece of skin from her hip area to cover the raw, burned tissue on her abdomen.

Monday morning Porter and I were assigned to one of the baby rooms, a large room that resembled a nursery. I walked into room 16, with butterflies scooting around in my stomach. Porter shuffled in beside me as if she still wore her pink, sloppy slippers. "I'm going to faint," she said. "I don't think I can deal with babies." She leaned over to me and whispered, "If we make a mistake ... it's over."

"Don't even think of making a mistake," I whispered back. "And leave your glasses on."

We crossed our fingers for good luck and walked over to our doll-like patients. Barely a few days old, they required tiny medications, tiny amounts of fluid, and tiny bottles of formula. They were the smallest babies I had ever seen. My babies had spina bifida, Porter's had harelip and cleft palate.

Baby Keeler, my first little patient, was in a bassinet as high as my waist, with clear Plexiglas sides. He lay on his stomach over a triangular, foam-rubber support, buttocks in the air, arms flailing, whimpering and turning his head from side to side. His legs did not move, they could not move. The impulse from his brain that ran down his spinal cord to tell his legs to move was abruptly aborted at the opening in his back; the spot where his vertebrae never finished fusing. Nor did the skin close, which left the raw spinal cord partially exposed. I lay my hand on his tiny shoulders and gently rubbed his back.

"Shh, sh, little baby," I whispered. "I'm going to bathe you now. You're not alone. Shh, sh."

I bathed baby Keeler with small gauze sponges dipped in warm water and Phisohex, an antibacterial liquid soap.

Glucose and water slowly dripped into the tissue of his scalp through a tiny needle. Finding a vein in a baby is next to impossible, and the small amount of fluid flowing into the scalp tissue (interstitial) is quickly absorbed into the baby's body. By the time I had finished bathing all of my babies, their screaming had reached a crescendo, which forced Porter and me to discontinue our chatty conversation. Our patients were hungry.

Feeding my patients went surprisingly well and I finished much quicker than I thought I would. But Porter was having a dreadful time with her four babies and was way behind schedule.

"Hey, Yates, can you help me feed my babies?" she said in her soft naive voice. She crooked her little finger, pushed her glasses up on her nose and squinted at me. "They're having trouble swallowing the formula, can't seem to get it down the right tube."

"Sure," I said feeling a little cocky. "Mine are all asleep."

I sat down on the chair with Porter's little girl who had been born with harelip and cleft palate, a deformity in which the palate or the roof of the mouth and the upper lip had not joined, and which left an opening or a split in the center. She had jet-black hair, much longer than normal for such a young baby and Porter had brushed it into a big curl on top of her head. I tipped the bottle into her mouth ~ her lips did look like a hare's ~ but with her deformed lips, she had trouble sucking on the nipple. When she finally managed to draw some milk into her mouth she gave a snort and sent the milk surging up through the opening in her palate and out her nose ~ straight into my face.

"You'll get the hang of it," Porter said, trying not to smile. "Hold the baby more upright, and don't tip the bottle back so far."

How had she mastered the trick so quickly? Porter, who was often clumsy in other areas, had found her niche. After several attempts at sucking, the baby managed to get an ounce of milk and swallow it. "Here we go," I teased, waving the bottle of formula. Baby smiled and I clucked to her until her bright blue eyes shone and she cooed back, kicking her legs, demanding more.

As I lay my last sleeping babe in the crib Porter glanced at me. "Oh, my God, Yates, look at you!"

I looked down. My crisp, white front was covered with sticky, yellow formula. Then I examined Porter and I began to laugh, too. She stood dripping like a snowman that had been in the sun too long.

We flopped down on our chairs, the room was finally quiet and our babies slept with full stomachs. I was dying to wash the formula out of my hair. But our quietude was only a brief reprieve.

After lunch, the clinical instructor took us to a room to see Mary, a little five-year-old girl who had been born with a harelip and cleft palate. She was recovering from her second reconstructive surgery. The palate and lip change so dramatically in the child's early years, they had to wait for the growth period to be stabilized before the first surgery. Mary's first operation closed the opening in her lip and this time the surgeon repaired her palate. Now she could eat and drink normally, and her appearance was dramatically improved.

Some of the older children with spina bifida had also undergone surgery. At times surgery was successful in restoring partial movement of the legs, but in most cases the nerves were irreparable and the surgery unsuccessful. It was not unusual for these children to spend most of their childhood in the Children's Hospital.

"What causes this deformity?" Porter asked.

"We're not sure at the moment," the clinical instructor said, "but research is being carried out on several medications women take while pregnant. And the DDT used on farms is being investigated. How tragic if *that* was indeed a cause."

My two-week rotation on nights flew by. All night long I made incessant trips to the ice machine to fill the croup tents and ice collars for the many children who had had tonsillectomies and who continually whined for ice chips to suck.

The children's bedside lockers overflowed with goodies their parents brought ~ candies, chocolates and cookies. But most of the children didn't want junk food after surgery, so Porter and I helped ourselves each time we made our rounds. If the night was particularly long and boring, we made more trips to check the sleeping children than were ever necessary for their well being. By the time we said good-bye to Pediatrics, Porter's uniforms had become tight and I had gained back a bit of the weight I lost after Mark Birch died.

When I left Pediatrics, my dear little friend, Angela, was recovering from yet another skin graft and I made a trip to her room to say good-bye. "I know you will make a great recovery," I said.

"Yup," she said with a grin. "If this graft takes, I'm going home in a week."

"That's wonderful. Your brothers and sisters will be glad to see you. I bet they miss you."

"Yeah, miss fighting with me," she laughed her special little laugh. "Want a chocolate? Cookie?"

"Nixo, Angela. Next time I see you, you'll be good as new." I waved as I left her room, and my mind flashed back to the first time I saw her eight weeks before. Now, after many grafts, she was almost restored to her former self.

The following Sunday was just what the doctor ordered, a lazy day at home. White came home with me for the weekend and tossed the football around with Allan out on the back lawn. Having two brothers, she was at home with boys. My father sat in the living room reading a new book, *To Kill A Mockingbird*, by Harper Lee. A column of smoke rose from his cigarette resting in the floor ashtray beside his chair.

I coloured Mom's hair with Nice'N Easy, Warm Brown, as she sat on a chair in the middle of the kitchen. The aroma of Sunday's roast beef cooking wafted through the house. We almost always had roast beef on Sunday, with mashed potatoes and Yorkshire pudding. Allan would pick up Grandma at five and we always ate at six o'clock.

As I set Mom's hair in pin curls with bobby pins, she said, "I've got a package for you to take back to the residence, Donna. And one for White, too. I made Rice Crispy squares, and chocolate chip cookies. Don't let me forget to give them to you when you leave."

She got up and slipped her arm around my waist. "You're getting too thin, dear," she said with a concerned look.

I chuckled, and gave her a hug. "I can't stand the hospital food any more, Mom."

"But you have to eat your meals, dear. Something tells me you're still upset about the death of your patient. What was his name ~ Mark Birch?"

My heart clutched at his name. I nodded. "I feel so sad that he had to die. I guess one day I'll get over it."

"Oh, Donna, I hope for your sake you do. That was a long time ago. Just put it behind you, dear. Promise me." She gave me an intense look. "I worry about you."

"Don't worry, Mom. I'll get over it. I promise." But I wondered if I ever would.

"I can't believe this is our second Christmas in this place," White said. We were sitting in the lounge watching the girls decorate the windows for Christmas. It was her supper break on the afternoon shift. She sat in her uniform, feet propped on a chair, savouring her last few minutes of repose before going back to work. Priestnall, still in her white nylons, was at the stovetop hotplate in her red duster, heating vegetable soup.

"Looks like the probies are doing most of the decorating," I said, as Rudolph's nose was transformed into glistening, bright red.

"That's the caste system," Niven said without looking up from her romance pocketbook. "I'm going to get all the slave-work I can from these guys. Got to make up for all the shit I've taken in the last two years from those bloody seniors."

"By the way, Niven," Priestnall said, pouring a glass of milk. "I keep getting complaints from the faculty about your whistling. I'm tired of making up excuses for you." She gave me a nod. "You're going to Obstetrics with her, Yates. It's your turn to keep an eye on her."

"Aw come on now," I whined. "I can't be Niven's keeper."

Niven gave me a quizzical look, raised her eyebrows, pursed her lips and gave her three-note, signature whistle ~ all on the same note.

Suddenly Guenette flew into the lounge. "Riley's gone," she said, breathlessly.

Niven's pocketbook hit the floor with a thump. "Riley? Gone?" she said.

Speechless, we all watched Niven pick up her book. Then she said exactly what we were thinking. "Bet she got kicked out."

Kaufmann's eyes filled with tears. "Why?" she whispered.

"I heard they caught her sneaking out." Guenette said matter of factly, as she kicked her shoes off not bothering to untie the laces. "It was bound to come."

"Well, we tried to warn her," Priestnall said, "but oh, no, she wouldn't listen to us. She knew everything." Priestnall blew on her spoonful of hot soup.

"But the girl had only a little over a year to go," White moaned. "Why the hell didn't Sister do something before she got this far?"

"Hell, they don't give a shit," Wolkoff snapped. "Riley was a damn good nurse and it's a shame if they tossed her out ... like ... like an old rag." Wolkoff's deep-set, blue eyes flashed angrily. "But we're only guessing. Maybe she quit. Sister's been on Riley's back for months."

"Hey, we all know that Riley thought the rules were made to be broken," Priestnall said. "She said so herself ~ many times."

"But she was a good nurse. Everyone loved her. She was my best friend. I can't believe they'd kick her out after all she's been through with that polio and stuff. God, if anyone would make a good nurse, it was Riley." Wolkoff's eyes darted wildly around the room. "It's a conspiracy that's what it is. Sister was definitely out to get her. She's probably going to kick me out, too."

"Come on, Wolkoff, you're losin' it, now," White said. "Don't compare yourself to Riley. She made up her own rules as she went along. She thought life was a big joke. You can't do that here. Break the rules, and you're out. You know that."

Wolkoff began to sob. "You don't know how mean everyone is to me. All the instructors ~ and Sister. They hate me. I'm Riley's best friend and I don't even know where she is."

To me it was a shock to hear Wolkoff say that. Wolkoff had been so ebullient and confident when we were in the diet kitchen. She had kept me from going out of my mind from boredom. Now she was floundering.

"You're not alone, Wolkoff. We're all in this together," Armbruster said softly. "We're all with you, praise God."

White got up and moved over to sit beside Wolkoff. "You don't have to love Sister, but you have to play the game. You're a damn good nurse, Wolkoff, and I'll tell you what ~ you *are* going to graduate."

"So Riley's gone," Guenette said pensively. "Another one bites the dust." Now we were 18.

Priestnall had finished her glass of milk. She rinsed the glass under the tap and stuck it up in the cupboard. "Eighteen is a far cry from the 36 we started with," she said. "We'll have to be careful. We've come too far to throw it all away now."

"Poor Riley, I'm going to miss her," Kaufmann sighed into her coffee cup.

"Amen," whispered Armbruster.

Not Always the Gift of Life

My skin tingled with excitement as Niven and I followed the signs that led us to Maternity.

Maternity was divided into three sections: the maternity floor, for women after delivery or if they had complications before delivery; two nurseries, one for normal and one for premature babies; and the Case Room, where the babies were delivered. Niven was sent to the normal nursery and I to the maternity floor.

Maternity was a whole new way of hospital life. The happy voices of new mothers, screeching babies ~ and lots of chocolates to eat. But best of all, the patients went home with a big smile and an extra little bundle in their arms.

I was assigned five rooms, a total of 14 patients. A heavy assignment for other wards, but on maternity the patients were generally not sick. Nursing care was primarily teaching the new mother about her baby. At 20 years of age, I found this a little intimidating, especially with mothers who were counting their children on both hands.

"Good morning," I sang to my patients when I entered the room. "Time to get up, the breakfast carts are here."

"Boy, what a treat to sleep in," said the woman in the first bed. She had four small children at home and was taking advantage of a rest in the hospital.

"I'm dying to get home," said the young woman in the corner, who'd had her first baby the night before.

The older woman tied a bow at the neck of her powder blue duster. "Wait 'til the next one comes along; you'll see what I mean. You'll take advantage of all the time you can get in the hospital."

I was thoroughly enjoying myself, chatting with my patients, making beds and looking at pictures of their other children when the grad poked her head around the door.

"Yates, get a move on! The babies will be here soon."

Yikes, the babies! They were delivered to the mothers at 9:30 and I had to have all the beds made and give peri-care to the new mothers before they arrived. Sterile perineal cleansing was ordered routinely four times per day to cleanse the episiotomy, the surgical incision of the perineum.

Just as I finished my last lady, I heard a chorus of crying from the hall. I rushed to the door and glanced out. Two long carts stood in the middle of the hall, each divided into six tiny cubicles, a newborn baby in each compartment. The nurses from the Nursery had started giving out the babies. I spied a frazzled Niven, her red hair drooping from under the white surgical cap, dashing down the hall with a screaming baby in her arms.

I raced across the hall, tossed my peri-care tray in the utility room, then flew round my rooms trying to make them look tidy. The clean linen ~ I had to get it out of the way. I stuffed it in the bedside locker beside an empty bed. I was desperate. The babies were on my heels.

The two nurses from the Nursery flew in and out of the rooms, delivering babies to mothers like card dealers in poker games. The patient in the blue duster skilfully held her baby to her breast and he began sucking. I was mesmerized. This time yesterday, he had been floating in a sea of amniotic fluid. In just a few short hours he had mastered breathing, crying and eating. The mother carefully studied her baby, savouring every limb, finger and toe. Suddenly I understood what a nursing bra was for. My mother had been right, it wasn't for nursing students.

"Nurse! What is this?"

I jolted to attention. A white billowy form filled the doorway. Her face, though pretty, had a beastly twist to it. Oh God, Sister Garneau, the troll of OBS, was waving my clean linen at me.

"I, ah, well ... you see this is my first day. I didn't get the beds finished before the babies came out," I said lamely. I felt the eyes of my patients on me and my ears burned with humiliation.

158

"This is never to happen again. Do you hear? Never!"

"Yes, Sister." I hung my head.

She spun around and flew through the door, robes swishing, veil streaming out behind her.

"Don't worry, nurse," the new mother said sympathetically. "She treats everyone like that."

The mother in the blue duster raised her baby to her shoulder and gently patted his back. He gave a tiny burp. "I don't know how you girls take all this abuse," she said. "I would never put up with that."

I paused for a moment, then said, "It's not so bad."

"The Calgary General is not as strict as The Holy," said the new mother.

"I've heard that," I said. I knew the nuns had a reputation for being tough but I had come to The Holy because of the nuns. We celebrated every milestone with prayers in the chapel and a sermon from Father Flanagan who told us we had a calling. We *were* different ... a notch above ... *because* of the nuns.

"The nuns turn out good nurses," I said, "and I want to be a good nurse."

"I told you obstetrics was tough," Perry said as we sat on my bed eating my mother's chocolate chip cookies. "Stay away from Sister Garneau; she's bad business. Have you seen her attack the doctors yet? You're in for a treat."

"But I felt so tacky, Perry. I didn't think I made that big a mistake. I mean, after all, it was my first day."

"Wait 'til you hear what I did in Ponoka last week. Promise me you won't tell a soul."

"I promise," I said raising my hand. "Scout's honour."

"I was playing Scrabble with my patient who was manic-depressive. Well, my turn came, and all I could make from my letters was CRAZY."

I snickered.

"I can't believe I did that."

I wanted to laugh but the look on her face stopped me. I realized how terribly upset she was. "Oh, Perry, I'm sorry," I said trying to look serious. "What did the patient say?"

"She was so nice about it. I said I was sorry, but ... " Perry's face turned pink and the little vein over her temple bulged. "Wasn't that a stupid thing for me to do?" Perry began to bite her thumbnail.

"Perry, you promised!" I said. "You've got nice nails now, don't start again."

She tucked her arms round her middle and we both began to giggle.

Then Perry began to cry. "Can you imagine how awful I felt? I felt terrible," she blubbered. Then she laughed again, and so did I.

"I know it's dreadful to laugh about this, Perry," I said after we'd calmed down, "but it feels so good to have a laugh once in a while. My cheeks hurt and my stomach's sore, but honestly, laughter is so good for the soul. Don't feel bad. I'm sure your patient understands."

The week before Christmas, Niven and I changed places. I began my rotation in the Nursery, the normal or big nursery as we called it, and Niven went to the maternity floor. Miss Small, the head nurse, showed me the procedure for bathing these "itty-bitty darlings," as she called them. Rows of babies lay in bassinets labelled with the family name in big bold letters on pink or blue cards. Venetian blinds covered a large window in the wall and opened only to show the babies to the fathers, grandparents, uncles and aunts.

Under the windows, against the back wall stood a row of ten lonely bassinets - - the unlucky babies. Commonly called the back row, the feed-ins, or the illegits. These babies never made a trip to the viewing window or to the maternity floor at feeding time. They never saw their mothers. These babies were up for adoption. Their destination ~ the Crèche.

Begrie, the senior student, and I had to bathe and change all the *legit* babies before they went out to their mothers for feeding. I changed baby after baby, assembly line fashion. The door near the large viewing window banged open and the grad from the case room barged in pushing a bassinet.

"Big baby boy," she said through her mask. "Nine pounds fourteen ounces, at 9:14, can you beat that? Dr. Bogart's the man of the hour."

"Oh shit," Begrie whispered to me. "That Bogart's a prissy ass if ever there was one."

I looked into the bassinet and for the first time beheld life's debut ~ a round pinkish-purple baby covered with a mixture of white paste and bright red blood, emitting a healthy cry of protest from his scrunched face. A tiny bath-blanket was thrown lightly over his nude body, his arms and legs beat the air. He stopped momentarily, took a hiccoughy breath, his chin quivered, his little body tightened, he gave a shudder and began his rhythmical cry again.

"I'll take care of this little precious. You girls get the babies out," Miss Small said, whisking the new baby over to the bath counter.

"Come on, Yates," said the senior. "We've got to get the babies to the mothers by 9:30. You take the west hall. I'll take the east. Grab a cart."

I suddenly realized that the babies knew it was feeding time. I could barely hear Begrie above the racket. I filled my cart with the vociferous bundles and pushed them gingerly down the hall. My knees were jelly. I couldn't stop shaking. God, please help me, I asked. I have to be careful. Check the band on the baby. Check the band on the mother. Check, check, check!

Don't drop the baby, I prayed as I clutched the screaming bundle to my body and tiptoed into the first room. I matched the name and room number on the baby's armband to that of the mother's, flashed a quick smile and rushed out for another baby. I delivered a wriggling mass, each with a healthy pair of lungs, to every room down the west hall.

When I returned to the Nursery, Begrie was sitting in a big chair giving Doctor Bogart's new baby some warm water from a small bottle. It would help remove the thick, gucky fluid from the newborn baby's mouth and esophagus. Begrie nodded to a rack on the counter. "The bottles have arrived from the formula room for the feed-ins. You'd better start feeding the back row."

The back row choir belted out fortissimo. I searched for the one I thought might be most hungry, picked up a baby girl and sat down on a chair beside Begrie. The baby quickly guzzled down the bottle and promptly went to sleep. My heart ached for this little life, just beginning, so all alone. There would be no mother to comfort her or rock her when she awoke at night. I glanced down the row and wondered, what would become of these babies. I asked Begrie how many would be adopted? She guessed about 10 percent.

"Most of them live in the Crèche until their 16th birthday, then they're pushed out into the world to earn their living."

I knew this was true. I was 9 and Julieanne was 13 when she had moved in with Mrs. Collins, just three blocks from us, as a foster child. She had lived her life at the Woods Orphanage in Olds.

Every morning Julieanne knocked on our door and she'd say the same thing, "I feel like I've died and gone to heaven." She stood on our back porch, her legs long and skinny under her over-washed blue cotton skirt. One day she wasn't smiling. "Things are not going very well for me. I keep dropping the toilet seat and Mrs. Collins said if I drop it one more time she'll send me back to the orphanage. She's very strict, you know."

It wasn't long after that when Julieanne came crying to my mother early one morning, her long black hair looking like a scraggly horse's tail.

"She's going to send me back," Julieanne sobbed. "I dropped the toilet seat cover. I couldn't help it ~ I'm so nervous. I tried not to drop it but I did. And now I'm going back!" She pushed her stringy bangs from her swollen red eyes then threw her arms around my mother.

Mom paid a visit to Mrs. Collins who answered her door in a brown knit suit, her hair the same colour and in tight waves. "Come in," she said through pursed lips, barely above a whisper. Mom and I stepped into her empty looking house with shiny brown floors. We sat on hard chairs. Mom begged and pleaded with Mrs. Collins, but the next day we said good-bye to Julieanne on our back porch. "Please stay in touch with me, Mrs. Yates," Julieanne said, "I need you."

Although I begged my mother to let Julieanne share my room, she had to return to the orphanage.

The rule was that Catholic babies had to go to a Catholic home. But most Catholic families had children, many children. So most of these castaways were doomed to a life in the Crèche. My eyes traveled down the row of helpless newborns. I knew something of what their lives would be.

My baby finished his bottle, I turned him over, waiting for him to burp. He let out a loud one.

"Look at this bruiser," I laughed. "What a little toughie he's going to be." I gazed into his chubby face. His clear blue eyes looked back, confident, secure, content. My throat felt thick. He had only just begun.

"I hope you get a good family," I said as I nuzzled him. "I pray that you won't spend your life at the Crèche. You wouldn't like it."

I lay my little orphan baby in the bassinet and bent over his sturdy little body. His dark blond hair stood in bristles over his head like a cartoon character. I laughed and cooed at him. He gurgled back, his arms and legs fanning the air.

"I'm going to call you Tommy," I said. "Tommy the toughie."

"Don't give them names," Begrie warned. "It makes it too hard to say good-bye." She was right.

Ten days later, a small, curt social worker arrived. She strutted over to the head nurse with the clothes for Tommy tucked under her arm.

"I've come for baby Clemens," she said

I dressed him in a white flannelette nightie that tied at the bottom, and wrapped him in the bunting bag Mrs. Snip had tossed on the stool beside his bassinet. Then I picked him up and held him close to me. "Bye-bye, Tommy the toughie," I whispered in his ear. "I hope you get a good family. Good luck. I love you."

He gazed at me with his steady blue eyes and straggly wisps of sandy-blond hair that poked out from under the hood of his bunting bag, a broad, toothless, trusting smile spread across his round face. I leaned down to kiss him just as Mrs. Snip snatched Tommy out of my arms and rushed for the door.

"I can't stand here all day while *she* makes her good-byes," she muttered.

I picked up another little bundle from the back row and held her close and I turned to the window to bury my face.

As soon as I got off duty, I telephoned my mother. "Please, Mom," I pleaded. "You and Daddy can adopt him. You would love him, Mom, I know you would."

"No, Donna. The answer is no. Your father would never hear of it."

"You can talk Daddy into it, Mom. You're good at that."

"I also say no," she said sternly. There was a long pause, then her voice softened. "Listen, dear, I know how hard this is on you, and I wish I could help, but I can't start looking after babies. Not at this stage in my life."

"But nobody will adopt him, Mom, I know he'll end up living his whole life in the Crèche. People are going to adopt the cute, pretty babies with curly hair and big blue eyes. They're the ones that families choose, not tough little Tommy. Please, Mom!"

"I said no, Donna, and I am not even going to mention it to your father. Besides, we're not Catholic."

"Maybe Sister can make an exception in our case."

"I know this is heartbreaking. I feel for those babies, I really do, dear, but we can't adopt them. And that's final, Donna. Just pray that he will go to a good home."

I realized there was nothing I could do to change the destiny of these babies. But I always wondered what happened to Tommy and the other babies in the back row.

The following week Niven and I were working together on Obstetrics, OBS, as we called it. There were three sections to this ward. First, the admitting room on the right where the student nurse gave the patient a shave-prep and a high soapsuds enema to cleanse the bowel. This would promote a clean delivery and hopefully increase the contractions. Then the labour room where we watched the patient closely as her contractions increased and the cervix gradually opened until fully dilated at ten centimetres. And there were two delivery rooms, similar to the operating room, where the anaesthetist's equipment stood at the head of the table and an empty bassinet waited in the corner.

A tiny nurses' station sat between the admitting room and the labour room. It was more of a rest area, with a long counter and tall stools where we sat and scratched quick notes in the patients' charts as their labour progressed. Though sparsely equipped with only a kettle for making tea and coffee, it had the all-important autoclave in an alcove at the back of the room.

Mrs. Baruta, the clinical instructor, gave us a thorough orientation. She had an attractive face, red cheeks and lips, and an incredibly stiff, wrinkle-free uniform. Though she was not fat, she was endowed with generous curves. Her piercing eyes sat behind dark-rimmed glasses that swept up to a point at her eyebrows. I gathered from her stiff attitude that her reputation for intolerance was well earned and I vowed to get off on the right foot. I had my doubts, though, about Niven, given her bristly attitude towards women patients.

The first two days, Mrs. Baruta kept Niven and me busy with shave-preps, enemas and changing the beds. Two grads in charge of OBS taught us how to use a fetoscope, much like a stethoscope, which we placed on the patient's abdomen to hear the fetal heartbeat. And we had to determine the degree of dilation of the cervix by inserting our finger into the rectum to feel the rim of the cervix. Only doctors were allowed to use the vagina to feel the cervix. I thought it felt very much like the rim of the condom that my girlfriend's brother had shown off to us. It had made a permanent ring in the leather of his wallet.

By the third day, I had done so many shave preps I felt that I could do them with my eyes closed. As I was inserting a new blade into my razor, ready to begin my fourth shave of the day, Simpson, the grad, rushed in through the curtains.

"Yates, come with me." Her words cut through the calm atmosphere I had painstakingly created for my first-time mother-to-be. Then I felt her yank the shoulder of my uniform. "Now!" She spit in my ear.

I threw the tray on the bedside locker, tossed a sheet over the woman and dashed out of the room.

"Over here!" Simpson shouted from the door of the Case Room. "Scrub-in for the delivery."

My heart pounded as I rushed to the sink beside the theatre. I lathered my hands and arms up to my elbows with soap and began scrubbing with a brush, almost the size of my hand. I tried to remember my duties for assisting with a delivery but my mind drew a blank. Simpson sailed by me with a stretcher. The patient was screaming every two minutes, obviously close to her last stage of labour. The anaesthetist arrived, rushed into the theatre and helped the patient on the table.

"Yates, get in here! Forget the scrub!" shouted Simpson.

I dashed into the room, gowned and gloved so quickly that I was sure I'd set a personal record. Then I began to prepare the small table of sterile instruments for the delivery.

"Hi, Carol." It was Dr. Beverly Humphrey standing at the door, bubbles of soap billowing from her arms as she scrubbed.

"Getting close," the grad said, anxiously. "Contractions about every 30 seconds."

Dr. Humphrey immediately rinsed the soap from her arms and walked in the room. I helped her into the gown and gloves.

"Everything is fine, Carol," she said in a business-as-usual voice as she examined Carol's perineum. "Just keep pushing. Baby's almost here."

Carol yelled and grunted. The opening for the baby's passage became larger with each contraction.

"Come on, Carol. Keep pushing." Simpson urged.

There was another long scream and a guttural groan from Carol, even louder than before. Splash! The sac that held the baby in its watery chamber burst. The amniotic fluid gushed to the floor soaking Dr. Humphrey and me. I saw something round and black inside the birth canal. The head. Crowning. Exactly as it said in the textbook. The mother's labia stretched like a crown around the baby's head.

Carol's legs were up in stirrups, draped with a white cloth, but I could see that she was up on her elbows, pushing, grunting. Her face red, her eyes glazed. She was in another world. The black head moved closer. Her vulva opened wider. I was spellbound.

Dr. Humphrey held out her hand. "Scissors!"

I snapped them into her open hand. She gripped the perineum with her left hand, the scissors in her right, and made a cut several inches long. During the delivery a zigzag tear in the perineum was almost inevitable and difficult to heal. But a clean straight incision made by the doctor was easy to suture closed and the straight edges healed quickly.

Carol gave one long, loud grunt. The baby's head popped out, face down, then slowly rotated to the right. Restitution, I thought, just as the textbook said. The spontaneous turning of the fetal head to the right or left after it has extended through the vulva. How absolutely amazing!

Dr. Humphrey inserted her forefinger and eased out first one, and then the other little shoulder. The baby was out! Dr. Humphrey held it up securely by the ankles. It dangled upside down.

"It's a girl!" the doctor said.

The baby had made a successful trip down the birth canal. Now she must make the traumatic transition from warm aquatic to human being. She would feel her movements restricted, the air cold on her body ~ but she *had* to breathe. The

164

baby cried. She screamed! Dr. Humphrey placed the baby girl smeared with bloody paste on Carol's chest, then cut the umbilical cord.

"Shh, shh, my baby," whispered Carol, smiling at her new baby. "Mommy's here."

Simpson quickly picked up the baby and laid her on a tiny scale. "Seven pounds, four ounces," she said, placing the baby in the bassinet. The grad then put two drops of antibiotic into the baby's eyes, a precaution to prevent infection or blindness in the baby if the mother unknowingly carried gonorrhea. She covered the baby with a bath blanket, and whisked her to the Nursery.

"Is she okay, doctor?" Carol asked in a weak voice. "She doesn't have any problems does she?"

"She looks fine," Dr. Humphrey said. "I'll give her a good going-over when I get to the Nursery, but from what I saw, she's perfect. And beautiful too. Did a good job, Carol. Now just rest."

Carol gave a deep sigh, smiled and drifted off into an exhausted, blissful sleep.

Dr. Humphrey had just finished suturing the episiotomy when Simpson returned.

"Yates, take the patient to her room and get back here as quickly as possible, Simpson said. "Bed four is ready. You're going to scrub in again."

I delivered Carol to the maternity ward and rushed back, anxious to see another delivery. I scrubbed in. The mother pushed and the baby's head came out. Okay, I said to myself, let's see if it is going to turn. And it did. It turned to the right. The baby came out all paste and blood. She was upside down, screaming, protesting, *breathing*.

"It's a girl!"

"Is it okay?"

"Perfect."

It was the same miracle.

"Okay, Yates, go for lunch," said Simpson. "Niven's going to clean up here and then she'll scrub for the next case. There's another one ready to deliver. She's eight centimeters."

It was 2:30. The cafeteria had closed but my lunch was waiting. A pencil-thin woman with a brown net covering her fine hair stopped cleaning the empty pock-marked pots and shoved my tray across the glass counter. She had deep plum circles beneath her sad eyes, and she looked very tired. I wondered if she was sick. I sat down at the first table in the cafeteria and stared at my lunch ~ dried up roast beef, cold, lumpy mashed potatoes, and beets in a shiny, sticky sauce that had coagulated. I shuddered, pushed my plate aside and gobbled down the generous square of lemon meringue pie.

When I returned to the delivery room, Niven was still in a mess. But the patient had already had her baby, she told me. It was the mother's tenth child. "She popped the kid out so bloody fast Dr. Bogart didn't even make it to the delivery. He arrived just as we were taking her to the ward." Niven chuckled through her mask.

"You should have seen that pompous ass freak out. He was royally pissed." Niven tore the bloody sheets off the table and tossed them on the floor. "Come on, Yates. Help me clean up this shit, will you?"

The next week on the 3:30 to 11:30 p.m. shift we had a nice steady flow of babies being born and plenty of time to relax between deliveries.

Wednesday evening, I checked the woman near the door in the labour room, she had been three centimeters the last time I examined her. I did another rectal ~ she was seven. I dashed for the grad.

"You're right," said the grad when she checked. "She's a *good* seven centimetres, and she's para five" (fifth time pregnant), "gravida five" (fifth pregnancy carried to term or viability). "Better get her into the Case Room, pronto!"

I quickly moved the patient to the case room and helped her onto the table. The grad checked her again.

"Start scrubbing, Yates," she said. "She's eight centimetres now. I'm calling Bogart."

Yikes. Bogart again! He had a reputation for taking only very wealthy patients, and this patient did look wealthy. She looked as if she went to the beauty parlour every week and she had a hair-do to prove it. Though it was a bit messy now you could tell it had been puffed-up to its limit and sprayed in a very professional way.

By the time I set up the instruments and draped the sterile sheets over the woman's legs hanging in the stirrups, Dr. Bogart arrived, or rather graced us with his presence. He slowly made his entrance with such affect and smugness that I smiled under my mask. He sauntered over to the patient, slowly pulling on his mask, and dramatically took her hand.

"Everything will be fine, my dear," he said in his British accent. "I'm here." Oh, brother, I thought. He glanced at me from the corner of his eyes without turning his head, I suppose to see if I was in a swoon, then slowly walked out of the room to scrub. He was a fairly tall man, much too conceited and pretty to be my type. Thinks he's God's gift to woman, Niven once told me. She was right.

His skin was peaches 'n cream. He did not have a trace of a five o'clock shadow though it was now almost six. His jet-black hair, parted just a touch to the left of middle, was combed back in even waves and a splash of grey at his temples added a look of maturity. His black eyebrows sat above big dark eyes like bushy hedges, and he wore glasses trimmed in gold. He never smiled, so his pencil moustache remained straight. But his left eyebrow hedge was constantly raised in a questioning way that said, "Like what you see?"

Gowned and gloved, he joined me at the foot of the delivery table. We stood in the sterile position, arms bent upward from the elbows, and waited. But with the patient's legs up in stirrups our only view was her vulva, enlarging with every contraction. I coolly glanced around the room trying my best to appear nonchalant. The woman had several large hemorrhoids ~ big varicose veins around her anus. These purplish-blue veins had become turgid with the pressure of the baby moving down the birth canal and were rhythmically enlarging and receding with every contraction.

"How would you like to have those on your nose?" Doctor Bogart said snidely. He stared straight ahead with indifference, as if those words had come from someone else.

I felt mortified. How I wished I could be anywhere except standing in front of this hemorrhoidic patient with this beastly arrogant man. But I had to answer. He was my superior. *The doctor.*

"No," I whispered. He did not respond.

We stood in silence for several minutes until I realized the hemorrhoids were no longer swelling and the woman no longer moaned. Her contractions had simply stopped.

"I am going out for a cigarette," Dr. Bogart announced in a perturbed voice. I waited. The woman waited. Everyone in the room waited. The grad brought me a chair and we waited some more. But the contractions did not begin again.

"I'm taking the patient back to the maternity floor," the grad finally said after 30 minutes. "Clean up the room."

The woman did not come back into labour until the early hours of the next morning, and I was happy to have missed the occasion.

The next day when I arrived, I checked the big blackboard in the hall between the two case rooms. The board was full. The name of each patient, para and gravida ~ number of pregnancies, number of babies born ~ were noted, as well as the dilatation of the cervix and the fetal heart rate.

"Yates, help Niven clean the case room and then get scrubbed," the grad said as she rushed past me.

As I finished scrubbing, the grad moved the patient into the case room. Dr. Cole joined me at the scrub sink and waved to the patient.

"Hi, Ann," he said through his mask. "Looks like we're having a baby."

Ann grunted and yelled. It was getting close. I set up the instruments.

"Keep up the good work," Dr. Cole said, drying his hands on the sterile towel. He slipped his hands into the sterile gloves I held. "Ann's my neighbour. Best friends with my wife, eh, Ann?"

Ann was past the point of answering, now grunting and pushing for all she was worth.

"Good, Ann. Good." The grad held Ann's hand and was stroking her forehead.

"Here it comes!" said Dr. Cole. But then his voice quickly changed as the baby's head began protruding through the vulva.

"What's going on? Doesn't look like the head, Bill. We've got a different presentation here."

The anaesthetist, Dr. Bill Dahl, was administering small whiffs of nitrous oxide, a gas that provides a light anaesthetic to take the edge off of the contractions but doesn't put the mother to sleep.

"A breech?" asked Dr. Dahl.

"Can't tell, it might be. It looks a little...."

Dr. Cole's voice trailed off as the head emerged through the vulva. But it was only half a head with squiggles of brains bulging out of the top.

"Oh, my God," gasped Dr. Cole.

"What is it?" Ann asked. "Is it okay? Is my baby okay?"

"Put her out." Dr. Cole screamed, waving his hand at Bill. "Put her out!"

Dr. Dahl slapped the mask on Ann's face and shoved the valve on the gas cylinder up higher. Ann's eyes rolled back. She was asleep.

"Oh, no. Oh, my God. No!" cried Dr. Cole as he pulled the baby from the mother. It was a boy. Dr. Cole held him up by the shoulders, I suppose thinking that the brains might fall out if he was upside down for there was no top on the baby's head. He hung limply, gave two short gasps, but did not breathe. "It's not going to breathe," Dr. Cole said placing the baby on Ann's chest. But then the baby gasped ... again ... and again, and then began to whimper, more like a low wailful drone. His face was formed only to the level of his eyebrows. No forehead. No skull. Dr. Cole cut the umbilical cord. The child lay like a baby gremlin on his mother's chest, mourning. Dr. Cole quickly placed the baby in the bassinet.

"Take it to the preemie nursery," he said to the grad. "Don't put it in an incubator. It's not going to live."

A heavy silence filled the room as Dr. Cole sutured the episiotomy.

"How am I going to tell Ann?" he said to the anaesthetist. "She's my friend, my neighbour. I see her every day." He glanced at Ann sleeping peacefully. "That's the damn trouble with taking a friend as a patient, Bill," he muttered. "Should never have done that. Came to me when she was first pregnant and I told her to find a doctor who wasn't a friend." Dr. Cole finished tying the knots and paused, waiting for me to cut the suture he held. He dipped a piece of gauze in the basin of clean water and began to clean the blood from the incision, now sewn together in a neat, straight line. "I knew I shouldn't take her," he said as he moved about automatically. "But she insisted, and I couldn't say no. That's the damn trouble. I couldn't say no."

Dr. Bill Dahl's mask covered his face but sadness filled his eyes. He nodded sympathetically.

"Well, that's it," Dr. Cole said with a deep sigh. He threw the dirty gauze into the metal pail on the floor. "I'm going to see Phil, her husband." He slowly shook his head and walked to the door, then turned. "Keep her asleep for a while, Bill, the baby's anencephalic. Can you believe it? First one I've ever seen. This is something you only read about, right?" His eyes met mine. I quickly looked down. He left murmuring to himself, "God, what am I going to tell Phil."

Dr. Dahl pushed Ann, still in an innocent sleep, towards the door. "I won't be back for a while," he said to the grad. "I'm going to sit with the patient until she wakes up."

I stood in a numb fog. "Did you ever see a baby like that before?" I asked the grad.

She shook her head sadly. "Never in my life."

"Gosh, that's like something from a horror movie." I felt a riveting shock creep over me as though I was waking up from a bad dream. Reality then began to sink in. I stood staring at the messy room ~ the bloody sheets, the empty stirrups, the used anaesthetic mask tossed on the delivery table, the umbilical cord attached to the life-giving placenta lay in a silver basin, waiting to go to pathology. A baby had been born. The room said so. We were supposed to feel happy.

"I feel sick." I said.

"So do I, Yates," the grad said, softly. "But that's life. Sometimes things go wrong. Pray for the baby's soul." She lay her hand on my shoulder. "Clean up the room, then go for supper."

A New Life

Monday morning I began working in the Preemie Nursery. Miniature babies lay in heated incubators. These were clear Plexiglas boxes with tiny tubes connected to outlets on the wall that controlled the heat and level of oxygen.

A senior nurse was caring for the smallest baby I'd ever seen. She slid her arms through the flexible covers of two large holes on the sides of the incubator that closed automatically when she withdrew her arms. Three of the larger babies, between three and five pounds, were in heated incubators without a cover on top, and one of them began to fuss.

My assignment was to feed the babies in the open incubators. My hands were shaking when I reached in for the first baby, but try as I might, I could not figure out a safe way to pick him up. My hand looked so large beside the tiny baby, I hesitated.

"Just pick him up normally," the head nurse said as she bent over and whisked the little fellow up and out of the incubator so fast that I couldn't see the way she held her hands. "He's tough as nails. He'll go home after he gains another three ounces." She thrust him into my arms. My heart almost stopped.

I gingerly held the baby and sat down beside the senior student who was feeding another one. I sat the baby facing me and eased the surprisingly large nipple into his tiny mouth. His eyes widened, he stared at me. Then he began greedily sucking on the nipple that covered most of his face. After a few minutes his eyelids began to droop, he had lost interest in the bottle. I made an effort to jiggle him, but he didn't move. I whispered, "I can't wake him up."

The senior reached over and flicked the bottom of his feet with her index finger, then his ear lobe. "He has to take it all," she said. The baby began to cry. I quickly shoved the bottle in his mouth, and he finished it.

"Good boy," said the head nurse as she picked him up from the scale. "You're almost five pounds. Another couple of ounces and you'll be able to go home to mommy and daddy."

But baby didn't wake up. He was busy gaining weight.

The tiniest babies were too small to wear diapers. They weighed from two and a half to four pounds, and except for the absence of eyelashes and eyebrows were perfectly formed. One baby, though, had not yet formed fingernails or toenails. The senior fed that baby through a tube in the baby's nose because it didn't have enough strength to suck on a nipple.

Midway through the morning Dr. Cole appeared in the nursery and spoke briefly to the head nurse. He glanced in my direction. His eyes were heavy and bloodshot, with dark circles beneath. He ran his fingers through his messy hair, turned and shuffled out of the nursery.

Miss Sutter, the head nurse, called me over to a bassinet in the corner. "This is the baby born the day before yesterday. I believe you were scrubbed for the delivery."

"Yes," I whispered, my eyes fixed on the baby.

"The parents have not seen the baby yet. Dr. Cole just informed me that the father wants to see him now. The mother is absolutely devastated, rightly so, and insists her husband see the baby before it dies."

Shock began working its way through my body again. The baby lay perfectly still. A head like Humpty Dumpty, but nothing above his eyes ~ a hard-boiled egg with the top taken off. The insubstantial brains that existed only from the level of his eyes to the skull base sat exposed ~ a mass of grey matter that glistened under a shiny transparent membrane, curving, twisting ~ going nowhere. His thick tongue kept protruding from his mouth, in and out, in and out in a nonsensical way. His blue eyes were fixed in a lifeless stare. Though the rest of his body appeared normal, it lay motionless, inert.

Miss Sutter stood silent beside me as I tried to absorb the reality of the tragedy. Then she put her hand on my shoulder. "Dr. Cole has ordered that the baby not be fed. There's no use prolonging the suffering of the baby or the family."

"The baby will die," I said, alarmed, but I knew death was the only option.

"Do you know what anencephalic is?" she asked.

"Well, no brains, I think."

"In effect, yes. You see, when the baby's brain was forming in the womb, hydrocephalus developed. That's literally water on the brain. The brain eventually became so enlarged that it ruptured. Because this happened before the skull finished forming, the skull became permanently damaged, and ceased to grow."

"The baby doesn't have a chance?"

"Doesn't have a chance," she repeated as she lowered her eyes. "You see, he has no sucking reflex. It would be cruel to tube feed him. We've tried to give him water ... we even had an intravenous running until this morning. Many doctors have seen the baby. I think their decision is humane." She took a Kleenex from her pocket and blew her nose under her mask. "There's no hope for this baby. My heart goes out to the parents."

A knock came from the viewing glass along the front wall.

"That will be the father." She returned the Kleenex to her pocket under her gown, pushed the bassinet to the window and opened the Venetian blinds.

I pretended to be busy with another baby as I watched the father look at his son through the viewing glass for the first and last time. Though he did not show any emotion, his body looked limp. He had surrendered. He knew his baby could not live, should not live. He turned and slowly walked back to his waiting wife. I knew he had relinquished his baby to God.

His parents named him Thomas, and the nuns baptized him. Thomas died four hours after his father saw him. The next day his parents gave him a private funeral.

"Do you believe Thomas had a soul?" I asked the girls in the lounge after work.

"Of course," Guenette said. "All babies have a soul. But they're born into fundamental sin. We all are."

"Oh come on, Guenette," said Perry, "how can a little baby commit a sin?"

"He doesn't have to commit a sin, he's born into sin. That's how it works."

"Is that what Catholics believe?" I asked.

"Yes," Kaufmann said, defensively, "Guenette is right."

"I don't believe Thomas was born into sin," I said. "And I don't believe he is floating around somewhere waiting to go to heaven or hell."

"So where did he go then?" said Kaufmann.

"I don't believe babies like Thomas, or any young children who die early, have only one chance," I said. "I believe their soul goes into another baby. A healthy one that has a life ahead of it." I stood up and looked over at the hospital. "Somehow Thomas has to be given another chance."

"Dream on, Yates," Guenette chided. "That's not how life works."

"Now you don't know that." Perry said, shaking her finger at Guenette. "I kind of hope Yates *is* right. I want to believe Thomas will be given another chance."

"I'll drink to that." Tanner raised her coffee cup.

Shortly after, Blackwell and I began working the day shift on the maternity floor, which we called the mat floor. It certainly was a welcome relief after all the nights I'd been working. Each student had to give a baby bath demonstration to the new mothers before they went home, and mine was due on Thursday.

Mrs. O'Reilly, my patient who'd just had her fifth baby, insisted on coming. At two o'clock sharp, she and the six other mothers gathered in the Demonstration Room. Of course, Mrs. Baruta was there. She had planted herself against the back wall. She would grade me and give the result to Sister.

The props were waiting on the table ~ a rubber doll, a basin of water, oil, powder, lotion, and diapers. Everything was ready. My fingers began to quiver and my knees shook. I took a deep breath, and began.

"Immerse the baby in the water. Be careful to support the head so the baby will not drown." I soaped the doll from head to toe. "Get into all of the little creases. Be sure to soap his head. Then we rinse." I carefully lifted the doll out of the water, placed it in a towel and dried it. Then I began with the lotions and powder. As I

171

rubbed oil on his scalp I said, "Oil is very important to prevent cradle crap. Those are the trusty scales babies sometime get on their scalp...."

Mrs. O'Reilly began to laugh, a real belly laugh. I paused. What I had just said had a funny ring to it, but I didn't know exactly what. Another woman joined Mrs. O'Reilly, and soon the whole room rocked with laughter. Even Mrs. Baruta laughed!

Cradle crap, what's wrong with cradle crap? Then I realized my mistake. "Oh, I mean cradle CAP. And they're CRUSTY scales." I smiled sheepishly.

Later, Mrs. O'Reilly was still laughing as I dressed her baby to go home. "This is my fifth baby bath demonstration, Miss Yates," she said. "But I have never had such a good time as I had watching yours. I'll never forget it."

"Neither will I," I muttered.

When I got back to the residence after work, humiliated and exhausted, I pulled off my uniform and went straight to bed. At 4:15 p.m., my buzzer rang.

"Miss Yates, you have a little visitor," Mrs. Schriefels said.

A little visitor?

Mrs. Schriefels smiled as I approached the reception desk. There stood Angela, my little burn patient from pediatrics.

"Angela!" I cried. "What a nice surprise."

Angela beamed and wagged her hand at me. "Hi, Miss Yates."

"How are you? How did your surgeries go? You look wonderful!"

"Oh, I'm all better. Look!" She hiked up her sweater to show me her scarred abdomen.

"That's great, Angela."

"Want to show me where you live?"

"Sure. Come on."

I gave Angela a tour of the residence and she gave me beige and pink candy-coated almonds wrapped in a blue net sack. I had never seen candies like that before and thought they must be something Italian. We went to my room and sat on my bed, chatting for at least an hour about the hospital, the nurses and Angela's long list of surgeries.

"How are your brothers and sisters?"

"They hate me. I get all of the attention now. I'm very spoiled, you know." She grinned, and then began to giggle.

"I'm glad to see you haven't lost your sense of humour. You're still the biggest tease I know."

Angela pulled a piece of paper out of the bag she brought. It was a self-portrait of her in a hospital bed with a nurse standing beside her.

"That's you, Miss Yates," she said, pointing to the nurse.

"It's beautiful. Thank you, Angela. I think you should be an artist."

She shook her head. "I want to be a nurse, like you."

I smiled. "You'll make a wonderful nurse."

I carefully pinned the picture on the cork bulletin board above my desk, then I gave her a hug. "I'll always treasure this picture. I'll look at it every day and think of you."

She smiled. "I hope so."

Sunday night, Niven and I began three weeks of nights in the case room.

"Remember, Niv," I said as we walked through the dim tunnel on our way to work, "No whistling. I hear these night grads in the Case Room are nasty."

"Yeah, yeah," she said in her offhand manner.

Our first two nights were quiet. But the third night was a full moon. When we arrived, the blackboard in the hall was covered with the names of patients who had come and gone, and messy stretchers lined the hall.

The two aloof night grads began shouting orders at us: "Niven get into admitting, and be fast." Then one turned to me, "Clean up the Labour Room. And keep an eye on those patients. There are two very close. Come on. Hustle!"

The Labour Room was in a shambles and unusually crowded. Two wide-eyed patients waited on stretchers in the hall, while I cleaned and remade the empty beds. I spied a bundle of dirty linen on the floor. Ye Gad! I thought, who left that there? Before I could pick it up, the tall skinny grad with a pointy nose flew in the room to check the woman in the first bed.

"She's ready!" She called breathlessly as she ran to the telephone to call Dr. Cole. "Get her to the Case Room!"

I moved the patient onto a stretcher and rushed her to the Case Room. She was panting and grunting. I left her with the other grad, but I could hear her screaming,"I want to push," as I hustled back to the Labour Room.

I didn't know where to start. I knew I should get the dirty linen out of the room, but thought I'd better check the patients first. That's what I had been told, always start with the patients. I had just inserted my finger into the patient's rectum to feel her cervix when I heard a sharp voice on the other side of the curtains.

"Nurse, come here!"

It sounded like Sister Picher, the night supervisor.

With my finger I quickly circled the cervix, which was definitely large. Close to nine centimeters, I thought. She's ready! I dashed out of the curtains, colliding with Sister Picher who was attempting to enter.

"Look at this!" She motioned to the linen on the floor. "This place is a mess!"

"Yes, Sister."

"Clean it up."

"Yes, Sister. Well, you see, I've been very busy. We've had so many...."

"That's no excuse. And don't talk back to me!" With a swish and a flip of her veil, she motored off to the other side of the room and began to straighten the magazines.

What a time to straighten magazines, I thought as I struggled under the weight of the dirty linen I had picked up from the floor. Darn, I muttered to myself. I knew better than to try and answer a nun. Just say "Yes, Sister, No, Sister," and wait for them to go away. That's what Guenette told me; she was Catholic and older, she knew. I squashed the linen into the linen chute and dashed for the grad.

All night, patients quickly circulated through the department, from the admitting room to the Labour Room, to the Case Room. I spied another woman waddling down the hall, her suitcase swinging from the arm of the admitting clerk beside her. Where are all these women coming from? I never knew there were so many pregnant women.

I dashed into the admitting room, but another patient was being admitted. High above the drawn curtains, I saw an arm holding an enema can.

"Oh, God, I can't hold it, I just can't," the patient cried in a weak voice from behind the curtain.

"You'd better!" It was Niven's voice. "I'm going to finish this can and I don't want it all over me!"

I peeked in through the curtains. Niven was giving her patient a soapsuds enema; she stood on a chair, holding an enema can full of warm, sudsy water high above her head.

"Niven!" I called in a coarse whisper.

She had finished giving the enema. The woman struggled up as best she could and ran to the bathroom. There was a moan, a grunt and then an explosive splash.

"What on earth are you doing?" I whispered. "Niven, that's terrible!"

"I've got a system," Niven said. "After these ladies get one of my enemas, they pass go, head directly for the Case Room and never see the Labour Room. I don't have to change any beds, and it saves my back, too."

Four babies were born in 80 minutes. The first was Niven's patient who sailed straight into the Case Room after that enema. My back was killing me. I had to haul the dirty linen off the beds in the Labour Room, sling it over my shoulders like a man delivering coal and carry it down to the linen chute. But I could never resort to Niven's tactics. Although we were supposed to give a high soapsuds enema, I drew the line at standing on a chair.

Every new baby was my reward for the hard work. When the head began to crown, it was like seeing birth for the first time. This was a thrill. A charge. Each time a new life entered the world I watched with reverence and awe. We all did.

For some reason, it took me all morning to fall asleep. Then a knock on my door woke me up. Perry walked in.

"Time you were up. It's six o'clock."

I moaned.

Perry flopped down on the chair. "It's our second anniversary. Want to come to the Lotus Café for a butterhorn?"

"No kidding?" I said sleepily. "It's February 10th?"

"Yup."

So six of us, Perry, Niven, Andresen, Blackwell, Hawkins, and I, celebrated at the Lotus Café with a butterhorn and a Coke. I did feel proud that I had successfully completed two years, but I wondered if we would all make it through the remaining year.

PART THREE

In the Garden

A twiggy man in a tweed cap drove up to the residence in a van to take us to the Catholic retreat house in Cochrane. Our chauffeur didn't introduce himself, but I was sure he wasn't a priest ~ he looked more like a hermit. He gave a half-smile from the side of his bony face as he lifted our small suitcases into the van. He legs were short and quite bowed which gave him a bit of a waddle.

"Rickets," Blackwell whispered confidently in my ear as we squeezed into the back of the van.

As we drove through the sparsely snow-covered foothills, the wind shifted from the cold north to warm west. Shafts of honey-coloured prairie grass, bowed in winter posture, swayed to the wind's whispers like Sunday-morning gospel songsters. Now at the crest of Cochrane hill, we had an awesome view of the western valley and the town that lay below, tucked in the fabric of the Bow's riverfront. The hill, once called "Manachaban" (the Big Mount) by the Stoney Indians was now famous for runaway cars and trucks whose brakes failed. We began to descend this treacherously steep, winding hill, two and a quarter miles long, which posted frequent warning signs "Danger! Steep Grade," "Trucks ~ Gear Down," "Sharp Curve!"

My father always delighted in telling the story of ascending Cochrane hill in reverse gear because his 1929 Model T Ford couldn't make it up going forward. And then at a very dangerous curve he had to stop and brace the wheels with heavy stones, jack up the car and change a flat tire.

Now Cochrane had a population of almost 300 and two streetlights on the main road. The Rockyview Hotel on the corner had a separate Men's and Ladies' Beer Parlour and guest rooms on the second floor. Next to the hotel was Mackay's Ice Cream Shop where my father had always stopped to buy Allan and me an ice cream cone on our way to Banff for summer vacation.

North of town we ascended another hill and drew up at Mount St. Francis, several quaint brick buildings facing west, overlooking the yawning Bow Valley.

As a Catholic, Blackwell was required to retreat every year. But Sister encouraged Protestant students to attend too, saying, "It is important for all of you as nurses to spend time each year in your own quiet way with God. Renew your commitment to serving the sick."

For two years my world had revolved around illness and death, and little else. I felt exhausted. I needed to be close to God.

The driver had not said a word during the entire trip. Blackwell and I, happy to be out of the car, walked over to the ridge near the buildings. I took a sharp breath as the ground at our feet seemed to drop away, opening into a vast valley. A quiescent landscape of endless ranch country ~ grazing cattle, snow-crusted prairie, dark patches of Alberta Spruce and Mugho or Mountain Pine, here and there a hill almost completely tree-covered. And deeply carved through the prairie foothills, the Bow River, grey-blue and cold looking, swiftly snaked its way east under thin patches of blue ice. It would join the Elbow at Calgary, the Oldman River at Medicine Hat and two more rivers in Saskatchewan before finally flowing into Hudson Bay.

I felt I was standing at the very edge of the world. Sparse ranches nestled in the folds of the rolling prairie. Beyond the fields and river and trees there stretched a mass of indigo swells and peaks draped with a blanket of snow that softly settled into mountain crevasses. Above, a Chinook arch illuminated the horizon in quiet shades of pale yellow and peach, joining the slate sky in a fuzzy fuse. These muted colours foretold the approach of the Chinook, that phenomenon of warm westerly wind that swept regularly over the Rockies. These Chinooks provided brief but welcomed interludes to the blustery Calgary winters. As a child it was not unusual for me to waddle off to school in 25 below zero snow only to trudge home at noon sweating in the spring-like warmth, dragging my heavy parka behind me.

The wind had indeed increased considerably since we left Calgary and was now strong and gusty ~ but it was warm. It swirled around us, playfully snatching at our bandanas knotted under our chins, before rushing off into endless space.

As we entered the large stone monastery I felt I had stepped back in time. The retreat was run by religious brothers, who did all the cooking and cleaning. Wearing large brown robes tied at the waist with rope, they moved quickly and easily around long wooden tables. Beneath the broad-beamed ceiling, hung huge iron chandeliers that seemed more suited to candles than electricity.

Blackwell and I mingled with the others, perhaps 15 people, mostly middle-aged couples and men dressed in business suits. Retreat was supposed to be a private, soul-searching experience, and although the participants knew that we were student nurses, they never spoke to us about their lives.

We each had a small room with a single bed, a wooden chair and a small wooden bedside table with a Bible and some religious prayers on top. A crucifix hung above the bed and Christ bearing his bleeding heart looked down on me from above the wooden door. The brothers allowed us to talk during supper, but after that, the rule of silence prevailed until the end of retreat. Our only interaction was at mealtime, when we communicated by using discreet sign language.

Each morning at 5:30, a huge bell from a tower in one of the buildings rang for four minutes to awaken us. It rang every few hours, all day long, our cue to move from meditation to lunch, to rest period, to meditation, to supper, to vespers, to bed. I was impressed that the brothers hustled off to prayers even more often than we did. I wondered how they ever found time for cooking, cleaning and serving us.

For my meditation hideaway, I followed the trickle of a path down the mountain and picked out a secluded, dry spot among the evergreens where I had a glorious view of both the valley and the mountains. I sat on a bed of pine needles, sheltered by a canopy of entwined bows, and began to contemplate the vast beauty of it all.

How lucky I was to be alive ... and healthy. I found myself ruminating about *why* I was so lucky, while others, like Lisa Lane got leukemia, and Mark Birch got Hodgkin's. Nature surrounded me, so beautiful, so peaceful, so perfect. Perhaps I'd had my share of suffering in another life. Perhaps those philosophers were right and we'd all lived several lives before ~ working our way up the ladder of life. Perhaps.

The Chinook breeze whispered past me rousing some dry leaves on the floor of the forest, they floated like little butterflies towards the gorge and fluttered into endless space. It reminded me of that beautiful fall day, my first day of school when my mother took me to Balmoral School, two blocks from home. I had not yet had my sixth birthday. Mom had made me a new outfit, a plaid pleated skirt and a white blouse with a ribbon around my collar. She curled my long, thick, unruly brown hair in ringlets, and tied it back with a ribbon in a big bow on top of my head.

Balmoral consisted of three buildings in a triangle, two small buildings at opposite corners, and a large brownstone building in the middle, at the top of the triangle. My classroom was in the small yellow clapboard building on the right, where there was one room of grade one, two rooms of grade two, and a principal's office.

At noon I meandered home for lunch along the same route my mother had taken me many times during the summer to teach me the way home. After lunch she waved good-bye to me and I started back to school. But as I walked past Carol's house, two doors away, Carol called me in to see her new kittens. She would not start school until next year, and because her newborn kittens were more interesting than my morning in school had been, returning to school quickly slipped from my mind. Carol and I dressed the kittens in doll clothes and pushed them around in the doll buggy. Mom happened by on her way to the store and heard my laughter from Carol's back yard.

"Don't you know you have to go back to school?" she said clutching my arm as she briskly whisked me home. I had to run at times just to keep up to her.

"I did go to school," I insisted. "But I would rather play with Carol." I didn't know I *had* to go to school.

The next day, the teacher was waiting for me, and asked for a note.

"What note?" I said.

"Were you sick?"

"No."

"There is a Truant Officer, who is a lady policeman. She will pick you up off the street and put you in jail if you are away from school and you are not sick."

"Me? In jail?" I was stunned, and very frightened.

"You played Truant," she said with her big mouth and large white teeth. Her glasses glinted in the light ~ she seemed to have no eyes. A real witch.

"You don't have a note!" she bellowed. "Donna, you played Truant!"

The class laughed.

I didn't tell my mother.

The insistent chatter of a sparrow on a branch above me now caught my attention, and I looked up at him. *God sees a little sparrow fall /It meets His tender view / If God so loved the little bird / I know he loves me too.* The song I sang in Sunday school when I was in grade one. I don't thank God often enough, I thought. I wished I could be more like Armbruster who thanked Him all the time.

That night as I was getting ready for bed, Blackwell snuck into my room, her dark hair up in rollers.

"Hey, Yates," she whispered in sotto voice. "Did you get a load of that brother at my end of the table? You know, the one that serves the meat."

"No. What does he look like?"

"He's cute. Such a doll in those robes. And I think he's our age."

"Do you think he's taken his final vows?"

She shrugged. "Don't know."

"What a waste."

Blackwell nodded in agreement, then put her finger to her lips and quietly closed the door.

Each day I moved about silently in the shadows of the others, all of us deep in our own thoughts. The warm breeze of the Chinook stayed for the whole weekend and blew my heart peaceful. Back at the residence on Sunday night, I called my mother to tell her I was in a place very close to heaven.

The next morning Niven and I set off for the nursery on our first day as a senior student nurses. Sister, with her usual stone-face, nodded to me as I passed her after prayer. Suddenly I realized Niven wasn't behind me. I turned to see Sister pointing to Niven's shoes. Her shoes hung together by a thread. Cracks in the creases had become gaping holes and were now impossible to mend. Even the adhesive tape couldn't disguise the wear and tear. They were falling off her feet and poor Niven didn't have any money to buy another pair until after graduation. I motioned to Niven to meet me upstairs.

Up in the nursery locker room, I quickly slipped into the white gown. Warm air enveloped me as I stepped into the room full of screaming babies. After the preemies the normal babies appeared gigantic.

"Here's baby Woods," the grad from the case room said cheerily, as she bumped the door open and pushed the bassinet into the nursery. "He was a tough one, a breech. Dr. Cole had to use high forceps and wants to keep him in an open incubator for three hours."

I wheeled the heated bassinet over to the counter used for bathing and changing. The grad, with her expertise and keen eye to spy any deformities, always gave the first bath and initial examination to the new baby. But she had to leave to attend a meeting.

"Yates, bathe baby Woods," she said to me as she rushed out the door.

The baby looked a little odd, I thought; a small head, round face and slanting eyes, not to mention a pushed-in nose and big lips. But it was his thick tongue that awkwardly moved around in his mouth, as if he was unable to find a comfortable spot, that gave me concern. The long forceps used in breech births to pull the baby from the birth canal had left a red streak on both his cheeks, which did nothing to improve his appearance. He looked as though he had just fought ten rounds and come out the loser. I wondered if he might have "mongolism" (Down's syndrome) and I quickly checked to see if he had a transverse crease ~ one straight crease across the palms of his hands and the bottom of his feet. It was difficult to know for sure as I examined his little hand, then checked mine to see if it was different. Mine had several creases, baby Woods' hands were questionable. I had never seen a transverse crease before, so I called the intermediate over to look.

"I'm not sure, Yates," she said, studying her own hands, then the baby's. "But I agree that baby Woods' crease is questionable."

Then I remembered the words of our instructor who had warned us about checking for birth defects. "Before you jump to any conclusions," she'd said, "look at the baby's father. Some unusual characteristics run in families, and if baby looks like father, then baby is probably normal."

"I hope Dr. Thomas will arrive soon to check the baby and make a proper diagnosis before the father arrives," I said.

At that moment, there was a knock on the window. The intermediate opened the door, spoke briefly to someone then returned. "Mr. Woods wants to see his baby," she said.

I pushed baby Woods with his stubby hands and feet and flattened face to the window and opened the Venetian blinds. There stood Mr. Woods, with slanting eyes, a pushed-in face and a tongue that seemed too big for his mouth, cooing and gooing and waving at his baby. I stifled a giggle. Baby was the spitting image of Daddy. Baby Woods was normal.

The following week I was back on nights in the Case Room. I admitted Mrs. Palmer to the Labour Room. Her contractions were not severe, but her water had broken and her doctor thought she should be near the Case Room. As I wrote her vital signs on the large blackboard in the hall, the intermediate from the Nursery walked by with a bottle of lemonade.

"I see you have Mrs. Palmer," she said. "She was my patient on maternity."

She checked the board. "Fetal heart rate 144. What do you want to bet?"

"Bet you it's a boy," I smiled.

"Okay, you're on. I'll bet a buck it's a girl."

"You're going to lose your money. If the heartbeat is in the 140s, it's a boy. Above 150, it's always a girl." I waved as she walked away. "Keep that buck handy. It'll be mine tomorrow."

Mrs. Palmer's contractions, however, petered out and they sent her back to the maternity ward to wait until her labour began again. The sac surrounding the baby ruptured when her water broke. There was now a hole, a dangerous opening to the outside ~ an entry for bacteria. If Mrs. Palmer remained upright, the umbilical cord might drop down through this opening, twist, and cut off the oxygen to the fetus. Thus Mrs. Palmer had to remain in bed.

The next night I stopped at the Nursery to speak to the intermediate. "Mrs. Palmer's contractions have stopped," I said. "We're going to have to bet on another baby."

We did. I won.

A few days later I met Mrs. Palmer walking down the hall, still obviously pregnant. She had an intravenous running in her arm and was pushing the I.V. pole. She looked upset and I thought she had lost weight.

"Having a baby is supposed to be a happy occasion," she moaned. "Mine has turned into a nightmare." Her face tightened and she began to sob. "My baby's dead."

"Dead?" I repeated, my eyes fixed on her bulging body.

"One minute he's okay, and the next he's gone." She covered her face with her hands and wept uncontrollably.

I flinched, in shock. She pulled a Kleenex from the pocket of her housecoat and blew her nose. Then, through her sobs, she told me her contractions had stopped in the Labour Room and the doctor sent her back to the maternity ward.

"The next day the nurses couldn't get the baby's heartbeat," she said. "It was gone." She bit her lip and lay her head against the intravenous pole as if somehow it would console her. "Gone ... " she whispered.

"I'm so sorry, Mrs. Palmer. So very sorry," I said as I lay my arm on her shoulder. My mind flashed back to the excitement we'd had charting the baby's heartbeat on the blackboard. My eyes began to burn but I clenched my teeth and fought back my normal reaction to cry. I had to keep talking. Empathy. Support the patient.

"I see they are inducing you," I said, noticing that pitocin, a drug used to induce contractions of the uterus, had been added to the intravenous bottle.

"But nothing is happening," she moaned. "All I want is to get this over so I can go home." She looked straight into my eyes. "How can I give birth to a dead baby? The thought is unbearable," she began to sob. "Just unbearable!"

Her words numbed me. I desperately tried to hide my horror. I stood helplessly staring back into her questioning eyes but unable to find an appropriate response.

"They told me to walk," she said taking a deep breath. "It's supposed to help restart my contractions."

"Can I get you coffee, juice, some toast?" I had to do something for her ~ *anything*.

"No, thank you. My husband will be here soon." She turned away from me and continued down the hall, dragging the intravenous pole with her.

For the next two days I watched Mrs. Palmer walk up and down the hall, silently grieving as her baby decomposed in her womb. A sticky putrid fluid oozed out of her, drop, by drop.

I spied Dr. Humphrey in the hall, and rushed over to ask her why Mrs. Palmer had to endure such misery. Couldn't she do a caesarean? Was it so difficult to deliver a dead baby?

"Yes," Dr. Humphrey said. "It is *very* difficult to deliver a dead baby. A caesarean is out of the question. You see the baby is decomposing. That increases the risk of infection and could even cause septicemia, which would be fatal to the mother." She shook her head sadly. "Cases of petrifaction of the fetus inside the womb have been reported. In some instances the fetus was not passed for years. But fortunately Mrs. Palmer has already begun to slowly dilate."

And everyone prayed that she would deliver soon.

The next night, we had just sat down for coffee at 3:00 a.m. when Dr. Humphrey walked into the nurses' room and said, "Mrs. Palmer is in strong labour. She's ready to deliver but I'm going to leave her in her room until the last minute. I don't want her to be with the other women in the labour room. Just get her in and out of the case room as quickly as possible. It's bad enough that she has to pass the Nursery with all those babies crying."

The skinny grad turned to me. "Yates, go scrub."

Mrs. Palmer arrived in the Case Room on a stretcher. She was beginning to push. Her contractions were severe and she groaned in pain. But there would be no reward at the end of this painful struggle. No little baby to cry. And when it was over, she would not ask if her baby was normal.

It was a long ordeal, and although the anaesthetist was present, he could do nothing to ease her pain. Any anaesthesia or sedatives might reduce the contractions or even cause them to stop. Mrs. Palmer had to do this alone. All we could offer her was encouragement until the baby was out. At times Mother Nature is rough, even downright cruel. Mrs. Palmer's baby was not pushing down the birth canal searching for life, fighting to take its first breath, its first cry. Her baby would never feel its mother's gentle embrace, nor taste the warm nourishment that filled her engorged, overripe breasts.

The room was hot. Even though we wore two masks to block the odour, the stench of decaying flesh was nauseating. The wretched fluid kept pouring out of this woman and her pain continued and continued. Soon she became exhausted. At one point I began to worry that this thing might never get out.

"Keep pushing, Betty," urged Dr. Humphrey in a kind but stern voice.

"I can't. No more ... "

"You have to. Come on, Betty. Push!"

"No, I can't," she wailed. "I want to die."

"Squeeze my hand," said the grad, stroking Betty's forehead. "Harder. Squeeze. Good girl."

"Push, Betty, that's a girl," said Dr. Humphrey earnestly. "It's coming. Good girl. Push!"

With every groan and thrust that Betty had the strength to muster, the fetus slowly inched out. The head ... an arm ... and another ... until with one final enormous splash of putrid fluid it slithered into the silver basin the doctor held.

I tried not to look but my eyes were drawn to the fetus. It was the shape of a baby, but it had macerated. Layer after layer of skin had sloughed off taking the baby's distinct features with it. The anaesthetist immediately strapped a mask on Betty's face and pumped the welcomed gas into her exhausted, empty body. Betty's difficult task was over. Now she could sleep.

I looked up. Sister Dakota stood in the doorway fingering her rosary, her lips moving in prayer. Holding a little cup, she went to the sink for some water. Then to the grim basin. She poured the water over the fetus' head, and as she did so, mumbled, *"Au Nom Du Pere, Du Fils, et Du Saint Esprit, Amen."* In the name of The Father, The Son, and The Holy Ghost, Amen.

We Protestants had been taught how to baptize a fetus if one of the Sisters or a Catholic was unavailable. It must be performed immediately.

Then the grad whisked the silent basin with the fetus away to pathology. The Sisters had a little corner in their garden reserved for burying fetuses. They adamantly refused to allow pathology to put them into the garbage. And I felt better knowing that.

The next day, with only two hours of sleep, I was awakened at noon to an unbelievable ruckus. I charged down the hall to the lounge like a groggy bull. Everyone was in a huddle around someone in a chair by the window.

"What's all the noise about?" I shouted. "I'm working nights. Have a little consideration."

Ingraham, whom I had worked with in Emergency, quickly turned to me. "Sorry, Yates," she said, "we're celebrating ~ Simm's engaged!"

"Again?" I said.

"Some people have all the luck," said Standish, whom I had hardly seen since we left Ponoka. "I probably won't even get one proposal and Simm gets two before we're finished training."

"I'd sure the hell like to know where you find the time," White said to Simm. "I only have time to work and sleep."

Simm certainly had managed to find the time, all right. She now had a huge rock on her ring finger. "Patrick is a Catholic," she said. "I'm going to convert, but not until after graduation. There's no way I'm going to give up my free hour while we're in block, to go to religion class." Simm spoke with the conviction of a true Protestant.

That evening I went home for supper and fell asleep while waiting for the meal. Falling asleep anywhere at any time was the defining characteristic of a student nurse. When my mother woke me, she said, "You have to get more sleep, dear. Every time you come home you fall asleep on the couch."

"I could fall asleep while a war went on right here on the living room rug."

I was still groggy when my brother, Allan, dropped his bomb at the dinner table. "I've enrolled in medicine at the university. I want to be a doctor," he said.

Everyone gave a little gasp of surprise. Then we felt a silence while Dad finished chewing his roast beef and swallowed. "What about your music?" he said, angrily. "I thought music was going to be your career."

"I've written Leonard Bernstein, the conductor of the New York Philharmonic Orchestra," Allan quickly said. "I asked Bernstein what he thought my chances were of becoming a conductor. He wrote a letter back to me. I have it right here."

Eyebrows went up as Allan pulled the letter from his shirt pocket and began to read:

Dear Allan,

... There are many good musicians as qualified as I am to conduct an orchestra. But it's a matter of getting the breaks, being in the right place at the right time. I was lucky, but there are a lot of musicians playing in my orchestra who are as good or even better than I am.

So I guess my advice to you, Allan, is if you think you can't be happy playing your trumpet in an orchestra then I suggest that you choose another profession and play trumpet for pleasure.

Best of luck in your future profession.

Sincerely,

Leonard Bernstein

Allan carefully folded the letter, slid it into his shirt pocket, then looked up at Mom and Dad and said, "So I found another profession. Medicine."

"Hey, that's great, Allan," I said. "You'll make a good doctor. Maybe I can work for you one day."

The night before the orthopedics exam, I was cramming in the lounge with Perry, when she asked, "Hey, if a patient is in neck traction, do you lift the weights before you change his bed?"

"Yes," I said. "But it takes two people because one has to support the head."

"Yeah," Porter said. "Especially if his neck is broken."

"Damn," I said. "I can never remember when *not* to lift the weights."

Just then Niven strutted into the lounge, pocketbook in hand. "Who wants to go to a movie?" she said in a breezy manner.

"Movie?" gasped Perry. "Are you kidding? We're going to write orthopedics tomorrow, Niv, in case you've forgotten."

"So, who needs to study for that crappy exam? It'll do you more good to get out and relax at a movie. Look at this beautiful spring evening going to waste," she motioned to the window.

I turned and looked out onto the early spring evening. It was beginning to stay light longer ~ 6:15 and the pale-yellow sun had only begun to set over the Rockies. The streets were almost dry and I could smell the exciting freshness of an April evening. The same freshness that had lured me as a child after supper out into the streets to play kick-the-can with the other kids until the streetlights turned on ~ our cue to head for home.

"So," Niven said, jolting me back to orthopedic-bed-frames and traction.

"Niven," I said, this is an important block. If you fail ... well ... look what you've thrown away, almost three years. I think you should stay home and study."

"You know what I think?" Niven sneered, "I think you're all a bunch of chicken livers." She turned and stomped to the elevator. Then she was gone.

"Far be it from me to say anything about studying," said White. "Have you ever noticed that Niven never studies but always manages to pass? ~ and with good marks!"

The next morning we gathered in the lounge before going down to write our exam. As we sipped our coffee in the solemn silence, Andresen suddenly slammed her cup down, turned to Niven and said sharply, "You little sneak." We all jumped, wondering at the cause of her outburst. Her bright blue eyes flashed violet and her Norwegian colour flared.

"I couldn't sleep last night, and I came out here for some milk." Andresen said, her face even flushed. "Your light was on, Niv. It was on the whole night. What the heck are you trying to prove? Who cares if you study or not. We sure don't. But don't give us all that bullshit about going to a movie and not studying."

White turned to Niven. "Is that right, Niv?"

"I didn't study the *whole* night," Niven mumbled with a silly, guilty smile. "Well, okay, I might have looked at my notes." She glanced around the room. "So what? What's it to you guys?"

White burst out laughing. "Niven, you are a goddamn little sneak."

The truth was out. Now I knew that Niven had to work for her marks like the rest of us.

To celebrate the completion of our senior classroom block, we hit the York for a beer.

"Onwards and upwards," Andresen said, as she stood up and held out her frothy glass of beer. "Here's to our final exams. Oh, God, they're just around the corner."

"Yea!" we shouted, even Kaufmann.

"Hey Andresen," I said, "how did you ever convince Kaufmann to come?"

"I told her she could drink tomato juice."

"Oh-oh, Kaufmann," I said holding up my frothy glass of beer. "That's how I started."

Dreams and Demons

From the nursery, I was immediately rotated to St. Anne's, the orthopedic ward, where every day was a new challenge. Being a senior meant additional responsibility of helping the juniors and intermediates.

Pressure intensified. In addition to new ward responsibilities, I would be responsible for supervising and supporting the junior student nurses. I hoped I could give them the courage and confidence I had so readily received from my seniors. Soon I learned that not only could I take charge of my juniors, I could also nurse patients in traction with fractured legs and hips, fractured back, neck and even a fractured skull ~ and I could remember when to lift and when not to lift the weights.

That I could lift a 200-pound woman in a full plaster body cast onto a bedpan myself in the dead of night when help was not available. That I could help the grad turn a patient with pathological fractures of almost every bone in her body, and then weep because her pain could not be eased by any drug ~ and when she died, I caught three buses on my day off and trudged a mile in the spring mud through a new development to attend her cold, Greek Orthodox funeral.

It was a perfect week for the Calgary Stampede and I was working the day shift on St. Anne's. When I arrived on the ward on Tuesday, the second day of the Stampede, the patients' radios were blaring out reports of Monday's infield results ~ the bull riding, steer decorating, calf roping, chuck wagon races and of the tragic bucking horse event casualty, Chris Knight.

"Look, Dad," he shouted in his delirium as I approached the Stryker. "There's a beautiful chestnut. How much is she? Goddamn that's too much! Tell the bugger it's too much for that horse."

Chris Knight was the cowboy with the broken neck. He lay on a Stryker frame, a bandage covering his neck incision where the surgeon had repaired and fused his fractured cervical vertebrae. A strap across his forehead immobilized his head, and body straps bound him tightly to the narrow Stryker bed, which was a tight canvas hammock fixed between two metal frames. It kept Chris immobile and his spine stable.

"What the hell do *you* want?" he shouted when his eyes shifted to me as I and an intermediate prepared to turn him over in the Stryker. "I'm not selling that mare. Do you hear me?"

Every two hours we placed the top frame over his body, screwed and strapped it to the bottom frame then safely flipped him over without disturbing his spine. The top frame, with a hole for his face, became the bottom frame and he lay prone staring at the floor. Two hours later, we sandwiched him between the frames and flipped him back.

Chris Knight was paralysed. His tragic fall had not only fractured his neck but also severed his spinal cord, rendering him a quadriplegic ~ forever.

Two bottles of intravenous fluid dripped slowly into his arm. His family huddled in the corridor trying to comfort one another. His mother and father, older brother and young fiancée were waiting for the surgeon, hoping against hope for some positive news. The surgeon arrived and spoke to them. They cried and embraced … and they mourned their loss. Not for Chris Knight, the person, for he would never change. They mourned the vibrant, active Chris Knight who walked, ran and gestured. The man who held his fiancée tightly in his arms and rushed off to work to stand in front of a class of students, the Chris Knight who drove his truck to rodeos and climbed on wild, bucking horses.

As I approached his bed I worried … what would I say to him? My paralysed patients had been old people. Chris Knight was young and healthy and now all he could do was talk and blink his eyes … and breathe.

My mind whirled when I thought of that fraction of a second that had changed Chris's life. His normal, every-day-taken-for-granted-life was gone, wiped out by just one of the thousands of falls he had taken from a horse. The sudden transformation was such a shock to his body that his mind couldn't keep up. And so his mind left his body.

"I'm not selling that mare. Do you hear me?"

He lay motionless, eyes fixed on the ceiling and he shouted orders to imaginary people as scenes from his former life flashed by, that life now bidding him farewell.

Again and again I would quietly tell him he had an accident.

He was in Holy Cross Hospital.

Was he in pain?

But he would be back with the auctioneers, his Dad, or anyone else in his imaginary world. His father stood helpless by his bed and begged him to answer, begged him to come back to the real world. But for the moment, Chris's delusions protected him from the cruel, agonizing truth ~ he would never walk again, never embrace his mother or fiancée or feel their arms about him, he would never feed himself or dance, never feel the grass at his feet or a horse beneath him. That now was his reality.

I glanced at my watch; it was 2:00 p.m. Yesterday at this time, Chris Knight had been preparing to ride. He had drawn a big Appaloosa and a time of 2:03 p.m. The horse was a mean one, known for its malicious twists, the kind that make cowboys happy; they can ride for the big bucks.

Chris was a teacher in a rural school and it was summer vacation, a time when he always rode the circuit. Not only for the extra money, but because he loved the thrill of the rodeos. Like all cowboys, he loved the smell of the animals, the dusty infield, and the sound of the horn at the end of a vicious ride from a spiteful horse.

A month before, he had become engaged to Shauna. They planned a December wedding to tie in perfectly with Christmas vacation and a honeymoon skiing in Lake Louise. Shauna had bought her dress and arranged for a two-week vacation from her job as a dental assistant. Now she stood with the Knight family in the waiting room shrouded in uncertainty, wondering what turn their lives would take, what turn *her* life would take.

The next morning Chris continued to rant and rave deliriously. The doctors juggled intravenous solutions in an effort to balance the electrolytes in his body and bring him back to reality.

I gave him injections regularly to relieve his pain, but Chris would sleep only briefly after each injection. The other three patients in the room spent two long sleepless nights listening to his ranting, but the only one to complain was the large man in the bed kitty-corner to Chris.

Mr. Mario Marino had fractured several vertebrae and he continually, as Miss Deitz politely put it, *broke wind*. At times he would give forth a squiggly squeak, like air being slowly let out of a balloon. At other moments he dropped a bomb.

Always done without batting an eye, as if he were about to say, "Please pass the potatoes."

One morning as I approached Chris in the Stryker bed, his ocean-blue eyes shifted to me.

"Jesus Christ," he shouted. "Here comes that farting nurse again. Every time she comes near me, she farts!"

I buried my face in my hands to hide my laughter and dashed out to tell Miss Deitz. She always enjoyed a good laugh.

On the fourth morning I walked over to Chris, ready to give him his bath. He was quiet, staring at the ceiling. "How are you feeling?" I asked.

"Not good." His eyes turned to the window. "Dr. Newman was here," he said in a whisper.

Chris's delusions had played themselves out ... he now knew his fate. Oh, God, how will he cope? What could I say to a man who was active one moment and totally immobile the next? What could I say to a man who thought he was no longer a man?

"This must be very hard for you." I said quietly as I knelt down to the Stryker bed and rested my hand on his arm. He had no feeling in his limbs but I wanted to show him that I cared. What else could I do?

"I'm so sorry. It's terrible ... what you've been through." Another few moments passed silently. "Dr. Newman has ordered physiotherapy," I said trying to sound encouraging. "It will start today. It will help your circulation. Your fractures will heal soon and you'll feel better."

"I'll never feel better," he said slowly, his eyes defiant, yet defeated.

"Your family is pulling for you. They love you very much. You haven't changed, Chris. You're still the same person."

I tried to feed him breakfast. "Just take a little Cream of Wheat. It will help you get strong."

His eyes turned back to the window, and closed.

We talked very little as I bathed him. I felt that he wanted to be with his own thoughts and there was nothing I could say that would make him feel better. I washed his heavy limp arms and legs and massaged them with alcohol and powder. There will come a time, I thought, when he would want to talk. But right now he needed space and silence to grieve, to regret, to be angry. In time he would accept the unacceptable.

His parents and fiancée arrived during visiting hours. Dr. Newman spoke to them in the waiting room. "It would help Chris if you come at mealtime and try to feed him," Dr. Newman said to Shauna.

Shauna did. After she fed Chris, she sat for long hours on a chair beside his Stryker bed, or stretched out on the floor, looking up into his face as he lay on his stomach. At first he was despondent. The following week his eyes tightened and flashed anger and frustration.

"Go away, Shauna. I don't want to see you. Go and find someone else. I'm no good to you any more. Don't you see? Don't you understand?"

But Shauna was not to be dismayed and continued to come each day, quietly trying to convince him that he was still the same person she loved. Still the same man with whom she wanted to spend the rest of her life.

Slowly Chris began to smile. His eyes brightened and he laughed with her once again. And I hoped they would find a way to continue their lives as a couple.

On Monday, I started working a short-change shift ~ eight hours on, eight hours off. I worked days then went back at 11:30 and worked nights.

When I returned to orthopedics on my first night, I met 68-year-old Ron Davies. He had fractured his hip that afternoon. His shoulder-length stringy, grey hair was terribly smelly and I had to scrub his fingernails for ten minutes to get rid of the embedded dirt. I made a great effort to clean his grimy feet, but there was not enough time to whip him into shape before the end of my shift so I had to leave him for the day staff to finish.

Mr. Davies was to go the OR mid-morning for a hip pinning. When I returned to work at 1:30 p.m. Tuesday, the evening nurse reported that he had become confused during the day. "Perhaps the effects of the anaesthetic," she suggested. "Be sure to watch him closely."

Mr. Davies' condition became considerably worse. By Wednesday night, his body shook violently, he perspired profusely and he was unbelievably confused. At 3 a.m. I called Mrs. Noseworthy, the night supervisor, who came to see Mr. Davies.

He shouted and flailed about in the bed. "They're going to kill me. Help! Snakes! Get back. Get back!" Then he spied the intravenous tube in his arm and began to pull it out. "Help ... they're attacking me!"

Mrs. Noseworthy and I both jumped to hold him but he was too strong. I ran for the orderly. The three of us had to wrestle with him for several minutes before we could tie his arms down. The restraints would keep him from harming himself but they also increased his agitation. His hallucinations worsened.

Mrs. Noseworthy motioned to me to follow her into the corridor. "I think Mr. Davies is exhibiting a full-blown case of delirium tremens," she said. "In other words, the d.t.'s. I'm going to call Dr. Newman. Stay with Mr. Davies until Dr. Newman arrives."

"It's certainly the d.t.'s." Dr. Newman yawned and gave his head a quick scratch, then turned to me. "What are the symptoms of d.t.'s, nurse?"

"Delirium, agitation, disorientation."

He nodded.

"Perspiration, hallucinations."

"Good, good. And now, what causes them and what's the treatment?"

"Alcohol withdrawl. Ah ... give a Molotov cocktail." I raised my eyebrows, "You think he's an alcoholic, Doctor Newman?"

He nodded again. "I'm going to give him that cocktail and a sedative, and I hope it will help him to settle." Another yawn. "We see many people, especially destitute, alcoholic men like this who fall and break their hips. While they're in hospital and can't continue drinking, their bodies go into withdrawal." He threw his hands in the air. "*Voila!* d.t.'s."

I mixed the cocktail, a combination of vitamin B, electrolytes, and a small amount of alcohol that I added to a bottle of glucose and water intravenous fluid. Dr. Newman also ordered a dose of paraldehyde per rectum, always effective for quieting elderly, confused patients.

The combination hardly worked on Ron Davies. He screamed while the phantom snakes slithered over his bed. He was terrified. He cried, begged, pleaded. "Take them away. Get me out of here."

Although he frightened me, I tried to calm him, but he was unaware of me. He had to somehow fight his demons alone, with his arms and legs tied down. My heart ached for him. I wondered how long he would, or could continue in this state. But his life of alcohol would not surrender easily and for three more days he thrashed about in Dante's Inferno.

The short change shift tormented me with insufferable insomnia and for three nights I stumbled about in sleep deprivation. When I crawled into bed on Thursday at 9 a.m. my eyes burned as if they had been prodded all night by hot pokers, yet I couldn't fall asleep. Then just as I finally dropped into a deep slumber, shouts from the girls thumping down the hall awoke me. Wearing only the green operating room top, I jumped out of bed and flew into the hall like a ruffled nest-hen. I almost slipped on the pool of water that came streaming down the corridor.

Then I felt the stinging blast of water on my face. A probie welding a rubber hose from the tap in the laundry room, aimed it at her classmate who darted in front of me. She ducked the stream of water ~ I received it ~ full force. It was the famous water fight.

"What the hell are you brats trying to prove? I'm working nights! I have a red tag on my door. Don't you have any consideration?" I turned and paddled down the hall, thinking that I now understood how the seniors had felt when we, as probies, invaded their floor.

"Just wait until you get on nights," I muttered as I slipped back into bed after changing into another green top. "Hope some stupid probies wake you up. Then you'll know what it's like." And I thought, God, I'm going to be tired tonight.

And I was. That night when I dragged my weary self to report, I suddenly perked up on receiving an encouraging report from the evening nurse. "Mr. Davies has been quiet, and even ate a little supper," she said. "I didn't remove the restraints, but you can evaluate him and see what you think."

When I made my first round at 12:15 a.m. he was quiet and looked comfortable.

"Do you know where you are?" I asked.

He nodded and gave a weak smile. "The Holy Cross. I fell and broke my hip." His voice was soft, his eyes downcast and he slowly opened and closed his hand which had become stiff and sore from the restraints.

I asked him the time and where he lived, to see if he was oriented to time and place.

"I think it's around midnight. I'm in Calgary. And I live on First Street Southeast." He looked a little embarrassed about having to answer childish questions.

I removed the restraints on his arms and said, "Don't touch the intravenous tubing."

Ron Davies was over the hurdle. He had successfully wrestled his alcohol withdrawal to the bitter end and would remain comfortable while his hip healed. But Dr. Newman told me that the odds that Mr. Davies would stay sober were not great.

"It's too bad for these old guys," he said as we walked out of Mr. Davies' room. "The minute they go home, they start drinking all over again. Their dependency on alcohol picks up where it left off."

Miss Greene, our clinical instructor, said the same thing in a lecture she gave one day. "It is a pity," she said. "Their courageous battle through the d.t.s was all for naught."

One night, just as Leo the lion roared from the zoo on St. George's Island, Mrs. Noseworthy sent me to St. Francis' ward at 4 a.m. "A new patient is having an acute schizophrenic attack," she said, "and the special can't handle him alone."

I had no trouble finding the room. I heard the man screaming all the way down at the nurses' station. I spied the grad sitting near the wall, watching the patient as I nervously entered the room. A floor lamp stood between them, which cast a gentle, yellowish glow on the patient's face. It produced a frightening effect, as if the man was wearing a mask like a madman. He grew strangely quiet when he turned his large, terror-stricken eyes in my direction. He lay in a tangle of sheets, his black hair dishevelled. I hesitated.

"Hello," the grad whispered. "Come over here. It's okay." She smiled, reassuringly and I cautiously made my way across the room.

"Now, first of all, this man can and may be very dangerous. He is in acute crisis. We're really not equipped to handle psychiatric patients, however, remember this: DO NOT TURN YOUR BACK ON THIS MAN. Is that clear?"

"Yes," I whispered, unable to take my eyes off the patient.

"If you need to handle the patient, make sure someone is with you."

I nodded, and blinked quickly. My eyes felt twice their normal size.

"I've called for the orderly to help us lift Mr. Werner into the bathtub. Water is soothing. It's good for anxiety. Let's hope it will calm him." She motioned to the bathroom. "Go and fill the tub with warm water ~ not more than 100 degrees. The orderly will be here soon."

My hands shook as I held the bath thermometer in the tub. This was a special tub, much larger than normal, with a little ledge inside at the end of the tub for the patient to sit on.

Harold, the orderly, arrived, a tall man much too thin, I thought, to lift this wild-looking patient. He lowered the bed rail and pulled back the covers. That is when I noticed Mr. Werner was in a straitjacket.

"Get away from me, you dirty bastards!" Mr. Werner shouted.

I wasn't expecting this outburst. I gasped and seized the grad's arm. She let out a terrifying scream. Harold chuckled and winked at me.

"I know the Queen, she's my wife. You'll all hang for this," Mr. Werner said, darkly. His jacket was white heavy cotton. The long ends of the sleeves were used to cross his arms and tightly bind them on his chest. It was impossible for him to move. The grad and I each took a leg, Harold was to take the top half but suddenly he let out a shriek of pain.

"Ouch," he cried as he slid his arms under Mr. Werner's shoulders. Somehow the patient managed to sink his teeth into Harold's index finger. "Damn!" he said, wrapping his finger in a Kleenex.

"Ha!" bellowed Mr. Werner. "That'll teach you. You don't believe me, do you? I am the King!" He cackled an almost inhuman sound.

"Let's get him into the water ~ fast!" said Harold, with a look that told me his finger hurt more than he cared to admit.

We got the patient in the tub. Harold quickly placed the canvas top, which was stretched between two metal rods, over him and secured it to the sides of the tub. Mr. Werner's head protruded through a small hole. He looked like a man taking a steam bath at an exclusive men's club, except that his eyes burned with raw rage.

"Where are my guards?" he bellowed. "Guards. Guards! Help!"

Harold hurried off to get a Band-Aid for his finger. The grad went for her break and left me to watch Mr. Werner. He sat on the ledge in his watery cocoon, eyeing me with suspicion. I sat bolt upright on my little chair, watching him. Could he hear my heart pounding?

"Think you're smart, don't you." He finally said in a low, spiteful voice. "I'm the one who will be laughing soon. I'll have you thrown into the moat and the alligators will eat you for lunch." He threw his head back and emitted a bloodcurdling, sadistic squeal.

I didn't answer. I was afraid to talk to him and I didn't turn my back to him. After a long 15 minutes of mumbling he grew quiet. He didn't close his eyes, but he seemed to be more comfortable.

"Must be the paraldehyde," said the grad when she returned. "It really helps to quiet these patients."

When I got to bed that morning I couldn't sleep. Mr. Werner was in an ambulance somewhere between Calgary and Ponoka, locked in that straitjacket. He was so sick. Would they give him those awful shock treatments? Would he ever be well again?

I flushed with excitement as I read the next schedule: Yates: Emergency, Two weeks, 7:30 ~ 3:30.

Monday morning I pinned my shiny senior pin on my uniform. It was a beautiful pin, *Semper Fidelis* (always faithful) H✠H written in gold across the red crest of the hospital. After morning prayer, I reported to emergency. The room was messy and still crowded with patients who had come in during the long night. I had just begun to tidy up when I heard a man's voice in the hall calling for help.

I dashed to the hall to see a man in his late 40s rushing towards me, his hand wrapped in a towel saturated with blood. It trickled down his arm like red lines on a road map. I steered him into the treatment room and sent his wife, who was circling round him like a wet hen, up to the admissions office on the first floor. "A useful way of giving hysterical relatives something positive to do," the head nurse had once told me. "And it gets them out of our way."

"Cut my hand with the meat cleaver," the patient said as I helped him up onto the examining table.

He wore a white apron that tied round his waist. It was heavily stained with dark blood ~ old blood.

"A butcher?" I asked.

He nodded.

I began to unwrap the towel that I was sure was holding his hand together. It was saturated with bright blood, fresh blood ~ his blood. What am I doing here? I felt squeamish, more than squeamish, actually, and I cast my eyes round the room for someone, anyone, to come and take my place. I can't do this. I don't *want* to do this. But every nurse was behind a curtain helping someone who had suddenly become victim of their own, or someone else's, carelessness. I had to unwrap the hand. Beneath that towel was another towel, and another. With each layer I unravelled, I expected his severed hand to tumble out, or maybe a finger or two. The last wrap was a cotton, flower-print blouse. I wanted to close my eyes but I had to at least *appear* confident, so I took a deep breath and tried to pretend that I did this every day.

"Oh, it's not so bad." I said nonchalantly when I realized all his fingers were intact. I tossed the bloody blouse-cum-bandage into the silver garbage pail on the floor. "I've seen worse," I added proudly.

The man received 30 stitches. As the doctor sewed up his wounds, the patient told us of the other times, and there were many, when he wound up in emergency to be stitched back together.

"The joy of being a butcher," said the patient with a half-smile.

"An occupational hazard, if you ask me," mumbled the doctor.

Wednesday, the middle of a busy week, I arrived at 7:30 a.m. to a messy room that told of another crazy night. A 22-year-old woman lay on a stretcher in the end room, head turned to the wall, both wrists bandaged.

I walked over to her bed. "Are you in pain?" I asked. She shook her head. I stroked her forehead, and my heart went out to her. Her chart told her story: the third time in a year she had attempted suicide by slashing her wrists. This time she had severed her tendon. The intern telephoned Dr. Hanson, the plastic surgeon, who would perform the tendon repair.

"You're going to feel much better after your operation," I said softly, trying to encourage her. She turned her head and raised her hauntingly sad eyes to mine. There was no sign of hope, not even a flicker. It had spilled out of her wounds in her warm, young blood. She knew I understood, and turned to face the wall again.

Dr. Hanson entered the room and walked slowly to her bed. "I'm sorry, Loraine," he said quietly, "but I have to report this to the police. This is your third attempt ... we have to make the report this time."

Loraine didn't answer, didn't move. She gave a slight nod indicating that she had heard the doctor.

"What will become of Loraine?" I asked Dr. Hanson as he sat at the desk writing in her chart. "What will the police do?"

"Probably nothing," he said, taking off his glasses. "But she will be started on a good program of psychotherapy and hopefully that will help. Are you aware that the law requires doctors to report all attempted suicides to the police?"

"Yes," I answered. "But I feel sorry for her."

"So do I," he said, replacing his glasses. "So do I."

That night was Home Night, an evening held monthly with entertainment provided by rotating classes. It was exciting and welcomed, a contrast to the sorrow of the emergency day shift. Tanner was a runner-up for the May Queen. Our class almost brought the house down with our cheering, and White and Niven did an outstanding job of whistling. Tanner looked so professional in her flowered print dress and white, high-heeled shoes. When we arrived back in the lounge after the celebration, a bouquet of 24 red roses sat on the coffee table amid old over-read *Cosmopolitan* magazines. The flowers were for Tanner. She read the card out loud.

To the love of my life. Congratulations!
All my love, Ralph

The pre-natal clinic took place once a month in Emergency. The intern and a gynecologist followed these young unwed girls throughout their pregnancy until the time they delivered their baby in the hospital. Sixteen-year-old Sally was very close to delivering her baby when she crawled clumsily up onto the scales for me to weigh her.

"I've been dreading this all week," she groaned. "Gosh, look at me, I'm as big as a cow."

"This is serious, Sally," I said, noting her weight-gain. "It's dangerous for you and the baby."

She threw a playful look at Trudy, a young girl licking an orange Popsicle and reading a Captain Marvel comic book. They both giggled as Sally sat down beside her.

"Just look at you girls," said the head nurse standing in the doorway, hands braced on hips. "You're drinking Cokes and eating those awful Popsicles. Didn't I tell you last month to stop drinking Cokes? First thing you know you're going to develop toxemia. Drink water instead. And think about calories, too. Eat only healthy food with lots of vitamins."

Trudy raised her eyes to the head nurse and gave a casual shrug.

Sally and Trudy were typical of the girls the nuns took under their wings. The Sisters housed the girls, provided medical care and made sure they received counselling before giving birth. The girls came to us from other cities to deliver their babies and usually gave them up for adoption. Then most of them returned to their families. This type of exchange took place among the nuns of Catholic hospitals across Canada. We sent the Calgary girls to British Columbia, or Saskatchewan, and the girls from those provinces came to us. When an unwed mother kept her baby, that was the exception. There was no assistance for these mothers and many were too immature to raise a child. The counsellors and nuns strongly encouraged them to give up their baby and get on with their own life. These girls were the mothers of many of the back-row babies, the feed-ins, the illegits.

When I arrived on Thursday, emergency was tidy and quiet. Just as I was going for lunch, the ambulance attendants rushed down the hall with a young woman on a stretcher.

"Cancel your lunch, Yates. You'd better admit this patient," I was told.

"We got a call from a friend of hers," said the ambulance driver as we moved her onto the hospital stretcher. "Must'a been her boyfriend. Said she had an abortion. You know, one of those back-street butcher types."

The intern helped to help move the patient onto the hospital stretcher.

"Accordin' to the boyfriend, about two days ago," the ambulance attendant said throwing a glance at his partner.

"Right," the other attendant confirmed.

"When we got there," said the first man, "well, she was barely conscious. Burning up with fever. Confused. Stopped answering us on the way here. She's bleedin' a lot, too."

The intern picked up the covers. Bright blood flowed from between her legs in a steady trickle. It had soaked her sheets.

"Call the OR," he blurted to the grad. "Tell them we have to do a D&C stat! I'll call Dr. Sullivan." The intern turned to me. "Get an I.V. going and get her blood typed and cross-matched as soon as possible. We've got to get some blood into her."

"I've got Sister Champagne on the phone from the OR," shouted the grad from the desk in the hall. "She wants to see some fetal tissue before she books the D&C."

"Christ Almighty," shot the intern. "What does she want, a direct consent from God?"

The grad had returned to the room. "Can't get past that nun without living proof that the fetus is dead and has been passed, or at least that the patient's passing *some* of it."

"Goddamn it to hell! I'm not going to perform an abortion. I'm going to try to save this girl's life after she's had an abortion ~ and a shitty botched-up one at that."

His eyes met mine. "These back-street butchers are criminal," he seethed through his teeth. "They murder the mother as well as the fetus."

"Do you think she is going to die?" I whispered.

He palpated the woman's stomach then walked to the desk, muttering, "Not if I can help it. But who knows. Who the hell knows ... "

The grad came back with a container and scooped up some blood from between the woman's legs. "I'll send this to the lab and you had better pray there's some tissue here."

We began to shave-prep the girl, but the intern shot his head through the curtains. "For God's sake, forget that. There's no time."

The orderly whisked her away to the OR. A few moments later, the phone rang. It was Sister Champagne demanding to speak to the intern.

"Sister, I just can't do that. I'm sorry Sister, but that girl is going to bleed to death." He was trying not to shout. A few moments of silence passed, presumably while Sister Champagne expounded the rules of performing a D&C.

"Yes, Sister," he said through his teeth. He banged down the phone then turned to me. "Try to believe this," he said straining to hold his composure.

"Sister isn't going to let the patient into the OR. 'Over my dead body,' she said. I suppose that saintly holier-than-thou nun is lying on the floor this very minute, stretched over the OR line to block the stretcher from entering her domain. This is preposterous," he said in a throaty whisper, wiping the sweat that glistened on his upper lip. "I thought nuns were supposed to be humane!"

Dr. Sullivan arrived and lay his hand on the intern's shoulder. "Larry, come on," he urged as he ushered him away and towards the stairs. "I know how to handle Sister Champagne. Don't worry, she always lets them in. She has to do this, Larry. It's her faith. It's her job. But she always lets them in."

The patient died several hours after her operation. She was 19 years old.

"I held the girl's hand and stroked her head until she went," Perry said in the lounge after work. "She was only a year younger than me, Yates."

Sunday night I went to bed early after an exhausting day in Emergency. I woke up at midnight, unable to get back to sleep. Finally, I got up and shuffled down to the lounge for a glass of milk. Through the soft amber glow from the light near the elevator, I saw Tanner sitting in the dark lounge, staring out the window. She was sobbing and I went to her.

"Tanner, what happened?" I said putting my arm around her shoulders.

"Ralph. It's Ralph," she said. "He was coming back from the bush up north. His plane took off and crashed into the lake." She buried her face in her hands. "He ... he's ... dead."

"Oh, my God, Tanner," I whispered. "I'm so sorry." I couldn't believe what I was hearing.

"Ralph was supposed to come home today." Tanner moaned, then she burst into tears.

"Oh, Tanner. Poor, poor Tanner," I said holding her close.

The elevator door opened and Hawkins stepped off. "What are you guys doing in the dark?" As Tanner turned her face to Hawkins, the gentle light from the hall revealed Tanner's anguish. Hawkins froze in her track. "What happened?" she asked in a quivering voice.

Tanner slumped and began to pick absent-mindedly at a loose thread in her duster. "He was going to make a lot of money for university," she said, barely above a whisper. "It was his last year. His plane crashed ... crashed in the lake. He's still there, somewhere in that cold water." Tanner burst into tears again.

Hawkins and I sat with Tanner for two hours until finally exhausted, we walked Tanner to her room and said, goodnight, promising to pray that Ralph would be found soon.

Late that morning, they pulled Ralph's body from that lake.

The day of the funeral, Sister gave Tanner the afternoon off. She was not entitled to the four-day compassionate leave reserved only for deaths in the immediate family.

After that terrible tragedy Tanner was never quite the same. Her bubbly effervescence had evaporated and left her flat.

Tapestry of Nursing

On Monday at 10 a.m. the ambulance arrived. Two attendants slowly pushed the stretcher down the hall, but it had not been extended to its full height, it was only inches above the floor. The patient lay on a wide board balanced on top of the stretcher.

"In here," said Dr. Newman, with a puzzled expression on his face. "Leave him on the stretcher. The less we move this man, the better. Now, let me try to figure this out."

I stood stunned with the intern and grad, staring down at the patient who stared anxiously back at us. From the position of his body, I wondered how this man had remained conscious. His legs were twisted and turned in a way that made me feel sick.

"Are you having pain?" I asked him, trying not to look at his legs.

He shook his head.

"He's 22 years old," said the foreman. "A Mormon missionary from Utah. Came to Calgary to work for the summer so as he can carry out his missionary duties in the evening. First darn day on the job, and this happened," the foreman moaned, folding and unfolding the grey cap in his hands.

Dr. Newman walked round the stretcher on the floor. He took his time, studying the patient, the angle of his feet and legs and the position of his arms.

"We were just standin' there, talkin'. I was explaining things, you know first day and all. All of a sudden, from nowhere, this here big sheet of metal that was leanin' up against the wall fell straight down." He made a motion towards the floor with his hand. "Don't know how it missed us. But it sure got this poor fella."

Dr. Newman walked over to the foreman and ushered him into the hall, away from the patient. I followed.

"Now the sheet metal fell," said Dr. Newman, "and then what."

"Fell right on top of Stanley here. Seemed to get him from his chest down."

"How long was he under the metal?" asked the doctor.

"Must'a been a good five, oh, maybe ten minutes. We got the crane ta lift it off as quick as we could . God, he was flatter'n a pancake. Squashed all ta hell." He shook his head slowly. "Took a while for him ta get all puffed up again."

I walked back into the room with Dr. Newman. Stanley lay still, only his lips moved. He was probably praying. But when he looked up at Dr. Newman, terror flashed in his eyes.

"Am I going to be okay, doctor? Am I going to walk again? Are my legs going to be okay?"

"I'm not sure, Stanley. I really won't know for a while. Give us time, son."

I was relieved that Stanley could not lift his head to look down at the tangle of the rest of his body. His legs had buckled under the weight of the metal ~ crushed beyond recognition. The toe of his right construction boot faced his right ear, and his left boot pointed into space at the level of his shoulder.

Stanley stopped praying and asked again. "Am I going to walk, doctor? Just tell me if I will walk again."

"We're going to take you to the operating room right now," Dr. Newman said gently, "and we are going to fix you up. Let's get through that first. Then we'll talk about you walking. Okay, son?"

Stanley closed his eyes and his lips began moving again in silent prayer.

"We need a few teams here," Dr. Newman said impatiently to the intern, who had been standing in a stupor beside him, staring at Stanley. I could tell from Dr. Newman's voice that he was nervous, overwhelmed. "Get David Decosta here as quickly as possible. Thompson, too if you can. And you, nurse," he pointed to me. "Get his boots off."

God, how am I going to do that? I knelt down and began untying the laces of his yellow construction boots. My face tingled and burned and I had that familiar ringing in my ears again. I wondered if Stanley noticed the position of his feet. But he seemed unaware, or perhaps consciously ignored the fact that I worked away at the laces very close to his neck.

Stanley gave me a distressed look with his big blue eyes. "Am I going to be okay, nurse? Am I going to walk again?"

"Dr. Newman is a wonderful doctor," I said, fumbling for the right words. "In fact you're going to have many good doctors working on you. That's the most important thing right now."

I had the laces untied, but I couldn't think of a way to get the boots off safely. I was afraid his whole foot would come off if I started to pull. I went to Dr. Newman.

"Never mind, never mind." he said with a sigh and a wave of his hand. "We'll get them off in the OR when he's asleep."

I helped wheel Stanley, slowly and carefully to the elevator and up to the operating room. A team of five doctors worked on him for many hours. But Stanley died there, on that operating room table, as the doctors and nurses tried to piece him together again.

That night I couldn't sleep. I saw Stanley lying alone on that stretcher on the floor, miles away from his family, fervently praying with blind conviction.

The next morning I tumbled straight into a rotation of night duty. I was posted to d'Youville, a tiny ward just off of the main lobby of the hospital, with eight private rooms.

The private patient rule prevailed in the hospital. Only registered nurses could care for private patients, with the exception of d'Youville, where a student nurse could replace the RN on her night off, but that student had to be a senior.

I would do the work of an RN. My newfound responsibility was exhilarating. As I hurried through the cool, dreary tunnel, I could almost feel the narrow black velvet band on the edge of my cap. But then terror struck. Me, RN? I shivered and pulled my white sweater round me.

After report, the afternoon grad and I made rounds together.

"You'll be just fine," she said as she threw her navy blue cape round her shoulders. "Everyone is sleeping, and Mrs. Wiggett has a special nurse. I see you've brought a book," she said pointing to the mystery I had under my arm.

"Well, yes ... someone told me to ... "

"Good, you'll have lots of time to read. If you do have any problems, call the supervisor, Mrs. Noseworthy, she'll look after you." And she left. Now I was alone with nobody to answer my questions, to help with my patients or to tell me what to do.

I soon realized I had brought the wrong kind of book. Sitting alone in the dimly lit ward, reading a mystery scared me half to death. I busied myself with paperwork, setting new sheets into the patients' charts for the day staff.

At 2 a.m. Mrs. Wiggett's special nurse appeared at the door of the nurses' station. "I'm going for my break," she said. "Keep an eye on my patient. She's been terribly burned. She reached across the gas burner of her stove while making Sunday breakfast and caught the arm of her housecoat on fire. Her housecoat went up in flames. Her husband wrapped her in a rug and put out the fire."

"Oh, my God."

"We're just keeping her comfortable and giving her intravenous fluids."

"What will I do if she needs something while you're gone?" I stammered.

"I don't think she will. The doctor says she might not make it through the night. Her husband's here. Wants to stay with her until the end. I feel so sorry for him." She shook her head. "He's devastated. So devoted to her."

I padded down to Mrs. Wiggett's room. A small light on a stand near the door cast a soft glow across her bed. She lay in a semi-upright position, asleep. I tiptoed over to her husband who was sitting in the shadows near the window.

"Hello," I whispered. "I'm the nurse on the ward tonight."

He nodded to his wife. "I think she's asleep." He sighed deeply. "You know, Minnie and I have been married almost 50 years. Her name is actually Marlene, but I've always called her Minnie," he said it with a soft chuckle.

"She's a very pretty woman," I whispered. Though Mrs. Wiggett's face had been badly burned, her bone structure was classic, and she had a serenity about her that suddenly made me wish I had known her before her accident.

"And a beautiful person, too." He sighed again. "My, my, my, to think we've come to this. And at this stage in our lives."

"It's wonderful you two have had such a good life together. I'm sure your wife is drawing a lot of strength from you right now."

"She was doing so well ... and then she took a bad turn this afternoon." He slowly shook his head. "To think we have come to this."

"You know, Mr. Wiggett, somebody once told me: one day follows the other, but they are not always the same."

He nodded. "True ... so true. You know, Minnie and I, well, we've always been around for each other. I want to be here for her."

"And you are doing a very fine job of that," I whispered.

"Thanks, nurse," he said, and he gently placed his hand on his wife's bandaged arm. "Minnie knows I'm here."

The next Monday, Arumbruster broke the news that Mrs. Wiggett had died during the day.

"Ah, poor Mrs. Wiggett," I said.

"And God bless Mr. Wiggett," Armbruster said. "What a kind man he must be. Mrs. Wiggett's safe in the arms of God now, Yates. She's not suffering any more."

How I wished I could be as kind and gentle, and have as much faith, as Armbruster did.

Yates: V.O.N. One week 7:30 - 3:30. Leaving the residence, I felt very important, ready to start the week with a home-nursing agency, Victorian Order of Nurses, the V.O.N. Since it was cool, I was allowed to wear my cape over my uniform.

Shirley Braithwaite, a small young woman with a friendly smile, sat at a desk scheduling her appointments for the day. She wore a belted, navy-blue shirtdress with shiny gold buttons down the front, and navy-blue shoes similar to my old lady shoes. She went over the patients we were about to visit, then belted her navy-blue trench coat, I grabbed my precious cape, and we were off in the V.O.N.'s little navy Volkswagen Beetle to visit our first patient.

Mrs. Pyke opened the door just as Shirley was about to knock.

"Hello, hello, Miss Braithwaite," she said. "Come in, come in. I'm all ready for you."

We followed her into the kitchen, where she had a needle and a glass syringe boiling in a small pot on her stove. A bottle of insulin sat on her kitchen table beside some cotton balls, and a bottle of alcohol for cleaning the top of the insulin bottle.

I took the pot, poured out the boiling water, carefully fished out the hot syringe and needle, and gave Mrs. Pyke her insulin injection.

While Mrs. Pyke hovered over us, wiping her hands on her gingham apron, we ate hot porridge with real cream and brown sugar then sticky cinnamon buns fresh out of her oven.

All week I traveled around Calgary, dressing wounds, counselling and giving injections and baths. This was home nursing: Teaching the elderly to care for themselves, sorting their mixed-up pills, visiting lonely and confused patients, and mothers with sick babies or sick mothers with babies ~ and eating ~ homemade vegetable soup, spinach quiche, hot apple pie topped with a hunk of cheddar cheese. It was a nice change, but by the end of my rotation I was looking forward to getting back into the hospital and acute-care nursing.

Payday again. "You've lost quite a bit of weight, Miss Yates. Do you feel well?"

"Yes, Sister." Despite my heavy feeding of the last week, I had lost 17 pounds since I had come back from Ponoka.

"Is anything bothering you?"

Mark is dead, I thought, but I said, "No, Sister."

I was still in shock. No appetite. A chocolate milkshake would never taste the same. I wanted to tell her all that, but she might kick me out.

"Miss Yates," Sister asked again. "Is something bothering you?"

"No, Sister ... well, just my final exams, Sister."

Sister gave me her barely-a-nod nod, and handed me my envelope.

As a senior, I replaced the assistant head nurses on their days off on all the wards, made rounds with the doctors, writing their orders and scurrying after them from patient to patient, and started intravenous infusions. These added responsibilities were a firm reminder that my goal was drawing closer, and what a sweet feeling it was. For this I received a whopping $15 every month.

Over the next three weeks I did the Cancer clinic and The Associate Clinic. At the Cancer Clinic I spent most of my time pushing patients in wheelchairs back and forth through the tunnel that connected the hospital to the clinic. Through thick glass walls, I watched patients receive radiation treatments, and I nervously nursed women who had cervical or ovarian cancer and had vaginal radium insertion. DO

NOT STAND AT THE FOOT OF THE BED was posted above each bed to remind us that a dangerous stream of radiation flowed from between the patient's legs. The head nurse's warning played over and over in my head: "Always protect your ovaries, girls."

The Associate Clinic was a medical building on Ninth Avenue where Walkoff and I were to experience working in a doctor's office. It was comforting to see Wolkoff's round, good-humoured face and playful dark eyes again, and she still had her Keeley Smith kiss-curls. We caught the bus to Eighth Avenue each morning and splurged on a Picardy tart and a coffee before walking the rest of the way to the clinic.

I was assigned to Dr. Manes' office. He was a general surgeon. It was a bitterly cold October and the Clinic was in the middle of renovating their offices. Chunks of the walls had been torn out and the stinging wind blew freely through the examining rooms. I could not wear my sweater, which was only permitted on the night shift. I almost froze to death, and so did the patients who had to undress in the breezy examining rooms.

"Most of the complaints seem pretty petty compared to what I've seen in the hospital," I said one day to Dr. Manes' nurse.

"You have to see the whole picture, Miss Yates," she said. "What you are seeing here is the beginning of what you end up seeing in the hospital. This is where the doctor picks up the patient's problems. This is an important part of the whole picture of patient care."

She was right, but I preferred nursing patients in the hospital. And I was relieved when my last day finally came. I made it through the two weeks without catching pneumonia.

With four months to go and at the urging of my brother, Allan, who was halfway through his first year of Pre-Medicine at the University of Calgary, I began studying for my graduation exams. Allan helped me chart a study program on the calendar, and I began a rigorous schedule of study. Because I had trouble staying awake after 9 p.m., I planned my study blocks early in the morning before I went to work. As Christmas drew close, I began to rise at 4:30 and study for two hours without interruption before I started my day. Every day I made a tick on the calendar, another step closer to those bittersweet exams.

The first day I arose early. to study it was Monday, ten days before Christmas. It was also my first day on affiliation at the Hudson Bay Company, where I would experience industrial nursing. I arrived early and joined a group of spectators at the Eighth Avenue entrance.

Each Christmas, employees sang Christmas carols from the store's main floor. The carols were broadcast on the radio. Half an hour before opening, crowds would gather at the entrance to watch the choir sing. In the ten years my mother had worked at Hudson Bay, she seldom missed a morning of Christmas carols. Her favourite person in the choir was Miss Mona Sparrow, the nurse who ran the health office.

Miss Sparrow was a formidable figure at Hudson Bay. "They call her Mighty Sparrow," my mother had told me. "She's tiny, but tough as nails."

Miss Sparrow was the troll of the health office to whom all employees had to answer when they fell ill at work. When my mother had suffered one of her debilitating migraines, she crawled up to the health office to face Miss Sparrow who gave her a piercing stare and growled, "And what's the matter with you?" Mom fluttered like a little bird and immediately vomited.

"And suddenly," my mother said, "Miss Sparrow's voice softened and she became an angel, a nurse." She sent Mom home in a prepaid taxi, courtesy of Hudson Bay Co. "She told me to stay home and rest for two days," Mom said, with a look of angels in *her* eyes.

It wasn't difficult to find Miss Sparrow; she was standing on a little stool in her nurse's uniform at the back of the choir. With a bell in each hand, her tiny arms lifted, one, then the other creating sweet, angelic music that merged with the choir's voices and floated over our group of winter-clad Calgarians, out into the crisp, dark snowy morning.

At the end of the performance, the bullhorn barked through the massive store ~ through the glittery jewellery department; the notions counter with a rainbow of buttons under glass; the delicate lingerie, hidden away in a back corner on the second floor; and through the milk bar beside the wide, white marble staircase. The store was officially open.

I jumped over the rope stretched across the entrance to the stairs and sprinted up to the health office on the second floor. I had learned this manoeuvre as a child from my mother, when she took me to the sales on Bay Day. She held baby brother Allan in one arm and, clutching my hand at the first blast from the buzzer, we hurdled the rope and did the 50-yard dash, with all of the other ladies, up to the women's department.

Immediately a fight would break out at the sale table. One time Mom lost Allan in the sea of mad shoppers and for a few frantic minutes, until she retrieved him, could only see his little tweed cap being tossed in the air again and again amid flying blouses and sweaters. Now walking through the empty women's department, I could hear Allan's tiny voice, rising from the floor, "Mommy!"

There was no one at the health office. From the doorway, my eyes moved around the small room ~ a narrow window, high, sterile-looking walls and two cots with white sheets. Suddenly I heard the ringing of bells. I turned to see the indomitable Miss Sparrow, who had graduated from Holy Cross in 1918, wearing the ancient cone-shaped Holy cap, ploughing through the Women's Department and ringing her bells at each employee she passed. When she finally arrived at the office, she walked past me without as much as a glance, sat down at her desk, locked her bells in the drawer and shoved the key into her pocket. She then checked her schedule, made a phone call to arrange a time to meet someone for lunch and, without looking up, said harshly: "For goodness sake, girl, don't just stand there. Hang up your cape in the closet." She pointed to a small door in the corner of the room, pushed her glasses up on her short, straight nose and studied the papers on her desk.

I hung up my cape and stood by the closet for several minutes before mustering the courage to approach her desk. "Hello, Miss Sparrow," I said, quietly. "I'm Miss Yates from Holy Cross."

"I know who you are," she snapped with her small round mouth, and brushed me away with her hand. "Go find a magazine to read." Her Holy cap was folded differently from mine. It was smaller and round instead of winged, and it sat on top of her black hair that was greying around her face.

I sat down on the chair opposite her desk and picked up *Cosmopolitan* magazine. Then the phone rang.

"Health office," she said sharply. Her mouth took on the shape of a little "o" again. Everything about her was small and round except for her large, piercing dark eyes.

"Well, what the hell's wrong?" Miss Sparrow barked into the phone. "Probably had too much to drink last night. Send her up!" She sounded like a general with a migraine.

Five minutes later, a pale woman walked into the office with dark circles under her eyes. "Miss Sparrow?" she said timidly. "I'm Bea Smith."

"I know, I know. Over there and sit down." Miss Sparrow motioned to my chair and I jumped up. "The student will take your blood pressure," she said, and thrust the apparatus into my hands.

I took the lady's blood pressure: 100 over 70.

"Go lie down on that bed for half an hour," said Miss Sparrow, gruffly. Out drinking last night?"

"No," the woman said almost in a whisper.

I helped her onto the bed and she threw up into the kidney basin I had thrust in front of her with polished proficiency.

"Hangover," Miss Sparrow said to me in a gruff stage whisper when I sat down beside her desk to wait for the woman to feel better. "She wants to go home and get paid for it, too."

Miss Sparrow gave the woman two aspirin, let her rest for two hours, then sent her back to work.

A second woman came in just before lunch. When Miss Sparrow read 101 degrees on the thermometer, she sprang into action.

"You are a sick woman," she said. "And you're not going back to work. Do you have anyone to pick you up? No? Well, I'm going to look after that. You drink lots and lots of fluids, you hear?"

Miss Sparrow quickly bundled her up and sent her home in a taxi, to be paid for by Hudson Bay Company. "We have to protect sick employees from those money-hungry managers," she said.

The next day, one of the money-hungry managers appeared.

"Too damn much wine, women and song last night," she barked. She thrust two aspirin at him with a glass of water. "Here, take these and get yourself back to work."

As I watched him walk out of the door, I said in a small voice, "He's a manager, isn't he?"

"I don't give a goddamn if he is the King of England," she snapped. "He's got a bloody hangover, and that's his fault, not The Bay's." She looked up from her desk. "And what's the matter with you? You look half dead on your feet."

"I've been studying hard, getting up at 4:30," I stammered. "I'm going to write my grad exams the beginning of February."

"Well get yourself onto that cot and get some sleep," she said. "I remember I was a bloody bundle of nerves before I wrote my damn exams." And I saw a flash of amusement in her eyes.

I slept then and every afternoon for the rest of my week at The Bay.

Painful Pleasures

Once again I requested my holiday time off the week before Christmas so that I could help my mother get ready. She always cleaned the house from top to bottom and baked her own elaborate Christmas cookies, fruitcakes and plum puddings. I wanted to help my mother with the last minute details at home and also to spend more time with my brother, even though I knew he would spend most of his vacation buried in books in preparation for his premedicine exams.

Christmas Day. My last Christmas at Holy Cross. "And what a glorious day!" Armbruster said at breakfast.

I loved the atmosphere in the hospital on Christmas Day and was happy to be working. Our prayer had an extra meaning because I was truly sacrificing my Christmas at home with my family. Although I would be home for supper, for the next eight hours I was going to bring happiness to those unfortunate patients in the hospital. This Christmas it would be the new mothers on maternity.

I was not surprised that Sister was not at inspection. She and all the other nuns would surely be spending the whole of Christmas Day praying in the chapel. I bounced up to the maternity floor, singing "Merry Christmas" to all I passed. After a quick report from the night nurse, I waltzed into my patients' room full of the jovial Christmas spirit as Bing Crosby crooned *White Christmas* on a patient's radio.

But Christmas also meant a skeleton staff and I had to rush to make my beds ~ the babies would be coming out soon. The linen hampers quickly became full. With no one in sight to help me, and confident that all the nuns would be in chapel all day, I began to hastily toss the dirty linen behind the door. As I did so, I hummed Christmas carols and beamed at the mothers as I made their beds. Just as I tucked in a perfect mitred corner on the last bed at the end of the ward, a sharp voice stabbed me in the back.

"Miss Yates, come here!"

Those words cut through *Joy to the World* like a hot knife through butter. I jumped a mile. Sister Garneau stood planted in the doorway. I tried not to be nervous. She most certainly would be in a good mood today. But the tone of her voice did have a perplexing ring to it.

"Yes, Sister?" I said with an extravagant smile.

"Get this linen off the floor!" she snapped, pointing to my stash behind the door. Then she spun around as she stomped out of the room.

"Yes, Sister. And Merry Christmas to you, too, Sister," I muttered as I picked the linen up off the floor. How ever did she find it?

With only nine weeks to go, White and I toasted in New Year's Eve, 1962 with a rum and Coke, or two, at a party. Finally 21, I was legal.

At 3:30 p.m. the next day, New Year's Day, White and I reported to the nursery with splitting headaches. After almost three years, we would work together for the first time. The nursery was hot, stuffy and the piercing cries of the babies were almost unbearable. We took two aspirin, stuffed our ears with cotton balls then mechanically changed the babies and delivered them to their mothers.

As we sat feeding the babies in the back row, White asked, "Where do you think you will work after graduation?"

I shrugged. "Don't know, but it won't be in the nursery. Can you imagine if I worked here? I would be adopting all of these babies." I held up my little nameless baby. I had learned my lesson about naming illegits. He burped with such force that White and I burst out laughing.

"Yup," White said, nodding her head. "You'd take them all home."

Six weeks away from final exams. We were all nervous and studying furiously. Even Niven, the-fly-by-the-seat-of-her-pants-right-into-an-exam girl, began to study overtly. We studied alone and we studied together, and when we asked each other questions, Perry always exclaimed: "Hey, I don't remember taking this!"

"That's because you were always sleeping," Kaufmann said one day with a chuckle, her chin tucked into her chest.

As we neared the end, we saw Kaufmann more often in the lounge.

"Atta girl, Kaufmann," laughed Niven. "Give her hell. Don't be afraid to speak up. Just let'er rip."

"Kaufmann isn't afraid to speak up any more, are you, Kaufmann?" I said.

She closed her eyes and smiled shyly.

My thoughts flashed back to the first time I had seen her with all of those shopping bags full of clothes. I turned to Perry and whispered: "Remind me, we've got to find a suitcase for Kaufmann before we leave the residence."

Countdown. Five weeks until final exams. One night as we sat in the lounge taking a study break and Niven was taping up the holes in her shoes, Standish danced in with Rosemary Martin, my classmate who came from Canmore, a small town west of Calgary. "We're off to Okotokes for a mushroom burger," Standish said.

"Now?" Andresen said, checking her watch. "You'll never have time to drive to Okotokes and back before 10:30. It must be over 30 miles away."

"I know where it is," said Standish, her eyes flashing. "I live in that area, remember?" As I looked at Standish, I realized I had hardly seen her since we had returned from our affiliation at Ponoka Mental Hospital.

"We're going with two farm guys Standish knows," Martin said as she tied her long brown hair up into a ponytail with an elastic band. "They've promised to get us back on time. Any takers?"

"You'll never make it back on time," Guenette said sternly, still mothering us even though we were seniors. "You'd better forget it."

"Hey, I'll go," I said jumping up. "I've been studying so damn hard lately, I need a break. It'll do me good to get out for some fresh air. Give me two seconds."

I ran down the hall to my room but as I started to change my clothes, my conscience began to take over. *You'll never get back on time ... don't take the chance ... maybe these guys are fast drivers ... dangerous drivers ... better stay home and study.*

"Changed my mind," I said, when I returned to the lounge. "And you guys had better stay, too. We're too close to the end to throw it all away for nothing."

"Na," said Standish, "gotta have a little fun once and a while. I wouldn't say that's *for nothing.*"

Martin gave a broad smile, revealing the silver braces on her upper teeth. "Yeah, God knows we need a little fun. Don't you guys spend all night worrying about us. See ya!" she called as the elevator doors squeaked closed.

"Damn fools!" White shouted after her.

It was the middle of the night when White shook me awake. "Get up, Yates," she whispered. "Standish and Martin aren't back yet and it's after midnight. Something must have happened."

I dragged myself out of bed and threw on what was left of my duster. We woke up Niven and Hawkins, then sat in the dark lounge watching huge snowflakes dance around the lights in the driveway. Finally a car turned in and slowly inched through the deep snow to the entrance. We couldn't see who got out, but soon we heard them giggling in the stairwell. Singing!

"Sssshowww me the wayyy tooo go hoommmme ... " Giggle, giggle

"Goddamn," snapped Niven, "they're drunk!"

We dashed down the stairs and met Martin and Standish clinging to each other, stumbling up the stairs.

"What a stupid, damn thing to do," said White, as we grabbed them and hauled them up to the fourth floor.

Niven and Hawkins struggled to support Standish down to her room. White and I helped Martin to hers. "I only had two drinks," Martin kept repeating like a parrot.

The next morning, I bounced out of bed on the first ring of my alarm, and ran into Martin's room to wake her. She was standing at the sink in her bra and panties, garter belt and nylons.

"Oh," I said, "I'm glad you're up. You can't miss work today."

"Yeah," said Niven, who suddenly appeared in the doorway. "You're in deep shit, Martin. Bet the housemother will report you to Sister. I saw the sign-in book. You took up the whole bloody page."

"Of course I took the whole page, I was trying to hold Standish up, she couldn't move! You think it was easy with Mrs. Schriefels staring my face off?"

I helped pin Martin into her uniform. She was sick with worry and trembling so.

"How am I ever going to work today?" she said. "I didn't sleep a wink last night. God, I feel like I'm going to throw up. I can't believe I was so stupid. Why did I go?"

We met Hawkins at the elevator who told us that Standish was in no shape to report for work. Hawkins stood like a statue. I had never seen such a stern look on her face.

Niven approached us with her cocky step-nudge walk. "God," she chuckled inspecting Martin. "You blend in with your uniform."

Kaufman appeared around the corner. "Leave her alone," she said. Then she tucked her chin to her chest and whispered, "It wasn't her fault."

"That's right, it wasn't my fault," whimpered Martin. "I'm sick because I'm scared. I'm bloody scared."

All the way over to the hospital Martin never stopped moaning: "Do you think Sister will find out? I can't believe I did such a stupid thing. Will the housemother report us? Do you think we'll get kicked out?"

At mid-morning, pale-faced White came to me on St. John's. "Martin and Standish have been called up to Sister! The disciplinary committee is having a meeting." She spoke in short, breathy phrases. "Those two might get kicked out!"

White turned on her heel and walked back down the hall with such a determined stride I thought she might take on the whole faculty. I dashed back to the residence without going for lunch. Wearing anxious faces, our entire class was crowded in the lounge.

"I can't believe they were so foolish as to throw their three years away for one night," said Priestnall.

Guenette nervously puffed on her cigarette. "Sister will kick them out."

"How can she kick them out when they only have six weeks left?" said Porter, who looked like she was about to cry. She had worked nights, and was sitting in her OR green top, underwear and pink socks; her fuzzy pink slippers had fallen apart months ago.

"Are you kidding?" Niven said snidely. "Sister would love to do something like that."

"Oh come on, Niv," said Porter. "Sister does have a heart, you know."

"Has nothing to do with a heart," Priestnall said, as she shaped her nails with a silver metal nail file. "Sister goes by the rules. It's black or white, remember the Grey Nuns? No grey." She held up one hand and blew on her little fingernail.

"Right," said Guenette. "If you're drunk in residence, that's immediate expulsion, whether it's your first day, or your last."

"Oh, God," gasped Kaufmann in a tiny voice from her corner chair.

I couldn't believe this was happening. I knew Martin and Standish liked having a beer or two. We all did. "Those boys railroaded them into this," I said. "They would never have done this on their own."

None of us could speak. We sat watching Simm, on a diet again, eat half a cantaloupe filled with cottage cheese. The elevator door opened and Martin and Standish stepped out. Pale and silent they sank into chairs hastily vacated by Porter and Armbruster. Niven was the first to speak.

"Well?" she taunted. "Do you have to start packing?"

Martin looked as though she had just been shot from a cannon. Standish didn't take her eyes off her shoes. I feared the worst.

"Sister wanted to have us expelled," Standish finally said, in short, choppy words. "But the faculty eventually convinced her to let us stay and write our exams. We're confined to barracks for four weeks."

"Yea!" We all exploded and jumped around the room.

"Yeah, we can't even walk from the residence to the hospital," Martin said with a thin grin. "Gotta go through the tunnel. But hey, I'm not going to complain. They're going to let me be a nurse."

We sat in silence and thought, four weeks locked in residence. Then Standish took a deep breath and said, "But I'm so bloody scared about my exams, I honestly think that's why the liquor went to my head. Has something to do with the body chemistry and excitement. That can happen, you know."

"Aw, who cares whether you had one drink or ten?" Tanner said, throwing up her hands. "The main thing is that you are both still here, and I think we should celebrate."

"No liquor!" laughed Andresen.

"God, no," said Martin. "I never want to see that stuff for the rest of my life. And I mean it! I'm making a vow right now, and all you guys are witnesses. I'll *never* touch that stuff again."

We all celebrated by ordering in hamburgers and french fries after work, but Martin and Standish missed their party. They were sleeping off their hangovers.

Standish had a stroke of luck when Sister made a mistake and posted her to the Alberta Children's Hospital for four weeks. Standish boarded the bus, laughing all the way to the children's hospital.

For the next six weeks we were all glued to the residence, especially Martin. Except for the odd trip to the Lotus for a Coke, we sat in our rooms or the lounge - -stunned little heads pouring over our Mosbey book of "Typical RN Exam Questions."

The night before our first exam we were having a huge snowstorm when my mother called at ten. "Just want to wish you good luck tomorrow, dear," she said.

"Thanks, Mom. I'm going to need it."

"I don't want you to worry, Donna. You've done so well these past three years, so well. I know you're going to be fine now. Please don't worry."

"Mom," I said, "do we have an extra suitcase? I would like to give Kaufmann one so she doesn't have to take her clothes out of here in shopping bags."

"Such a lovely little girl," Mom said, with a sigh. "I'll have a look in the basement. I think we have one she can have. Now go to bed and get a good rest. You have three days left, don't get yourself all worked up. Stay calm."

"I'll try."

My heart heaved the next morning when I awoke. My last three years hung on the next three days of exams. If I failed, I would fail my family ~ Mom and Dad and Allan, Grandma Yates and Grandpa Scorah and Auntie Violet. I would fail the world.

It was still snowing lightly as I rode the special bus up Centre Street that was taking us to the University of Calgary on the north hill. It turned west on Sixteenth Avenue and stopped at a red light in front of Balmoral, my old grade school. Through the frosted window, I faced the three silent buildings. In the first floor classroom of the building to the right, my grade two teacher, Miss Hatchet, had sat me on a tall stool in front of the class with a three-cornered cap on my head and told the whole class I was a dunce.

I began to rub my hands. I could still remember the burn from the stinging blows of Miss Hatchet's wide, leather strap. I had followed her into the cloakroom at the back of my grade two class where damp coats and parkas hung from low pegs that circled the room. I signed "Donna Yates" in the strap book below Hewey's crudely printed name. Hewey was the mentally retarded teenager who was a permanent fixture at Balmoral School. Mine was the only girl's name in the book. My crime was talking. After I received seven blows to each of my seven-year-old hands, I walked back to my desk, pressing my hands to my thighs so no one would see them beet red and swelling. I was a bad girl, with my name in a book of bad boys' names. I talked too much. I was a dunce, a girl Hewey, a failure. And of course, I could never tell my mother.

The bus lurched forward and I heard my mother's voice: "You've done so well these past three years, so well. I know you're going to be fine now."

We were all quiet, pensive. For the next three days there was suspended animation. Like in a dream, we tranced up the hill each morning to the gruelling exams. Each time we passed the Highlander Hotel on Sixteenth Avenue where we all had agreed to celebrate when the exams were over, White looked longingly up at the sign and said, "Boy, I can almost taste that Seagram's V.O. and ginger ale. And it's not going to come bloody soon enough as far as I'm concerned!"

But exams did finally end and we spent the whole evening at the Highlander crying because we only had three more days to be together. The last evening in residence we carried out the age-old tradition of visiting each instructor's house. They were supposed to give us a drink, no matter how late the hour. We scheduled our last visit at our most permissive instructor's apartment in the wee hours of the morning, arriving boisterous yet courteous. Miss Beckor had come to Holy Cross in our third year and was not much older than we were.

At 2 a.m. we arrived back at the residence for our last night together. But soon the problem of another ritual surfaced ~ dumping all the students out of bed. Two months before, Sister had given us a stern warning about dumping students out of bed. And she repeated the warning at the last Home Night. "I have instructed the housemother not to give out the passkey," Sister said. "Anyone participating in the ritual will be severely punished."

But as we sat in the dim lounge discussing our dilemma, White became more adamant about performing the ritual. "Have you forgotten how those seniors treated us?" she said. "Have you forgotten about how they dumped poor Kaufmann in the tub ~ twice? I've been waiting three bloody years to get even and *nobody* is going to stop me tonight."

"Ditto!" Niven said. "Who gives a damn about what Sister said?"

"Niven," Kaufmann said gently, her face in a full flush. "That's not nice."

"Yeah, I guess not. Sorry, guys. Anyway, from now on Sister's out of my life. Forever!" Niven tossed her empty coffee cup into the air and caught it with one hand.

White laughed. "You can say that again. What do we have to fear? That woman can't touch us now."

"Well, I'm not going to do it," I said. "I always hated getting dumped in the middle of the night and I'm not going to do it to anyone else. It's stupid and childish."

Niven puckered her mouth as if she had just tasted a lemon. "Oh come on, don't be a prude."

"Nope," I said sternly. "Sister will get even. I'll bet on it."

"Oh, garbage!" Niven said. "What can she possibly do to us?"

"You'll see. She'll think of something," I said, and went off to bed.

Sometime during the night, four members of the class of February '62 sang their last farewell ~ and dumped all of the students out of bed. I vaguely remember the faint chorus in the stairwell.

> We're graduating in the morning
> Ding dong the bells are going to chime
> Throw back the covers
> Roll out the buggers
> But get me to the church on time.

The next morning I rose early with butterflies in my stomach and pinned myself into my uniform. It seemed like yesterday that I had struggled with my bib and apron and here I was, graduating, registered nurse. Where did those three years go? How was I going to live without my classmates, my sisters now?

I gave one last glance in the mirror at my uniform, completely white. No more blue stripes. The precious black velvet band edged my winged cap, informing the whole world that I was a registered nurse!

A registered nurse ...

My mind rushed back to grade three, to Miss McNabb's classroom at Balmoral, musty, dark and dreary, except for the large tree with luscious green leaves that stood outside the window on the left side of the room. That tree was my refuge. As I stared at its branches reaching for the sky, my grade three agony melted into dreams of tree houses and birds while Miss McNabb's voice faded into a hypnotic babble.

I remembered the girl with blond hair who sat behind me. One day, she leaned forward and whispered something she'd found out from one of the older girls in the playground.

"When you get to grade six, you have to see a doctor," she said. "He makes you take off all of your clothes."

Horrified at the thought, I blurted out, "I hope I skip grade six!"

The whole class turned in my direction.

"Stand up, Donna, and tell me what you said," demanded Miss McNabb with the sneer over her face, saved only for me.

I stood. "I hope I skip grade six," I mumbled, barely above a whisper.

"At the rate you're going, you are never going to get to grade six," said Miss McNabb, snidely. And then she laughed.

The class laughed.

That laughter rang in my ears and followed me through the years. I would be six feet tall and still be in grade three, like Hewey, poor Hewey who hopped from foot to foot drooling and laughing while everyone made fun of him. I felt sorry for him; shame burned my cheeks. Now I would be the girl Hewey of Balmoral. I didn't tell my mother. But Miss McNabb did.

"No, you are not allowed to come with me," said my mother as she dressed for the interview. "You are so capable, dear, I don't know how I can get you to try harder." She leaned over and kissed me, and she left, dressed in her grey-striped suit, wearing her black felt hat with a gold pin on the side. It gleamed in the sunshine as she walked past Louie's store.

I followed her in secret, sneaking from bush to bush as she made her way up the long walkway to the brownstone building. This was a big meeting, held in the big building, all about me. I waited, crouched behind a bush, until she finally came out. She was crying ... she cried all the way home. As I followed stealthy behind her, I thought, I did this to her. I made my mother cry. But how could I behave differently? I was a bad girl. I was stupid. The teachers said so. Miss McNabb said so.

I made a vow to myself, if I ever made it to grade six I would go back to Miss McNabb and tell her she was wrong about me. But when I got to grade six, I decided to wait until I graduated from grade 12, and then when I graduated from grade 12, I decided to wait until I became a nurse. That would be my sweet revenge.

Suddenly I heard a bang on my door. "Move it, Yates," Perry shouted as she rushed by, "you're going to be late!"

I lifted my finger to the velvet band on my cap, soft and smooth as the fur of a baby kitten ... then I turned and rushed out to join the girls in the lounge.

We walked through the tunnel to the chapel for the graduation Mass. Father Flanagan believed in us, believed we were chosen to perform God's will, to care for the sick, to be good nurses. We had a calling, Father repeatedly told us. Now he was our friend forever.

After Mass, we hurried back to the residence Reception Hall where breakfast that was more like a banquet awaited us. The table was set with linen and shiny silverware, and the ladies in the kitchen served us royally. All of our instructors were present, and of course, so was Sister Leclerc, whose face looked more strained than usual.

It was a simple breakfast, with much laughing and crying, but no speeches.

"Come on," Niven said, as we all blubbered into our last cup of coffee. "It's not as if we aren't going to see each other again. After all, we'll get together for graduation in September. And remember what Sister said, 'Don't get pregnant!' It doesn't look nice to sit on the stage in your grad uniform with a big belly. That's for you, Simm, you'll be the only married one."

Then the moment finally arrived for us to make our final march through the hospital as students and sing our sweet-sorrow farewell to the nurses and patients. Silence descended on us as we walked through the dismal grey tunnel with its weary light bulbs. As I moved toward the hospital for the last time, my chest felt tight and a knot grew in my throat. Was I supposed to feel this way? I should be happy. But I was happy. I was also very sad. How could I live without my classmates, the girls I had lived with, laughed with and cried with for the past three years? I was an RN, but it was painful. I felt empty. I glanced at White, her face was twisted into an anguished smile. We all felt it, even Niven looked emotional. She seemed to glide down the hall like a true professional nurse; her defiant step-nudge had disappeared.

We ascended the grand marble steps, up which I had carried the milkshakes, one for me and one for Mark. Two nuns stopped to watch us go by. For once, they were smiling.

"Good-bye. Good luck!" said the intermediate standing beside the Sisters.

Her words hit me with a jolt. On the second floor, I looked up. Miss Horne, our clinical instructor, was standing at the entrance of St. John's ward, waving and smiling proudly. I passed the hopper room where she had held my head after I tried to help change Miss Quick's dressings.

My eyes fell on the closed door of the private room where all those beautiful young people had died, Lisa with leukemia, Sandra the one-armed Sleeping Beauty, Mrs. Mullens the Catholic denied birth control, and Miss Jackson who succumbed to her cancer as the Ink Spots crooned, *If I didn't care* ... I closed my eyes and smelled her Crepe de Chine perfume.

"Come on, come on. Let's hear you sing!" Miss Horne was shouting.

Guenette began slowly, to the tune *It's a Long Way to Tipperary*:

It's a long way to graduation,
It's a long way to go

We looked at each other and giggled, then began to sing as we increased our pace and fell into step.

It's a long way to graduation,
To the sweetest day I know

We moved around the corner to St. Joseph's. Mrs. Black, the witch, was standing at the nursing station, smiling. Our eyes met. She waved and her mouth moved, "Good Luck." My mind flashed to the day she had grabbed my ear and marched me to the medication cupboard where I had left the keys. Deep down in my heart, I thanked her for that lesson. I passed the room where I had nursed Mark through the night, his sweats and his fear, our fear, of death. Where we sat in the amber-glow of the late afternoon light talking jazz and sipping milkshakes. I would never forget him. We turned another corner to St. Charles. Mr. McPherson appeared at the door of his room. I thanked him for his brave battle and for teaching me about dying with dignity.

We marched up to the third floor to St. Mary's and St. Anne's, waving to the nurses and patients who gathered in the hallway. I took a deep breath; yes, I smelled it ~ the antiseptic odour. It was still magic.

Good-bye, Holy Cross,
Farewell, Sisters dear
It's a long, long way to graduation,
But, thank God, it's here!

The last "Good-bye, good luck!" was still ringing in my ears as I removed the few clothes from my closet and packed them in my little suitcase. I took a photograph of my bulletin board, then stripped it. I carefully lay my cheerleader pompom in my suitcase beside Allan's metal horse and placed the pictures of Cisco Kid and Lester Brennen, along with the dried up prom corsage, on top of everything. As I was tucking my burn patient, Angela's picture into the side, White walked slowly into my room looking as though she had lost her last friend. "Came to say good-bye," she said, flopping down on the bed.

"I'm going to miss you, White," I said.

I slid the picture little Angela had given me between the pages of my *Pediatric Medicine* book, and tucked it under my white nylons and garter belt at the bottom of my suitcase.

Perry appeared around the doorway. "Geez, guys, I can't stop crying.

I just can't imagine living without all of you." She walked in, her eyes brimming with tears, her mouth quivering, and threw her arms around me.

White stood up and joined us, one arm around Perry, one around me. Our sobs brought Niven to the door.

"Come on, you cry-babies, knock it off! Don't you know it's hard enough without you guys blubbering all over the place?"

I looked up at Niven, her eyes were red. She had been crying. I reached out and pulled her to us.

I picked up my suitcase and walked to the door, then turned to look at my room for one last time. It was empty. Waiting to receive another naïve young girl and turn her into a mature caring woman. The process would take three years. The nuns would prod and shape and mould these young women until they could proudly say: "I'm a *Holy* grad."

I suddenly began to realize that the nuns gave us much more than an education to become a good nurse. We had not become nurses just because we passed an exam. The Sisters, especially Sister Leclerc, would not allow that. They had to see something else, something deeper. With those piercing cold, blue eyes, Sister looked into the heart and soul of each student. If she saw a determined student ready to forfeit all to become a nurse, willing to forge on when the going seemed unbearable, aching to become a nurse more than anything else in her life, then, and only then, would Sister allow that girl to graduate. Each one of us had to be on fire with that one desire ~ to nurse the sick. There were no compromises. *Yes, Sister*, I was taking home more than my little suitcase full of treasures. I was taking home memories that would last the rest of my life.

I had friends to carry with me forever, not only in my heart, but *for-real* friends. Friends I could count on in good times, bad times, middle-of-the-night times, anywhere, on any corner of the earth. Friends I could drop in on and say, "Hi, I'm here!" and know that they would greet me unconditionally with open arms. Friends? No, they were more than friends, much more. Every single girl in my class of February '62 was my sister. I closed the door of my room for the last time. The lock clicked shut.

My parents proudly waited for me downstairs in our 1950 Chevrolet.

As I left the residence clutching my suitcase, I shouted. "Hey, Kaufmann! Do you want a lift somewhere?"

"No thanks," she said. "My sister's in town. She's coming to pick me up." Kaufmann pointed to the suitcase on the curb beside her that held her few simple belongings. "Do you want me to send it back to you?"

I turned to our car and glanced at my mother; she shook her head.

"Nope," I said with a wave. "Keep it."

Kaufmann smiled. "Thanks. See ya."

Getting Even

The following Monday morning, a letter arrived in the mail from Sister Cécile Leclerc.

Holy Cross Hospital
Calgary, Alberta
February 19, 1962

Dear Miss Yates,
The members of the Holy Cross School of Nursing wish to inform you that in view of the unprofessional behaviour displayed on your last day at the School, your Graduation Pin will be deferred for a period of three months.

I am sorry for the disappointment this decision will bring to you but this disciplinary measure has had to be taken because you have disregarded the rules and policies of the School.

Your pin will be sent to you on the 15th of May.
Yours sincerely,
Sister C. Leclerc, s.g.m.
Director of Nurses,
Sr.CL/iv.

What You Dare to Dream

Several weeks later, I received a telephone call from my father one afternoon while I was at home. "The results are in the mail from Edmonton," he said. "Yours are at the depot on Sixteenth Avenue. If you want to go and pick them up, Mr. Gus Stevens will give them to you, otherwise they will be delivered tomorrow."

I shot out of the house and dashed to the depot, two blocks away. Gus smiled and nodded his head, as he chewed on the butt of a half-smoked cigar.

"Thought you'd want these right away," he said, handing me the large envelope, University of Alberta, Department of Nursing, Edmonton, Alberta, typed in the left corner.

"Thanks." I smiled.

I walked out the door and round the corner of the building to a small, empty patch of grass between the Post Office Depot and Chisholme's Confectionery and opened the envelope. My heart drummed double-time. Across the street, Balmoral. I tore my paper out of the envelope. My fingers shook as I ran down the list of subjects: medical nursing, surgical nursing, psychiatry, obstetrics, pediatrics ... I took a deep breath, closed my eyes and whispered a prayer of thanks. I had done it ~ I passed.

On my way home, with the envelope containing my results tucked tightly under my arm, I walked past Louie's store. The same black cat with big yellow eyes was still smirking at Balmoral, and once again Miss McNabb entered my thoughts.

The moment had finally come.

I ran the water in the bathtub. As I soaked in the tub, I rehearsed the speech I would deliver to Miss McNabb. I would tell her how she almost ruined my life. And I would ask her in no uncertain terms about how many other lives she had ruined. What was the matter with her? Why was she so cruel? Always sitting the quiet little girls up on the piano for being good. I had wanted to run, run with the boys, not sit and play dolls and ball and jacks. Didn't she know how to handle children who could not sit still, chained to a desk hour after hour, children who had to be busy?

At three o'clock I dressed methodically in my new suit and high-heeled shoes and I walked back to Balmoral School, down the long walk and past the brownstone building that my mother had run crying from, because of me. I continued on to the small white building on the left. A wave of nausea hit me as I climbed the stairs. How I had hated it all. To the left was the small gravel area where the girls had played ball and jacks and scratched squares into the dirt with a stick for hopscotch. To the right was where the boys played touch football ~ my favourite side.

The building was smaller than I recalled, with shinier floors, but with the same musty smell of old books and ink wells. Miss McNabb's room was in the same place to the left of the entrance. And there she was; her back to me as she cleaned the blackboard with the same brush. I could see the class choosing their teams for the spelling bee, one on each side of the room ... and I still at my desk, the only one never picked for either side ... finally in the end given to the line that had the least.

I walked down the narrow aisle, past desks fastened to the floor by the same black metal plates. Desks with crudely carved initials in hearts, ingrained forever into the fibre of dead trees. Suddenly, like a crush of angry waves breaking in a stormy sea, it all came back to me; the sharp, dank odour of steamy, hand-knit sweaters after recess, dirty grimy fingers on hands cupped to cover stinging whispers that whirred from desk to desk ... I had trouble breathing.

Miss McNabb turned. I clenched my teeth.

"Miss McNabb?" I said.

"Yes."

I smiled. Darn! I didn't want to smile. "I'm Donna Yates."

"Yes, I know who you are. How could I forget you?" She smiled.

"I guess I gave you a rough time."

"Oh, you were just being a child. But I could never forget your smile, Donna. You always had a beautiful smile."

For a moment I was taken aback. She had thought that I had something beautiful? I cleared my throat and went on. "Are you still teaching grade three?"

She nodded. "This is my last year. I'm retiring in the spring. Just three months to go." Her glasses glinted in the pale light of late afternoon ... I shuddered.

Suddenly I was facing a younger Miss McNabb as I hung up my coat after recess. "Did you see the fly ball I caught?" I had asked her, proudly. And she answered, "I'm glad to see you can do something right, Donna."

Now I stood facing her again, I stiffened. She was a tiny woman, much smaller than I remembered her. She barely reached my shoulder.

A tiny, old woman.

I could not deliver my speech.

She was about to retire. How could I hurt her? And what good would it do at this point?

"I've just graduated from nursing at Holy Cross Hospital," I said proudly.

"That's nice. If I remember correctly, you always wanted to be a nurse. I'm sure you will make a good nurse."

I had gone back, given her proof that I made it past grade six. But she didn't seem to remember, or care. I was just one of her hundreds of students. She was old, and she was tired. I glanced at the familiar big tree standing outside the window, its bare branches still reached for the sky. In a few weeks it will sprout new leaves, I thought. And I left.

For You, Mom

YOU ARE INVITED TO ATTEND THE GRADUATING
EXERCISES OF THE HOLY CROSS HOSPITAL,
SCHOOL OF NURSING, CLASSES OF FEBRUARY
AND SEPTEMBER, 1962, TO TAKE PLACE AT THE
JUBILEE AUDITORIUM, OCTOBER 14, 1962
AT 5:00 P.M.

Graduation. The day I had dreamed of. Our class gathered in Waterloo Hall.

"Stand still, for God's sake," said White as she pinned Tanner into her grad uniform.

"I can't. I can't," Tanner said, dancing from foot to foot, her June Allyson face was serious but her blue eyes flashed mischievously. "I've got to pee. Gosh, I hope I can make it through the exercises. I have to pee every five minutes. I'm so damn nervous."Perry said as we pinned each other as always, "He made it. My dad made it, oxygen and all. That's the best present I could ever have."

I gave her a hug. "I'm so happy, Perry, for all of you, your mom and dad and Joan."

Miss Horne appeared looking pressed and said, "Sister says you are not to sit down before the exercises. Your uniforms must be absolutely wrinkle-free. So that means you have to stand on the bus."

Niven examined Simm with an impish grin and said, "Sister will be glad to see you've still got your figure."

Simm had converted to Catholicism and married Pat as soon as we had left residence.

White picked up several letters and said, "I've sent invitations to the instructors, and most of them are coming except Mrs. Meeres, who says, 'I'm very proud of all of you. It seems like only yesterday that I helped measure you for your first uniforms ... I really do have a soft spot for each one of you in my heart (or should I say "Myocardium").' And Father Malo says, 'I shall be with you in spirit and know that you shall have a salubrious and scintillating gathering regardless.'"

"Hey look, here's a telegram from Guenette from California! I'll read it."

=VANNUYS CALIF 12=
GRADUATING CLASS OF 62=
HOLY CROSS HOSPITAL CLGY=
CONGRATULATIONS AND SINCERE BEST WISHES TO EACH OF YOU ON THIS GRADUATION WEEKEND STOP I PRAY EACH OF YOU WILL HAVE EVERY SUCCESS IN YOUR FUTURE ENDEAVORS STOP HOPE THE OLD CLASS SPIRIT IS RUNNING TRUE TO FORM THAT YOU ARENT IN AGREEMENT STOP HAVE A WONDERFUL TIME AND WRITE ME THE DETAILS=
GUENETTE.

"Gee, I miss Guenette," Kaufmann said in her small voice.

"Me too," Porter said, her hair shining like a mirror. "I hope Guenette likes working in Los Angeles. We'll just have to make a trip to California one day and visit her."

"I'm all for that," chuckled White.

Guenette was already gone and Wolkoff had to make up her sick-days before Sister would let her graduate. "It's a damn, dirty shame," Niven said, her freckled face turning its fierce pink. "Wolkoff passed her bloody exams. There's no reason to hold her up like this."

Niven was right. Wolkoff had worked hard and paid her dues. She belonged with us.

Outside it was a cool, clear fall evening, a huge, white full moon shone in the dark sky. The bus arrived and jounced us to the Jubilee Auditorium on the north hill. We stood all the way.

"Hey, Yates," White said, as we bumped over Tenth Street Bridge. "Take a look at the moon. Does it remind you of our hitching trip to Regina?"

I laughed. "Hey, come to think of it," I said. "I haven't heard from Lester for a while. I think he's graduating this year."

"Maybe he's found a cute Saskatchewan chick."

"I wouldn't be surprised."

We gathered behind the stage, whispering and giggling like child ballerinas at their first review, peeking out at our parents.

And suddenly it was time. A lonely silence descended on us as we marched two by two up onto the stage, just as we had done in our capping ceremony. Fifty-six of us graduated from the Holy Cross Hospital School of Nursing, 1962: 16 from our February class and 40 from the later September class. Each of us received our diploma, framed in an impressive red folder, along with a large bouquet of red roses from Mrs. Bland. We sat on the stage like stiff dolls in our white starched uniforms, black velvet bands crowning our caps. I chuckled as I looked down at my graduation pin on the left side of my chest: a large gold cross, artistically engraved with H✞H School of Nursing. Sister must have forgiven us by now, I thought, but she would probably never forget us. The glee club, dressed in their student uniforms and navy blue capes, sang Climb Every Mountain.

Calgary was very proud of their nurses. The *Calgary Herald* and the *Albertain* printed our graduation pictures, as they did for every graduating class, and the mayor of Calgary gave a speech. Mrs. Bland gave a speech, and a student from the September class gave the valedictorian address.

"Tonight is only the beginning of a promising and rewarding future ..."

"This is not an end, but a beginning ..."

"As an RN you will be called upon countless times by the community in which you live ..."

There were ten awards given to the graduating year, our class recieved six. At the end of the program, Sister Leclerc stood at the microphone and called the name of each girl who had won an award ...

General Proficiency ∽ Margaret Ingraham
Bedside Nursing ∼ Hazel White
Pediatrics ∼ Christine Andresen
Aseptic Technique ∼ Marie Guenette
Obstetrics ∼ Lucy Hawkins

I was jolted ramrod straight in my chair when I heard my name called out.

The Person Who Shows Most Promise in Her Profession - Donna Yates.
True to the very last, my name was at the bottom of the list.

We recited the Jeanne Mance pledge:

That I may be strengthened in my resolve to model my life of duty after that of Jeanne Mance, the first lay-nurse of my beloved Canada, I place myself in the presence of God and I pledge myself, with the help of His Grace, to be faithful to the following ideals:

I will be true to the practice of my Religion, which is the inspiration of my noble vocation, and while administering to the body, I will serve the soul by observing the principles of right Ethics and Nursing Honour.

I will be devoted to the Profession that is mine, obeying the physician within the sphere of his authority, and I will make my work a labour of love rather than of profit, whenever the service of God or Country requires it of me.

We ended the ceremony with the Florence Nightingale pledge, and my thoughts returned again to our Capping Ceremony, to Father Flanagan, our beautiful marble chapel and my proud parents ... the day when I had first read the pledge. I had an ache in my chest. Part of me wished that I was starting all over. But could I do it again? If I had known what lay ahead of me that spring day in our little chapel as I read the Nightingale pledge,

If I had known that I would come to love study, that I would be so proud of my uniform, that I would work nights with little sleep, and stay awake, that I would happily work overtime without counting the hours or expecting extra pay,

If I had known that I would throw up in the hopper after viewing a wound, that I would pin my finger to my patient's buttock with a hypodermic needle, that I would chase mental patients around a clover field, that I would weep helplessly as my young patients slipped into death, that I would drop an amputated leg in the operating room, that I would crack a doctor on the head with a heavy lamp, that I would look into the eyes of a dying young man and then send my parents to his funeral,

If I had known that I would delight at being left alone in charge of a ward through the night, that I would watch each birth with awe, that my heart would ache for every trusting illegitimate baby, that I would irrigate a colostomy and then without batting an eye, go for lunch, that I would cherish a little girl's crude drawing, that I would learn that 'Yes, Sister' was the only answer,

If I knew all this ... would I begin again?

Suddenly my eyes fell upon mother's face, uplifted, looking directly at me with admiration and grace, such happiness and fulfillment. I knew that my dream was her dream, and that our dream had come true.

If I knew all this ... would I begin again?

Yes. Oh, yes.

Photos

Holy Cross Hospital
Nurses' Residence

The hospital Chapel, Father Flanagan

Yates' room

First year
Nursing Arts

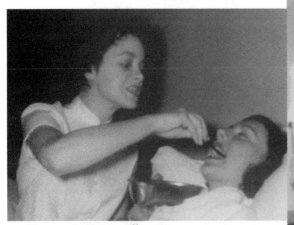

Tanner & Priestnall

(LtoR) Wolkoff, Porter, White, Andresen
(kneeling) and 3 Mrs. Chase Dolls

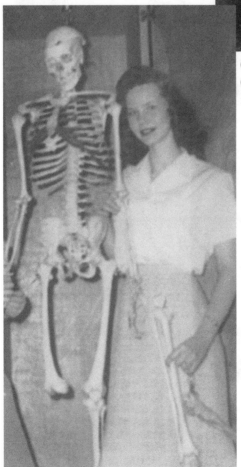

Porter with Jasper

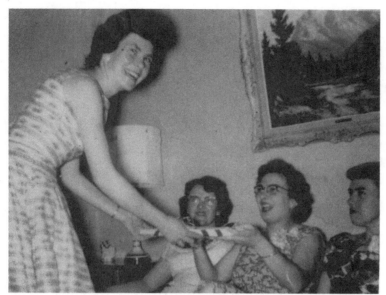

Mothers' Day Tea; Simm, Miss Horne, Mrs. Whitford, Miss Lynch

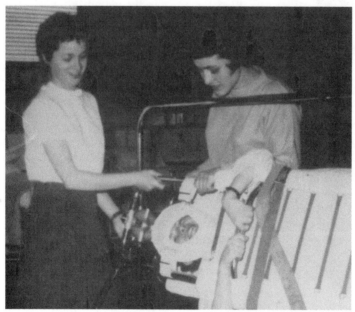

Tanner & Wolkoff turning the Stryker Frame.

The Capping Ceremony

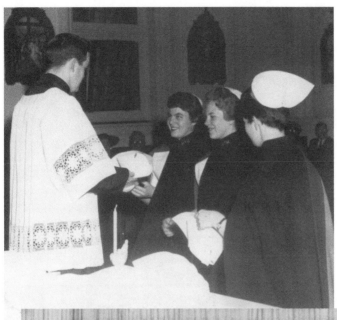

Capping
Father Flanagan, Yates,
Andresen, Senior

Class of February 1962
following Capping Ceremonies

Yates with
parents and
Grandma Yates

Post Capping
Lounge;
Yates, Perry,
Armbruster,
Andresen

227

Second year

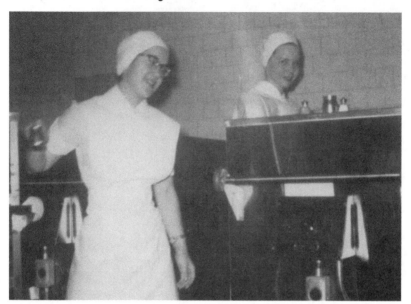

Diet Kitchen; Kaufmann, Porter

"Holy Terrors" Ball Team; (LtoR) unidentified student, coach,
Andresen, Tanner, coach, White.
For inter-hospital week.

Third Year

Class party at Blackwell's. Porter, Yates, Armbruster, Wolkoff, Hawkins, Andresen, Priestnall.

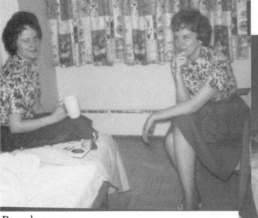

Perry's room.
Perry, Andresen

Standish & patient in hospital.

Porter, Standish, Yates,
White, Armbruster,
Andresen.

Blackwell's house Tanner, Perry, Andresen

Home Night Instructors; Miss Goodchild, Miss McLeod, Miss Greene

Home Night; Tanner & Wolkoff 'Ghost Riders in the Sky'

White at Blackwell's party

Graduation Breakfast; Miss Horne, Mrs. Cherry, Mrs. Meeres, Mrs. Bland, Mrs. Whitford

HOLY CROSS AWARD WINNERS. These are three of the award winners at the Holy Cross Hospital school of nursing's annual graduation ceremony Sunday night with Sister Le Clerc, director of nursing. From the left they are Sister Mary Jean, who received a gold medal for the highest standing in theory; Helen Ingraham, who was awarded the school's highest prize, the gold medal for general proficiency; Sister Le Clerc, and Elizabeth Jempson, who received the prize for professional ethics.

Faculty

MRS. A. CHERRY
Health Director

MISS D. GREENE
Orthopedic Nursing

231

MRS. E. BLAND
Associate Director of Nursing Education

MISS I. LYNCH
Assistant Nursing Arts Instructor

MRS. M. WHITWORTH
Nursing Arts Instructor

MRS. A. MEERES
Anatomy and Physiology
Instructor

MISS M. HORNE
Medical Nursing
Instructor

MRS. I. BARUTA
Obstetrical Nursing

Holy Cross Hospital
GRADUATING CLASS
FEBRUARY
1962

W. NIVEN
D. KAUFMANN
J. BLACKWELL
D. YATES
P. PRIESTNALL
PRESIDENT
FEBRUARY CLASS
H. WHITE
J. ARMBRUSTER
J. TANNER
C. ANDRESEN
C. SIMM
J. PERRY
R. PORTER
L. HAWKINS
E. STANDISH
M. GUENETTE
M. WOLKOFF

Absent from photos: M. Ingraham

233

Reunions

1984
(back) Porter, Blackwell, White, Priestnall, Hawkins, Kaufmann, Armbruster
(front) Wolkoff, Andresen, Ingraham, Yates, Simm

1985
(back) Ingraham, Perry,
Hawkins, Andresen
(front) White, Priestnall,
Yates, Simm, Porter

Ingraham & Hawkins

Montreal reunion 1984
Porter, Priestnall, Yates, Hawkins,
Simm

(back) Hawkins, Tanner,
(front) White, Andresen
1995

1999 reunion (back) Perry, Andresen, Porter
(seated) Hawkins, Priestnall

The Old Spice Girls
Doris Greene, Ruth Storey,
Phyllis Barry

235

Dear friends
Class of '62
Holy Cross School of Nursing

I had a dream, the most beauti-full dream. I was flying high above the clouds with Calgary as my destination, anticipating a most joyful homecoming. Suddenly the dream vanished and I was face to face with reality, particularly illness.

Believe me, I am sorry to miss this most important encounter for all of us. I have no doubts it will be the best meeting ever, carefully pre-pared and efficiently carried out. I shall miss each and everyone of you.

Thanks to Donna's kind devotion, my remembrances are kept well alive as she faithfully updates each one's memorabilia.

As ever I love you all very
dearly and I keep you in my prayers.
May our Foundress, Saint Marguerite
d'Youville. continue to guide you and
keep you all under her care.

Affectionately,

Cécile Leclerc P.J.m.

Montreal
October 29, 1996

Sister Cecile Leclerc; Montreal
reunion, Old Montreal.
September 1994

Yates' bulletin board, end of third year.

School Song (1954-1979)

Oh Holy Cross we owe to thee
Our future and our praise
Of high ideals and charity
This day our voice we raise.

Oh Holy Cross to thee we give,
Our future promise true
To love, respect, uphold and guard
The name we leave to you.

The day will come when each of us
Will bid our last adieu
In joy we feel these will reveal
The hint of sorrow too.

The happy hours we share with friends
The priceless times we know
Are treasures dear, Oh Holy Cross
That we all owe to you.

Tune *America*. Words by Monica Bruder
and Marian Jorgensen, class of 1954.
(They were awarded one extra late leave
for their efforts)

Epilogue

Montreal, Summer 1992

I wake up to the sound of my mother sobbing.

I lie still, wondering if she will go back to sleep, but she doesn't. I slip out of bed, gently close our bedroom door and hope I won't wake up my husband.

It had been very subtle, at first, after my father died, when Mom began to forget. First it was names, then recipes, then how to mix the colours of paints on her palette. Then one day I woke up, and I was her mother.

I arrive at the guestroom door; the one we now refer to as Mom's room. Her door is closed save for a narrow crack which I peer through. Mom is kneeling by her bed, hands folded in prayer. She's wearing her long, cotton nightie with pastel butterflies. The early morning light peeks through the white lace curtains behind her, casting a soft yellow glow across her delicate, wrinkled face, wet with tears. She raises her beautiful blue eyes to Christ on the wall ~ His face and shoulders, a healthy-looking compassionate Christ.

"Oh, God. What will become of me?" she sobs. "What? ... What will become of me?"

Montreal, Summer 1993

After all these years I'm still terrified of her. Terrified of being late. So I arrive half an hour early.

I park the car on Guy Street in front of the Mother House of the Grey Nuns. At ten minutes to two, as I walk through the parking lot to the front door, I imagine nuns critically eyeing me from the many windows of the massive building. I press the call-bell. There is a soft click. I push open the heavy door. Scenes of Mother d'Youville, founder of the Grey Nuns in 1737, and her early days in Montreal are sketched on the semi-circular wall before me. My steps echo in the austere stairwell as I ascend the wide, staircase that leads to the receptionist's desk.

"Sister Cécile Leclerc, *s'il vous plaît*," I say, nervously.

"*Oui.*" The receptionist smiles and tells me to wait in the second visiting room. It is small, with two windows opposite the door, an uncomfortable looking sofa and two chairs. A bouquet of artificial flowers stands in one corner. There is a crucifix on the wall over the couch and a picture of Christ bearing his bleeding heart above the door.

After several minutes, a small woman in a blue polyester suit and white blouse limps towards me. It has been 31 years; she does not wear her habit anymore, but I will never forget that limp. Sister Leclerc.

"Allo, allo," she says with an extravagant smile.

I reach my hand forward to shake hers but she leans towards me, I bend down awkwardly and she kisses me on each cheek. I never thought she would kiss my cheek, ever.

"Sit here," she says, waving me to the couch.

She sits beside me. There is a long pause, an uncomfortable silence.

"I was at The Holy's reunion last month," I say, quickly pulling some pictures out of my purse. "Do you remember White, Perry, Niven, Porter, Andresen?" I point to the middle-aged women in the picture.

Sister takes the photo from me and carefully studies each person. "My, my, my," she keeps repeating.

I've also brought the framed picture of my graduating class at Holy Cross School of Nursing, 1962, and I point out which girl in the class is the woman in the recent photograph. She takes a handkerchief from her pocket and wipes her eyes, under her glasses.

"Oh, my, this is wonderful," she says.

We talk about each girl-woman, about nursing then and now.

"I was too severe with you girls," Sister suddenly says, and dabs her eyes again.

This remark takes me completely by surprise. Her face is now tight with pain ~ pain she has been harbouring all these years. She *had* been too severe. But I find it hard to believe that Sister Leclerc is actually admitting it.

"No, Sister," I say. "You were doing your job. After all, we were wild girls. You had to keep a rein on us, watch over us. You gave us a good education, and you turned out good nurses. You had to be harsh."

And I wonder if being cold and inflexible was being harsh ~ if going over the line bordering on cruelty ~ *was* simply doing her job?

"I know I was too severe," she repeats. "I knew that when I became a student again. They sent me back to school in Minneapolis with two other nuns. We had so much fun playing pranks on the other students. That is when I realized I was too severe with you girls. I mellowed, you know, Donna, when I went to Edmonton General. I wasn't as harsh with those girls. I pray all of you will forgive me. I pray every day."

I sit beside Sister, remembering how she used to frighten me in her imposing habit. Now I see a tiny, old woman in a blue suit, her white hair beauty-fully coifed. I smile at the irony. I'm bald from chemotherapy and wearing a wig.

I have a hard time believing this is the same Sister Leclerc I knew in my prankish training days. But her eyes are the same. The same icy blue ~ steely blue, and now she is smiling.

"We're all grateful to you, Sister," I say. "You made good nurses out of us." I hoped I spoke for everyone in my class. I knew I spoke for myself.

The years of fear and resentment then begin to melt and I feel sorry for her. She was suffering. Sitting in the big empty Mother House, worrying about her crimes of severity. It was eating away at her. I want to embrace her and tell her we all forgive her. But I can't go that far. Not on the first visit. So instead I give her the new pen I've brought her, and I leave.

Montreal, September 1995

Our February, '62 class is having a reunion in Montreal, our 33ʳᵈ anniversary. White, Porter, Simm, Priestnall, and Hawkins meet in Calgary and fly to Montreal. When they arrive at Dorval Airport, I greet them like long lost sisters. We pick up a van at Hertz and drive out to my house in the country. There is constant chatter, laughing and teasing. Mysteriously we become 18 again. The grey hair and wrinkles disappear; it's just us ... as we were ... White, Porter, Simm, Priestnall, Hawkins, Yates.

On Tuesday I call Sister to invite her for supper the following night. She is overjoyed at the thought of meeting the girls. Then I tell the girls my surprise "We're going to take Sister Leclerc out for dinner tomorrow." Silence descends; I'm surprised they are not excited about seeing Sister.

"I never thought I would see that woman again," one girl says.

"Sister has been suffering," I say. "She thinks she was too harsh with us."

"She *was* too hard on us," White mumbles.

"But she's mellowed ... she's changed ... and she's old," I say.

"I bet those steely-blue eyes are still as sharp as ever," White says. "I bet she hasn't changed."

"Sister is so excited about seeing you," I say. "I showed her your pictures of our last reunion. She feels close to you guys, for God's sake."

They finally give in. I make a reservation at a quaint, French restaurant in Old Montreal. "It's a very special night," I tell the maître d'.

On our way to pick up Sister, White buys a beautiful bouquet of flowers from a young women vendor on the street, then we head for the Maison Mère. Sister is waiting anxiously in the doorway; I help her into the car. There are warm kisses all around and Sister is glowing.

I drop everyone off at the restaurant and find parking. When I return, they are sitting upstairs and I wonder how Sister made it up all those stairs. Everyone is chatting at once ~ "What did you do when you left The Holy, Sister?" ~ "What do you think of the separatist party in Quebec?" ~ "No, no, you were not too severe with us, Sister," ~ "Well, maybe a little, but that didn't hurt us," ~ "You made good nurses out of us, Sister," ~ "We're so grateful to you."

Sister keeps dabbing her eyes; They become brighter with each passing hour. We talk about nursing ... then and now ... and how sorry we are for the new nurses who have missed so much by not training in the hospital setting. All the while, I'm worried about getting Sister down the stairs. Going up is easy, but getting down is difficult for her, and there are so many stairs.

As we are about to leave, I have an idea. I ask the waiter if we can make a chair by crossing our arms at the wrists and carry Sister down the stairs. He grabs a real chair and another waiter. They hoist Sister, who is as light as a feather, up on the chair and carry her down; she looks like Cleopatra on her barge. Sister actually giggles. *"Merci. Merci."*

"C'est mon plaisir, ma Soeur," the waiter says.

Sister is elated ~ beaming, glowing with pride. We are her students, her children. She knows now that we are grateful for all she has given us. The waiters gently lower Sister to the floor and help her off the chair. White gently takes her by one arm, Hawkins, the other. I smile; I know Sister has found peace.

Montreal, April 1997
Beaconsfield Nursing Home

My mother is gasping; I know that sound well ~ the sound of the final struggle. "It's very natural," I used to tell families as they watched their loved one slip away. But now as I watch my mother, it seems anything but natural. I have long been praying for her suffering to end; praying for her to go ~ and now ~

For the last six weeks, my mother has not known me, and for six weeks before that I'm not sure if she even knew I was her daughter. When I would arrive and say, "Hi, Mom," she would always answer, "Hello, dear." But then so did at least three other women residents in the room.

I sit on the bed and stroke Mom's face. I hold her hand ... I know this is the end. I tell her I love her ... so very much. I thank her for all she has done for me ... for all she has given me. Then I tell her to go with it. Don't fight it, Mom. Fly away ... fly away to God ... and she does ...

Mom had made Allan and me promise to have an autopsy performed on her brain when she passed away. "To help science learn about this complicated brain disease I have," she said. So I go down stairs and call my brother. I begin to cry at the sound of his voice; he knows Mom is gone. He tells me to call his colleague at the Royal Victoria Hospital to arrange the autopsy. The colleague tells me to have the car from the funeral parlour transport my mother to the morgue at the Montreal Neurological Hospital.

I return to Mom's room, pull a chair over to her bed and sit and wait for the car to arrive. Mom looks different now. Not that Parkinson's look any more, but more like her old self, as if she will turn her head to me and say, "So how was your day, dear?" Her eyes are slightly open, bright blue as the Alberta sky. This vision, I know I will always remember. I sit and study her face. I don't close her beautiful eyes.

With Mom

Once again we are 18 years old, giggling and laughing as we pass around photos of our grandchildren.

Perry is worried that Kaufmann won't make it to the reunion. "I called her three times," Perry said, "and she promised me she would come. But she's so busy babysitting her grandchildren, she never has any time to herself."

Last reunion, Kaufmann arrived with bags of religious literature and preached pro-life to everyone. Priestnall came down hard on the side of pro-choice ~ the rest of us did our best to referee.

Andresen hasn't aged a day even though she was the first of us to be a grandmother. She is amazed that we all remember what we do about training days. "I think I was so scared that Sister would kick me out that it's all gone," she says. "I can only remember the great fear I had of failing."

Porter, dressed in pink, is still trying to get by without wearing her glasses and still working in the special nursery. "I just can't live without going in and holding those little babies," she says.

Blackwell is now Standish's sister-in-law, after marrying her brother. Standish is living near Cardston but unable to attend the reunion.

Ingraham sits across from me, her wide smile as innocent and contagious as it was 40 years ago.

Guenette is retired in Las Vegas; none of us have seen her since graduation, though Simm and Hawkins remain in touch with everyone.

Armbruster drove down from Burton, B.C., where she has lived since her marriage. "We are so truly blessed to all be together again," she says. "And such a beautiful weekend!"

Wolkoff now works in the nursery ~ nurturing plants not babies.

Niven worked until recent back surgery forced her into retirement. She is unable to attend our reunion. We all miss Niv.

Tanner ~ our beautiful June Allyson sister, never recovered from losing Ralph. Hawkins remained Tanner's friend and strength through her turbulent years after graduating. This year, Tanner is too ill to travel. We all miss her.

Hawkins drove down from Wetaskiwin with White, who sits beside me now as she always does at reunions.

We begin to talk about my recent hip replacement surgery.

"I feel terribly sad that nursing has changed so much since our day," I say.

"I read that the average age of nurses is 42," White says, pausing to sip her V.O. and ginger ale. "What's going to happen in five or ten years? All of the hospital-trained nurses will be gone, and the younger ones who want to be good nurses haven't the basic hands-on training to make their job fulfilling. They're scared to death in the hospital. I feel bloody sorry for them."

"I had one nurse in the rehabilitation hospital who came in the middle of the night like an angel," I said. "Her flashlight was pointed to her white uniform, like we were taught, reflecting a soft light, instead of pointing directly into my face like the others. I thanked her for answering my call light so quickly. She said 'It's my pleasure to serve you.' She brought my medication without delay, pleasantly, courteously, caringly. Just her presence made me feel better.

"I asked her where she did her nursing training. She was taken aback for a moment, but she drew a breath and said, 'I've worked over 20 years ~ a year in Vancouver to learn English, then in Hull, Quebec City, up north. I've been working a long time,' she said. And she patted my hand, and left the room. In a moment she returned and said, 'I just went into the hall to shut the light and it came to me: I had a calling. I trained in a college, but really, I was born to nurse.'"

I pause for a moment, then say, "Now that's a nurse."

Yes, the girls agree. That *is* a nurse.

Florence Nightingale Lamp

Afterword ... for Nurses

During the Crimean War, 1854-1856, Florence Nightingale's lamp brought hope to wounded soldiers on the battlefield. Working with nothing except cleanliness and attentive care, this one woman transformed medicine. For 134 years her lamp offered nurses a light to steer by. Nightingale's lamp is a call to remember our purpose and our history.

For those of you whose desire to serve burns true, know this: Nursing includes many unpleasant tasks that are simply part of the job, but dedicating your life to nursing the sick will bring you measures of joy you never thought possible. You will grow wealthy not by monetary standards but by the gold standard of satisfaction.

And so to those of you with a genuine desire to nurse the sick ... a passion to sustain life ... and a calling to care ... I pass to you this trustworthy and radiant lamp. Carry it high, with pride and dignity.

Excerpt from Father Flanagan's speech at 80th Celebration of Holy Cross Hospital School Reunion, Calgary, Alberta, 1987

... I think that truth gives a beautiful background for you to consider the 80 years of Nursing training that was carried on at Holy Cross. It certainly was the intent of the Grey Nuns and training school faculty, to impart that value to you regarding nursing.

Self-less service, to the sick ~ is the primary goal. Rewards of whatever kind came after. Such ideals of course, are manifested and learned in concrete situations, not in speeches or families ... and one such situation comes to my mind.

About 4 o'clock (long after the shift was over) I went into a ward on St. Ann's. A student was pleading with a reluctant orthopedic patient to drink a glass of juice. She was almost in tears. "Please take this," she said. "Miss Tenant won't let me go home until you drink it."

That's an example of learning that the welfare of the patient comes first, before our own convenience. I'm sure you have had many laughs this weekend, as you recall events from your training. We tend to mythologize the past, and most stories don't lose much in the telling. But really, you have much to be grateful for, and we will offer our thanks in the Eucharist today for the nurses training that helped you at an early age to be a caring person. But a caring person in a disciplined way ~ able to respond to Crisis situations in a calm, cool, principled way ~ imbued with a deep respect for life and dignity of and with each person.

...That you are grateful for all whose lives you have touched ~ and who have touched yours.

About the Author

Yates-Adelman was born in Calgary, Alberta. A graduate of Holy Cross Hospital in February, 1962, she worked for 26 years, primarily in surgical intensive care and coronary intensive care in hospitals in Montreal, Calgary and San Francisco. She was head nurse in surgical intensive care at Montreal's Jewish General Hospital before opening her own medical clinic, Doctor's Replacement Medical Clinic, which she owned and operated for 12 years.

Yates-Adelman lives in Montreal.